MAYA-BRITISH CONFLICT AT THE EDGE
OF THE YUCATECAN CASTE WAR

Maya-British Conflict at the Edge of the Yucatecan Caste War

CHRISTINE A. KRAY

University Press of Colorado

Denver

© 2023 by University Press of Colorado

Published by University Press of Colorado
1624 Market Street, Suite 226
PMB 39883
Denver, Colorado 80202

 The University Press of Colorado is a proud member of
the Association of University Presses.

The University Press of Colorado is a cooperative publishing enterprise supported, in part, by Adams State University, Colorado State University, Fort Lewis College, Metropolitan State University of Denver, University of Alaska Fairbanks, University of Colorado, University of Denver, University of Northern Colorado, University of Wyoming, Utah State University, and Western Colorado University.

∞ This paper meets the requirements of the ANSI/NISO Z39.48–1992 (Permanence of Paper).

ISBN: 978-1-64642-462-7 (hardcover)
ISBN: 978-1-64642-564-8 (paperback)
ISBN: 978-1-64642-463-4 (ebook)
https://doi.org/10.5876/9781646424634

Library of Congress Cataloging-in-Publication Data

Names: Kray, Christine A., author.
Title: Maya-British conflict at the edge of the Yucatecan caste war / Christine A. Kray.
Description: Denver : University Press of Colorado, [2023] | Includes bibliographical references and index.
Identifiers: LCCN 2023012992 (print) | LCCN 2023012993 (ebook) | ISBN 9781646424627 (hardcover) | ISBN 9781646425648 (paperback) | ISBN 9781646424634 (ebook)
Subjects: LCSH: Mayas—Wars—Mexico—Yucatán (State) | Mayas—Mexico—Government relations. | Mayas—Belize—Government relations. | British—Mexico—History—19th century. | Ethnic conflict—Yucatán Peninsula—History—19th century. | Land use, Rural—Mexico—Yucatán (State)—History—19th century. | Great Britain—Colonies—Administration—History—19th century. | Yucatán (Mexico : State)—History—Caste War, 1847–1855. | Belize—History—19th century.
Classification: LCC F1435.3.W2 K73 2023 (print) | LCC F1435.3.W2 (ebook) | DDC 972/.6506—dc23/eng/20230412
LC record available at https://lccn.loc.gov/2023012992
LC ebook record available at https://lccn.loc.gov/2023012993

Cover image: "Mr. Henry Fowler, Colonial Secretary, and His Exploring Party." Illustration for *The Graphic*, January 24, 1880, from Look and Learn (lookandlearn.com).

To Annalea—
who hadn't yet been born when I started this project
and is now old enough to ask for more pirates.

And to the memories of two taken by COVID-19:
Doña Mary Poot Tamay and my *padrino*, Don
Gabriel Cano Góngora. Dios kanáant a wóole'ex.

An Indian who finds his wife or child in the custody of another person can reclaim them if proof be given, and they will be turned over immediately without any obligation to provide compensation.
—1853 PACÍFICO-YUCATÁN PEACE TREATY

Every border implies the violence of its maintenance.
—AYESHA A. SIDDIQI

Contents

Illustrations

FIGURES

TABLE

Acknowledgments

I would not have started down this road had it not been for an invitation from Jason Yaeger, Minette Church, and Richard Leventhal. They had launched the San Pedro Maya Project in Belize, had begun archaeological investigations, and asked if I would conduct interviews with former residents of the region. My work benefited enormously from our collaboration over the years. Jason Yaeger had already tracked down many people in western and northern Belize who had once lived in San Jose and interviewed them in Spanish. The relationships he forged and the information he shared made it much easier for me to visit them (and others) and pursue additional interviews in Maya. Jason helped me get situated in San Ignacio, loaned me an SPMP truck, and introduced me to several Belizean academics and community leaders. Jason, Minette, Richard, and I exchanged ideas and information over the years, and their collective impact on this work is substantial.

This book might not have been written had it not been for the extraordinary generosity of Grant Jones. Jones had conducted extensive research at the archives in Belmopan, and when nearing retirement, he donated his archival notes and transcriptions to the San Pedro Maya Project. When I prepared this manuscript, he graciously confirmed that the notes could be put to that purpose as well. I will forever be in his debt.

At the University Press of Colorado, I am thankful for the expert guidance and assistance of Allegra Martschenko, Darrin Pratt, Daniel Pratt, and the entire team. Two anonymous reviewers offered keen insights and suggestions for revision.

I am grateful to the College of Liberal Arts at the Rochester Institute of Technology for a Faculty Development Grant and two Faculty Research Fund grants that supported a trip to the National Archives (UK), conference travel, and the acquisition of illustrations. My department chair, Uli Linke, offered endless encouragement for this project over the years and helped me trust my instincts. The university's interlibrary loan librarians tracked down several critical sources.

In Belize, several researchers and community leaders offered valuable advice: Filiberto Penados, Fernando Dzib, Alfonzo Tzul, Angel Tzec, and Davíd Ruiz Puga. For sitting with me for interviews, I am very grateful to former residents of San Jose: Felipe Puc, Jorge Tun, Ernesto Ortega, Tomasa Ortega, Pedro Ortega, María Torres, Angela Humes, Marcos Tun (in Santa Familia and Branch Mouth); and Emeterio Cantun, Valentín Tosh, Asunciona Pérez, Genoveva Pérez, Victor Cantun, and Dolores Velásquez de Pérez (in San Jose Palmar). Helpful suggestions and introductions were provided in Santa Familia by Israel Rivera and Narciso Torres, and in San Jose Palmar by Angel Cantun. I also benefited from the commanding knowledge and kind assistance of archivists: Marvin Pook and Mary Alpuche in Belmopan and Simon Fowler in Kew.

Richard Wilk undoubtedly planted the seed of inspiration for this work long ago when he assigned Nelson Reed's *The Caste War of Yucatán* and helped me locate materials so that I could study the Maya language as an undergraduate student. Many regional experts offered helpful feedback and support along the way: John Watanabe, Fernando Armstrong-Fumero, Alejandra Badillo Sánchez, Anne MacPherson, Paul Sullivan, Matthew Restall, Wolfgang Gabbert, Allan Burns, Ron Loewe, Michael Hesson, Christine Eber, and Cynthia Rivera. Nancy Farriss set the example for painstaking, theoretically oriented, and community-engaged historical research.

The enormously talented Emily Kray designed the maps. Sound editor Ryan Gaynor enhanced the interview recordings. Geidy Rodríguez Poot helped sort out some Maya vocabulary.

No amount of money can repay my debt to Lauren Beck and Ramona Walker, who spent hundreds of hours caring for my daughter so that I could disappear upstairs and work on this book. Academic work depends upon the cooperation and kind-heartedness of so many unsung heroes.

Finally, I am grateful to my parents for listening to me fret about the "Belize book," encouraging me to take risks, and celebrating my successes. Aunt Mary Andonov, the family historian, best understands my (obsessive?) compulsion to hunt down details. Annalea reminds me when it is time to go to work and motivates me to keep plugging away. Thank you for waiting. Now, let's go ride our bicycles in the sunshine.

Preface

A Note on Language

Decisions about naming and spelling are inherently political as they preserve or challenge existing social and political hierarchies and inequalities. Three goals guide my use of language, although they sometimes work at cross-purposes. First, I want to reflect historical perspectives, which can be achieved by using terminology then employed. Second, I want this work to be understood by various audiences, which prompts me at times to rely on convention. Third, however, I am conscious of the ways in which language use contributes to ongoing colonization processes, and I aim to avoid reproducing that cultural violence, insofar as is possible. Striking the right balance is no easy feat, and my choices will surely disappoint some readers (just as they have disappointed me, at times).

TERMINOLOGY

The Yucatán peninsula (northern Belize and the Mexican states of Campeche, Yucatán, and Quintana Roo) is home to speakers of an Indigenous language that they call Maya. To differentiate this language from the other thirty languages in the Mayan language family, linguists have termed it "Yucatec Maya." Since native speakers call it Maya, I generally do so in this work.

The term "Maya" as applied to a group of people, however, is not without its problems. While outsiders such as anthropologists, historians, and tourists use the term to refer to a presumed ethnic group that would include speakers of the

Mayan languages and their ancestors, in Yucatán, it has never been widely used as a self-ascribed ethnic term. As Matthew Restall and Wolfgang Gabbert discerned, the Maya-language documents of the colonial period and those from the Kruso'ob region in the nineteenth century reveal that the Maya speakers in the peninsula did not use any term ("Maya" or otherwise) that would suggest a peninsula-wide sense of ethnic identity.[1]

A more fundamental issue is how people identify themselves and their relations to others. It is not just a matter of pointing to a predetermined group of people and selecting the "right" label for them. If they do not identify themselves as a group of people with a shared past and common characteristics, then the term we use is beside the point. Since the nineteenth century was a tumultuous period characterized by war, flight, and various forms of exploitation and conflict, we should anticipate that how people decided to identify themselves and with whom they found commonality was very much a matter of concern for them. Moreover, ethnicity is just one dimension of identity, as are economic position or status, place of origin, residence, political affiliation, kinship, occupation or means of subsistence, religion, and many others. How people define themselves along any of these dimensions varies over time, and on a given day, one such identity may loom larger in a person's image of self. The historical documents do not give clear answers to questions of identity, of course, since—as is true for all utterances—they are communicated by one person to a specific audience for a specific purpose. A document would not reflect the whole of how the author imagined themself, although it would reflect something of how they want the recipient to view them. People may define themselves one way to one person, a second way to another person, a third way to themselves when they wake up in the morning, and a fourth way in their quiet thoughts at the day's end. Consequently, my references here to "the Maya" should be understood as a heuristic device, but not as a term that necessarily reflects their most salient identities at any given time. How they imagined themselves, how they sorted themselves out, and how they sought new alliances and severed old ones is a central question in this book.

In the Yucatán peninsula in the nineteenth century, government officials and people of Spanish and British descent referred to the Indigenous peoples in the peninsula as "Indians." The term "Indian," of course, is Eurocentric, a linchpin of European colonial rule, and it is frequently used as a racial slur in modern-day Belize and Mexico. Not wishing to reenact that violence here, I use the term sparingly—doing so only when I am referring to a group of people targeted by a specific Spanish, Mexican, or British legal framework or to specifically capture the perceptions and judgements of others whose actions, based on those judgments, bore consequences for Indigenous peoples.

While people of Indigenous, European, and African descent mixed, married, and bore children throughout the Spanish colonial period, nevertheless, differential rights

TABLE 0.1. Consonants in (Yucatec) Maya

	Labials	Dentals	Alveolars	Alveopalatals	Velars	Pharyngeals
Tense stops	p	t	ts	ch	k	'
Glottalized stops	p'	t'	ts'	ch'	k'	
	b[a]					
Voiced stops	(b)	(d)			(g)	
Spirants	(f)		s	x		j
Nasals	m	n	(ñ)			
Semi-vowels	w			y		
Liquids		l				
		r				
		(rr)				

Note: The phonemes enclosed in parentheses have been introduced into the language through Spanish loan words. Adapted from Robert Wallace Blair, "Yucatec Maya Noun and Verb Morpho-Syntax" (PhD diss., University of Chicago, 1964), 1–26.

[a] The b is always glottalized in Maya, but the apostrophe that would normally indicate a glottal stop is not included in this orthography.

and privileges under colonial law as well as social prejudices resulted in a situation in which, in the nineteenth century, Yucatecans often sought to distinguish themselves from others in racial and cultural terms. Those of greater Spanish descent at times called themselves *españoles* (Spaniards), *blancos* (whites), *criollos* (Creoles), and *gente de vestido* (well-dressed people). So as not to further entrench racialization, I generally use a descriptive label: "Yucatecans of Spanish descent." Those who fled to the British settlement during the Social War were treated by the British as minoritized immigrants, and they were called "Spanish," "Yucatecans," and sometimes "Yucatecos" (in contrast to the Maya, whom the British called "Indians"). The term "Yucateco" is useful since, as a Spanish-language term, it draws attention to them as a linguistic community. Consequently, when referring specifically to Yucatecans of Spanish descent within the British settlement, I sometimes use the term "Yucateco."

SPELLING

The Maya orthography used in this work is one that was developed by bilingual (Maya and Spanish) Yucatecan educators. It has been adopted as the official orthography by the National Institute for Indigenous Languages, and has facilitated a cultural renaissance of Maya literature, music, and political organizing.[2] The consonants are represented in table 0.1. The five vowels (*a, e, i, o, u*) vary by length (short, long, and glottalized) and three tones and are written as such, using *e* as an example: short (*e*), long low (*ee*), long high (*ée*), and glottalized (*e'e*).

This book includes some exceptions to the official orthography. Within quotations, the original spelling is preserved. For the names of modern-day political entities (states, towns, and counties), I use the official spelling within that country, even if it relies upon a now-antiquated orthography (e.g., Chichanhá, Icaiché, and Lochhá). This has the unfortunate consequence of creating an awkwardly hybrid text, as localities within what is now Mexico utilize accents; across the border in Belize, however, where English became the primary language of government and education during British rule, accents are not used. Consequently, a town in Mexico would be spelled San José, whereas in Belize, it is San Jose. A reader might prefer standardization of spelling within this book, but I could not impose a singular set of conventions without offending either Mexicans or Belizeans. Similarly, I use the conventional Yucatecan spellings for surnames, for example, Tzuc and Ek (which in the newer orthography would be Tsuk and Ek').

MAYA-BRITISH CONFLICT AT THE EDGE
OF THE YUCATECAN CASTE WAR

Introduction

Several months into the Social War of Yucatán (more commonly known as the Caste War), Maya rebels seized control of the colonial Spanish-era fort at Bacalar in May 1848. To the south, across the Hondo River, lay the tiny British settlement in the Bay of Honduras, with its superintendent seated in the town of Belize. The rebel commander at the fort wrote to the British superintendent—this letter being the second out of hundreds of letters penned by Maya leaders to British officials as the war stretched out over the next five decades. What was his concern? Weaponry? Official recognition of the rebellion? A promise of neutrality? No—it was timber.[1]

Mahogany—a resplendent, rot-resistant hardwood that grows in the forests around the Bay of Honduras—was then coveted in British and United States markets for use in fine-furniture making and shipbuilding. If the rebels were to sustain an effective defense against the Yucatecan army, they needed guns and a regular supply of gunpowder and shot—and for that, they needed both money and friendly relations with British merchants. British woodcutters had been extracting logwood and mahogany along the regional waterways for more than a century. If the Maya rebels could somehow gain access to timber profits, they could defend and expand the locations they had secured.

In his letter to Superintendent Charles St. John Fancourt in Belize, Comandante (Commander) Juan Pablo Cocom explained that "we already have won the large part of the state," that those were "our Indian lands," and that mahogany taken from those lands should be purchased at the price of two pesos per log. That money

https://doi.org/10.5876/9781646424634.c000b

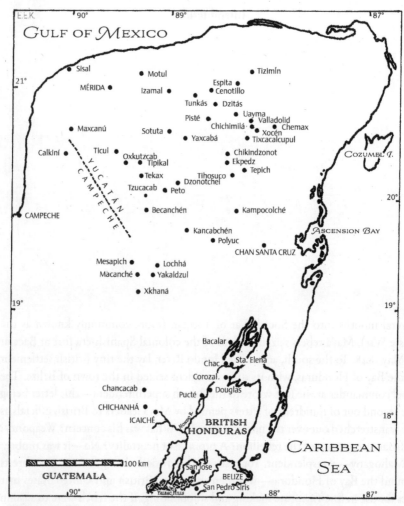

Figure 0.1. The Yucatán Peninsula, 1840s–1860s. Credit: Emily Kray

would subsidize their military costs and care for the widows and orphans of fallen rebel soldiers. One Bacalar resident who fled in the attack had absconded with logs, floating them out through the Chetumal Bay to sell to British merchants. The comandante needed the superintendent to ensure that the rebels would be properly recompensed for timber taken from "our Indian lands."[2]

This letter demonstrates that from the outset of the rebellion, land was valued first as a place to escape the exploitative conditions under which Maya peasants had been living, and secondarily as a form of leverage to achieve other goals (in this instance, timber profits). As we shall see, Maya leaders consequently aspired to be recognized as lords of the land and to maintain good relations with the British. At the same time, the British settlers had their own ideas about land tenure—seeking to secure British territorial sovereignty in a region in which they had never enjoyed it, and to establish private ownership of the land and of the enormously valuable mahogany trees thereupon. Control over land was also a means through which land-lords (regardless of ethnic background) could direct Maya tenants to pay rent and provide labor (in commercial enterprises or in military campaigns). Consequently, while the Maya and British were compelled to seek favor with one another, con-flicts deriving from the competition over land were inevitable. This book explores the ever-shifting political terrain as, during the first quarter-century of the Social War, one group of Maya (the Pacíficos) and the British at times cooperated with one another strategically, but ultimately fought in battle since an alliance could not withstand the accumulated insults, injuries, and resentments.

During the period that is our focus (1847–1872), relations between the Maya and the British had their own dynamic, but they were at every turn affected by the Social War of Yucatán (1847–1901). The fighting was concentrated mainly to the north of the Hondo River—that is, to the north of the region that the British called British Honduras (which later became the independent country of Belize). However, events at the geographical heart of the conflict were very much affected by developments south of the river, as well. The Social War has long been a subject of intense fascination and scrutiny, for a variety of reasons. It was a (primarily) Maya rebellion that lasted half a century, in which, in mid-1848, it appeared as if the rebels might successfully seize control over what was then the independent Republic of Yucatán. Since the uprising occurred on the heels of the wars of independence from Spain—within polities lacking established rules of governance and embroiled in a series of revolts and civil wars—the war fed upon the instability of the political landscape. The rebellion was transformational, as it pushed independent Yucatán to rejoin the Mexican federation (in 1848), and the war reduced the population of Yucatán by one-third through a combination of death and displacement.[3] The conflict fostered the creation of a new, syncretic, millenarian religion—worship of the Talking Cross—in which the Cross issued military commands to its follow-ers, and in the Maya language. Finally, it led to new political formations, as some Indigenous groups were able to parlay their military strength into new political, economic, and civil rights.

At the outbreak of the hostilities, Yucatecan elites characterized the conflict as a Caste War (*guerra de castas*).[4] The name has persisted, even though most con-temporary scholars acknowledge that it is problematic. This book's title employs the term for the purpose of recognizability. However, as some other scholars have

done, in the pages of this book I use the term Social War, because of three characteristics of the conflict neatly summarized by Wolfgang Gabbert. First, "Caste
War" implies a division rooted in ethnic descent. However, a fact which is central
to this account is that, over time, hundreds of thousands of people of Maya descent
resisted joining the rebellion, sought peace with the Yucatecan government, and/or
fought against the rebels. In addition, the rebels included—both as leaders and foot
soldiers—many people who were of mixed ethnic background and even some who
were legally *vecinos* (rights-bearing townspeople; in effect, non-Indians). Finally,
by characterizing the conflict as a race war, Spanish-descended Yucatecans could
blame "racial hatred" and draw attention away from the (legitimate) political and
economic complaints of Yucatecan peasants.[5] For these reasons, and to keep economic factors squarely in view, I use the broader term Social War.

OUR VANTAGE POINT

Another unfortunate consequence of the longstanding label "Caste War of Yucatán"
has been a statist conceptualization of the conflict. From the outset, however, the
conflict was regional in scope. Since most of the fighting took place within what
are now the Mexican states of Yucatán, Campeche, and Quintana Roo, most of the
existing scholarship focuses on that region. Special attention has been given to the
rebels who called themselves Kruso'ob (People of the Cross) and their devotion
to the Talking Cross. Don Dumond's *The Machete and the Cross* is the magnum
opus—the most comprehensive account of the Social War. He provides the widest
regional view, tracing developments both within Mexico and the British-claimed
zone, particularly the importance of competing land claims and British Honduran
sales of guns, lead, and gunpowder to the rebels.[6]

This book focuses on relations between the Pacíficos—those who brokered peace
with the Yucatecan government and thereafter became known as the *rebeldes pacíficos* ("pacified" or "peaceful" rebels)—and the British. Indirectly, it also illustrates
how the Social War both shaped and was shaped by arrangements of land, labor,
and migration within the region that is now Belize. Opportunities for illicit trade
and resource extraction, and the ability to escape military violence, forced military
service, debts, debt bondage, oppressive employers, and prison sentences by crossing from one region to the next (and sometimes, back again), built up resentments
and disputes that spun out into international conflicts, leading to a reshuffling of
alliances and a new round of boundary crossings and vexations. This work takes a
view from the south, revealing that, rather than being a distant "hinterland," the
area south of the Hondo River was the staging ground for rivalries and strategies
that had enormous regional consequences. We can see the transmutation of war:

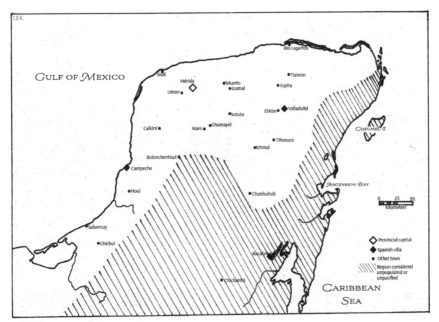

Figure 0.2. Yucatán Province, 1780. Adapted from Nancy M. Farriss, *Maya Society under Colonial Rule: The Collective Enterprise of Survival* (Princeton, NJ: Princeton University Press, 1984), 77. Credit: Emily Kray.

once people crossed the Hondo River into the region claimed by the British, emerging arrangements of labor, law, land tenure, policing, and trade set new strictures upon people's movements, autonomy, and hopes for security. Reactions to those new strictures generated new conflicts, which ultimately fed back into military conflicts to the north.

The regional scope of the conflict is not surprising, considering that for centuries prior to that, large numbers of people had migrated from the northern part of the peninsula to the south, as well as in the opposite direction. Throughout the Spanish colonial period, Spaniards effectively controlled the northwestern part of the peninsula, but the portion south of Campeche and the Bay of Ascension was considered "unpopulated or unpacified," with the exceptions of a small mission at Chichanhá and a military villa at Bacalar (see figure 0.2). Burdened, as northern Maya peasants were, with heavy demands for forced labor and church and civic taxes and fees, they would frequently escape by moving southward into the region that is now Belize.[7] In turn, in the eighteenth and early nineteenth centuries, Africans and African-descended people who had been enslaved by British woodcutters were escaping in the opposite direction (as well as westward into what is now Guatemala).[8] As we shall see, competition over land in the Social War was directly tied to the need for labor in military and commercial endeavors. Consequently, the ability of people to flee from one jurisdiction to another frustrated Maya leaders and British landlords, aggravating the political conflicts even further.

In the mid-nineteenth century, once the rebellion was underway, Indigenous people predictably moved back and forth across the Hondo River to maximize their safety and prosperity, in accordance with evolving conditions. One group of people who were a key link between Yucatán and the British settlement at this time—and who are critical to the developments described in this book—were those whom O. Nigel Bolland and Grant Jones identified as the San Pedro Maya. They were a group of Maya speakers who moved southward from Yucatán into the British-claimed zone in the late 1850s and early 1860s, settling several villages in the Yalbac Hills region, with a political center at San Pedro. The Maya rebels in Yucatán had by this time split between those committed to the rebellion (the Kruso'ob) and the Pacíficos. The San Pedro Maya subsequently broke away from the Pacíficos centered at Chichanhá, and therefore became a third group of Maya actors within a complex set of shifting political alliances at a time of intense insecurity and mutual apprehension.[9] This widespread insecurity was sustained and fed over time by a post-independence power vacuum in the early national period; successive waves of raids in Yucatán; a regional build-up of arms and ammunition; broken promises; brittle military alliances; disputed territorial boundaries; and a sparsely populated frontier zone that served as a safe haven for rebels, pioneers, commercial woodcutters, refugees, thieves, war profiteers, deserters, escaped prisoners, and runaway debt servants, alike.

How the San Pedro Maya were treated by the British at different moments in time had much to do with whether they were perceived as useful allies or treacherous foes. The San Pedro Maya entered a peaceful arrangement with the British in 1862, committing to protect the settlement in case of a Chichanhá Pacífico or Kruso'ob Maya attack from the north, only to be swept up later in a maelstrom of political scheming, accused of treason, and their villages burned by West India regimental soldiers in 1867. These events represented a watershed moment from the British perspective, ushering in a suspicious, defensive, hardened approach to racialized "Indians" by the colonial government. My initial questions were: Why did this unlikely alliance come about, why did it fall apart, and what was the aftermath of its collapse? Those initial questions led me down several rabbit holes of inquiry. Along the way, I came to see that in many respects, the San Pedro Maya were not unique, but had much in common with thousands of other Maya and mestizo settlers at the time, and factors that continued to trigger violence across time included contrasting and evolving visions of the land, strategies for the acquisition of people's labor, and the risks and damnable frustrations that inhere in borders.

VISIONS OF THE LAND

None of the various groups of regional inhabitants at this time demonstrated a singular view of the land. (There was no singular or fixed "Maya" view of the land, for example.) Rather, diverse conceptualizations of the land (as bridge, frontier, property, leverage, territory, and homeland) emerged over time in relationship to broader changes in material and political conditions. To explain: If one views a stretch of land as a bridge, one sees opportunity on the other side. If one views a region as a frontier, one sees low population density and limited governmental control, and consequently, opportunities for freedom from government interference, to exploit new resources, and safety from military conflicts. "Property" implies exclusive ownership, monetary value, ownership of the land's resources, the right to sell or lease the land and/or its resources, and criminal trespassers. A related concept is "leverage"; those who control the land can withhold access to it to secure desired concessions from others (such as labor, payment, or military service). "Territory" implies domination by a political entity, often through military victory, with citizens whose rights are secured through birthright or legal entry, and borders to be surveyed, mapped, policed, and defended with force. Finally, if one views a region as a homeland, one imagines collective rights to belonging by virtue of original occupation, "native" inhabitants, political and cultural autonomy, freedom to use (and safeguard) natural resources, and those who do not belong configured as "invaders."

Throughout the mid-to-late nineteenth century, various images of lands—as frontiers, bridges, property, leverage, territories, borderlands, and homelands—were articulated in Maya-British relations and fueled armed conflict. Just as in the Spanish colonial period, some Yucatecans looked at the region of Belize and saw a frontier, where they might escape war and oppressive conditions, and find some measure of autonomy, or simply exploit new resources. Others (particularly peasants of diverse ethnic backgrounds) looked at the Hondo River and saw a bridge, and they moved back-and-forth across it over time, cultivating fields on one side but living on the other—to escape the combination of rent payments, debt servitude, and military impressment. Others saw property and the profits it promised. Others (particularly British officials) saw territories, secured through military victory, and they pursued regulatory policing of the borderlands and the population. Others saw homelands, to which they had a special claim as original inhabitants, and the attendant rights to use and safeguard their natural resources.

Curiously, at the center of the conflicts around the Hondo River, two powerful groups revealed remarkably similar views. Both Maya leaders and British timber company managers viewed land as leverage. Maya leaders of the time styled themselves as lords of the land and used land as leverage to secure not only financial profits, but also the loyalty, labor, and military service of tenants. At the same time, British timber companies used London-based legal frameworks to lay claim to enormous tracts of land, which they could use to extract the valuable timber. In addition—acting as landlords—they used land as leverage to charge rent and compel the labor of their new tenants.

In the United States, two of the most intractable myths about Indigenous people are that they "do not understand the concept of property," and relatedly, that they "do not view land as property."[10] There is a kernel of truth in these myths, in that precolonial native North and Central Americans often used land in accordance with use-rights—that one could use the land by virtue of membership in a social group. The myth that Indigenous people "do not view land as property" is often repeated by well-meaning Americans who indirectly critique the logics of consumer capitalism by holding up Indigenous use-rights as an alternative cultural model. However, Maya people combined ideas of use-rights and ownership of land in the late prehispanic and early postconquest periods.[11] Moreover, they adapted new strategies of land tenure within the contexts of Spanish and British imperialism. It is worth noting that if one's romanticism leads one to appreciate Indigenous people for their supposed differences (e.g., egalitarianism and environmentalism), one denies them the opportunity to leverage resources for their own purposes.

During the Social War, Kruso'ob and Pacífico Maya leaders treated lands as (collective) property, charging rent from British woodcutters and small-scale farmers in order to finance their war efforts and achieve the sovereignty and political autonomy that were their end goals. Their demands, when backed with threats of and use of force, outraged British officials and woodcutters, ultimately triggering the British military campaign and demands of total surrender and relinquishment of land claims in 1867. At root, the British seemed reluctant to view Indigenous people as people who could legitimately hold and wield property rights. While they were willing to pay the Mexican government for timber harvest contracts, they found the Maya leaders' demands "absurd" and "Blackmail." They failed to envision the Maya as coequal parties in business transactions; this racist vision thereafter became enshrined in official policy.

THE CYCLE OF DEBT, FLIGHT, AND CONFLICT

Another pattern revealed through the events of this period is that the conflicts over land created a positive feedback loop through the elements of debt and flight. The conflicts over land and the exploitation of labor both spurred people to flee in search of safety and freedom. Flight, in turn, exacerbated the conflicts, and the cycle of war continued. This was a complex dynamic that requires explication.

In the mid-nineteenth century, Maya families could secure most of what they needed on their own, so long as they had access to forest lands to farm and from which to gather resources. (They could sell a surplus of their produce to purchase other desired goods.) Therefore, someone who wanted to compel their labor—in either military or commercial ventures—could do so more readily if the people's access to land were somehow restricted. As we will see in chapter 2, in the northern half of the peninsula in the eighteenth and nineteenth centuries, a series of laws facilitated the large-scale alienation of Indigenous lands and the expansion of larger hacienda estates. Work on haciendas offered an alternative for dispossessed peasants, and in addition, they could thereby earn at least some of what was needed to pay their substantial church and civil taxes. Hacienda owners benefited from the accumulated debt of workers since they could parlay those debts into debt servitude and be assured of a regular workforce.[12]

As we have already seen, throughout the Spanish colonial period, Maya peasants sought to escape the burdens of forced labor, heavy taxation, and related debts by fleeing. While some fled to the southern reaches of the peninsula, others simply moved from one town to another in the same area. They would begin to accrue new debts, certainly, but they could at least start anew.[13] In the first half of the nineteenth century, as sugarcane cultivation, the pace of land alienation, and the accumulation of workers' debts all increased, so, too, did the numbers of peons who escaped their debts through flight.[14]

Then, after 1847, the regional conflict ironically brought into being new opportunities for indebted servants. Runaway debtors might have guessed that they would be safest within the fold of the enemies of their "masters" (or landlords or other creditors). The master's adversaries—they might have assumed—would make no efforts to repatriate the runaways and would prevent the employer from entering the territory to capture them. Matthew Restall identified this regional dynamic of labor exploitation in an earlier period, specifically in the eighteenth and early nineteenth centuries in the peninsula. According to Restall, although slavery was employed in the British settlement and in the neighboring Spanish colonies at that time, the regional conditions of labor and social life varied, prompting African-descended people to flee from the British settlement to the surrounding Spanish colonies, from which they thought they would not be forcibly returned. A region relying upon similar, yet distinctive, types of labor exploitation would ultimately share overlapping pools of labor, since frontiers would be "avenues of human movement." "Borders between colonies were not obstacles but bridges, crossed by sailors and slaves in search of safety," Restall described.[15] In other words, the British and Spanish alike employed exploitative labor systems, but the very fact that borders separated their respective realms of control meant that laborers would maintain the hope that escape to the other side represented freedom. Thereafter, in the mid-nineteenth century, once the Social War was underway, indebted servants—as well as deserters—similarly likely would have envisioned that flight into a region controlled by their master's adversaries represented a chance to shed their burdens and begin anew.

However, these patterns of flight ultimately fed back into and extended the cycle of conflict. As Maya peasants moved back and forth across the Hondo River, they riled landowners, Maya groups who claimed lands by right of conquest or prior possession, and Yucatecan and British officials, alike. Those seen as giving succor to runaway servants or deserters exacerbated the political and military conflicts, just as did the frequent raids by irritated masters aiming to recapture those who had absconded. Consequently, movement of people from one location to another intensified competition among power centers for control over territories. While analyses of the Social War have often centered upon the political struggles—for autonomy and sovereignty—the events of this book highlight the economic substratum of land, labor, and flight. At that time, there were multiple centers of (economic and political) power. While Restall considered the colonial centers of Mérida and Belize (and hinted at Guatemala City), in the mid-nineteenth century, two Maya power centers were formidable: Chan Santa Cruz and Chichanhá (later, Icaiché). Each center possessed its own fluctuating constellation of resources, rewards, and pressures on people. With five power centers, there were (at least) five times five "borders" that people could cross in search of security and prosperity.

Furthermore, the fact that a river was the putative border between Mexico and the British settlement made it possible for people to move quickly on the water and cross to the other side, whether to get away from oppressive conditions or to pursue new opportunities. In the mid-nineteenth century, almost everyone in the region of Belize was in motion: escaping, scouting, trading, positioning troops, smuggling, putting animals to pasture, cultivating multiple fields, recruiting, raiding, hauling timber, pursuing criminal offenders, collecting rent, conspiring, delivering messages, and surveying. The opportunistic movement of people across the Hondo River created intractable problems for governments, landowners, Maya leaders, and mahogany companies that often could not be resolved without calling upon the aid of more powerful agents at a distance. The borderlands began to take on a life of its own, luring people across it, stymieing others, and frustrating the imposition of law. Small-scale, localized disputes would spin out into larger conflicts. What began as a fight over a mule or late rent could blow up and trigger an international incident, especially as emerging governments sought to affirm and exercise sovereign power.

NARRATIVE AND THE PROCESS OF BECOMING

In this work, I have aimed to capture Indigenous perspectives and experiences as much as possible. Rajeshwari Dutt's important book, *Empire on Edge*, analyzes how British Honduran officials, concerned with physical security, adjusted strategies in reaction to developments along the Hondo River throughout the Social War.[16] British views take center stage in her narrative. This is understandable since documents preserved in the official colonial records overwhelmingly were both written and archived by representatives of the colonial government. Here, however, I give priority of attention to documents authored by Maya people as well as what they were reported as saying and doing, and I try to understand what motivated their actions.

In addition to communicating information about a time and place, this book also represents an experiment in anthropological writing. This is not simply a creative endeavor, but also an attempt to align style and theory. Writing is theory, of course. The way we write about people reveals more about our theory of action than our explicit formulations ever could. How we write reveals what we truly think about such abstractions as agency, culture, ethnicity, conflict, influence, power, and structure. The form itself is content, observed Hayden White.[17] In this book, I use a narrative (storytelling) approach to best illustrate the social processes of becoming.

This storytelling approach emerges out of a sustained critique of conventions in anthropological writing and theory. In her now famous chapter, "Writing against Culture," Lila Abu-Lughod critiqued the concept of culture as highly problematic, as it erases differences within a group, erases difference over time, it distances and exoticizes ethnographic subjects, and in speaking authoritatively about others, it reinforces the global inequalities that permit ethnography in the first place.[18] Culture as a noun—as a set of shared beliefs and practices—is an abstraction. In the swirl of everyday life and interactions among people, a "culture" is not perceptible. One cannot reach out and touch a culture, and likely everyone would describe "the culture" differently. Moreover, the notion of a culture as an internally consistent set of beliefs and behaviors shared within an identifiable social group is, at least in part, an artifact of a century of a certain type of ethnographic writing. In the conventional approach, the ethnographer would conduct fieldwork that amounted to hundreds or thousands of interactions with various people, playing out over a year or so in time (diachronic). The process was often confusing, characterized by frequent misunderstandings, social blunders, and uncertainty about people's intentions. Thereafter, having returned home, the anthropologist would pore over the piles of fieldnotes and interview transcriptions, straining to see patterns. The polished ethnographic text that emerged a year or more later would typically describe a neatly organized system of belief and behavior that bore little resemblance to the ethnographer's diverse and confusing interactions and conversations "in the field." While the fieldwork was diachronic, the cultural "system" described was synchronic. Earlier ethnographic texts both assumed and reinforced an understanding of a culture as logically consistent, stable over time, and shared within a bounded social group.[19]

That approach has been thoroughly critiqued, and it is now generally acknowledged within cultural anthropology that the sociocultural world is always in the process of becoming. If ethnographers must strain to interpret the meanings that motivate people's actions and expressions, it is because all interlocutors are constantly trying to discern one another's meanings and motives while also trying to communicate their own. Culture, therefore, is negotiated in and emergent through every social interaction.

Moreover, in their interactions in the present, people communicate and take steps toward creating their idealized future. They aim to refashion the world to create the conditions that would promote and sustain the well-being, safety, and contentment of themselves and others about whom they care. If culture does exist, it is oriented to the future rather than to the past. Critiquing the notion that people follow a "way of life," which would entail "a prescribed code of conduct, sanctioned by traditions, that individuals are bound to observe," Tim Ingold described the person as a "wayfarer." What a wayfarer does, he wrote, "is not to act out a script received from predecessors but literally to negotiate a path through the world." We might say that action, therefore, entails both creativity and courage. If we accept this theory of action, the style of writing must align with it. Taking a series of diachronic events and reducing it to a synchronic system (a "culture") would contravene the nature of becoming. It would strip people of the creativity and courage of their wayfaring. If the social world is always in the process of becoming, emerging out of people's wayfaring and future-building activities, a storytelling (narrative) framework is most suited for its description. As Ingold wrote: "For the things of this world are their stories, identified not by fixed attributes but by their paths of movement in an unfolding field of relations."[20]

Attention to writing style is particularly important for this region of the world, since there has persisted a tendency to write about Maya people in ways that imply homogeneity of and continuity in thought and practice over time. This may reflect romanticism about the Maya—continuity of belief and behavior over time is often celebrated as a triumph. More than anything, though, the extraordinary tumult of the late nineteenth century—including the sustained armed conflicts, the frequent assassinations of leaders, the violent raids conducted in search of deserters and escaped debt servants—should be a signal that looking for continuity would be asking the wrong question. If anthropology cranes its neck to see what remains the same despite extraordinary pressures, it would be a bankrupt discipline—one that cranks out the same "answer" and thwarts discovery.

Rather than asking what of the past the Maya retained, we should be asking what kind(s) of future they (as individuals) were trying to create. In the second half of the nineteenth century, Maya people created and experimented with leadership, regional political alliances, regional identities, worship, notions of collective territory, and the commercialization of property and natural resources. Much of this book concerns land claims: how people asserted the right to access, use, control, and own stretches of land and how they did so on the bases of personal position and membership in a group. This was a tricky endeavor since—amid war, dispossession, debt servitude, and flight—people were on the move and often (quite literally) on the run. Successfully asserting belonging in a new location would have depended upon their ability to convince others—even complete strangers—that they had common cause. If the nineteenth century was an epoch of war and competing visions of belonging, it was also an epoch of creation, as people tried to create a space for themselves, even if those claims entailed enormous risks and thousands lost their lives in the process.

Abu-Lughod called for experimentation with "narrative ethnographies of the particular," which would narrate how individual people have—with agency, contestation, and deliberation—carried out their lives. These narratives would resist generalization about culture and preserve agency.[21] John Van Maanen similarly called for storytelling approaches in ethnography—what he called "impressionist tales." Interactions and events would be narrated in chronological order so that knowledge is revealed to the reader over time, and people are preserved as individuals with names, personalities, reactions, and words spoken. Such storytelling techniques, he believed, would highlight the "episodic, complex, and ambivalent realities" of social life.[22] When undertaken with respect to historical inquiry, such narratives might end up curiously looking a lot like the styles of writing associated with the discipline of history. They would track the actions of individuals, the resources and obstacles that structure their options, the difficult decisions laid out before them, and the costs and consequences of actions. Such narratives would have dramatic events, turning points, watershed moments, risks and rewards, and moments of crisis and resolution. Rather than learning about "Maya beliefs" about land, war, and leadership, the focus would be on individual actors, the choices they made, and how their actions affected others in turn. The subject would not be "Maya culture" or even "the Maya," but how this series of events unfolded over time through the decisions and interactions of individuals. Would this blur the boundary between anthropology and history? Perhaps, but if so, so be it.

Such an approach might be particularly important when writing about war. Carolyn Nordstrom's *A Different Kind of War Story* shows how a war is not constituted by two "sides" motivated by opposing ideologies. Rather, it involves a multiplicity of types of actors (such as civilians, voluntary recruits, impressed soldiers, civilian collaborators, spies, smugglers, war profiteers, healers, and visionaries), all of whom have different and shifting experiences and motivations under the umbrella term of "war." Anthropologists should be attuned to the myriad experiences of people on the ground, for ultimately, it is the sum of their actions that perpetuates the violence or brings it to a close.[23]

Rather than being abstract "Maya," "peasants," or "workers" steered by structures and inherited patterns of thought, nineteenth-century Maya people were multidimensional and often unpredictable.[24] Through their words and actions, they sought to persuade different audiences of courses of action, and they were also capable of changing their minds. For example, the picture of San Pedro Maya leader Asunción Ek that emerges from the historical documents is that he was sometimes humble, gentle, and conciliatory, sometimes frightened, sometimes angry and threatening, and sometimes cagey and inscrutable. In these pages, I will introduce you to many individuals in addition to Ek, including Luciano Tzuc, Florencio Vega, Marcos Canul, Robert Downer, Calisto Medina, John Carmichael, Basilio Grajales, John Hodge, J. Gardiner Austin, among others.[25] I would like you to know them as individuals, because that is how they knew one another. They interacted with one another over time and in different contexts, and consequently would not have known one another as stock characters or (solely) as representatives of one ethnic group or another. They knew one another as multifaceted—perhaps as both employer and courtroom magistrate, or as fellow soldier and political rival, or as military deserter and timber crew foreman, or as landlord and spy—and with distinctive personalities. While the historical documents are often silent about sensory details that would help us visualize certain pivotal interactions (such as settings, what a person looked like, the languages in which they communicated, the clothes they wore, whether they rode a horse or walked on foot, etc.), I will provide such details here and there and quote passages so that you can "hear" people's voices. Ultimately, I aim to animate the individuals whose excruciating decisions—within specific political and economic constraints—had fateful outcomes. I aim to track their wayfaring, as they charted their own paths and turned blind corners, across terrain strewn with pain, violence, abuse, selfishness, deception, traps, lethal indifference, suspicion, and glimpses of freedom. You may not like them all, but I hope that you will be able to envision them and the worlds they were trying to fashion.

HISTORICAL ETHNOGRAPHY

My research methodology could be called historical ethnography, as I approach the historical record from the perspective of an anthropologist, and I rely on both historical documents and interviews. I began with sustained attention to one place and time: western Belize in the period 1847–1872, between the initial uprising and the so-called "last Indian attack" on the British settlement. With my initial goal of understanding why the San Pedro Maya–British alliance was forged and why it fell apart, I sought to reconstruct as much as possible the minute details of the region of western Belize at the time and to reconstruct pivotal interactions. Then, in dialectical fashion, I moved ever-outwardly in concentric sweeps, looking across a broader expanse and further back in time to trace the larger processes, material conditions, and patterns of interaction that constituted the context within which people operated and the forces that might have steered their decisions. Tracing these changes over time requires a balance between a narrative framework and description of the details of community life.

The primary written materials consulted for this book consist of four types. Roughly half of the archival records consulted for this book were transcriptions of such documents most generously shared by Grant Jones from his research in the Belize Archives and Records Service in Belmopan, Belize, in the 1970s. I am profoundly grateful for his generosity. Using his notes in fact turned out to be essential, since some of the documents he transcribed can no longer be found in the archive.[26] Second, I consulted additional documents from that archive and the Colonial Office records in the National Archives (United Kingdom). Third, I utilized summaries and reprints of documents indexed in Governor-General John Alder Burdon's massive, three-volume *Archives of British Honduras*.[27] Finally, primary published materials such as treaties, colonial reports and handbooks, maps, almanacs, and narratives by travelers, amateur archaeologists, and military and colonial officers provided additional context for understanding.

Working with the colonial British documents requires a steadfastly critical perspective. One faces the typical problems of working with older documents in a tropical setting: fading of ink, crumbling pages, and damage from moisture and mildew. Some documents that were available a few short decades ago have since gone missing. Other obstacles are typical of records produced within the context of colonialism. For one, as the overwhelming majority are British-authored, events are filtered through those cultural and political perspectives. Given the frequent competition and conflict over land and resources, it is not surprising that British officials often offered dim views of Chichanhá and Icaiché moral characters and ambitions. One might read those assessments more critically, seeing them as often self-serving commentary within the highly charged atmosphere of war, border disputes, competition over valuable resources, and cross-cultural misunderstandings. Other problems of understanding stem from miscommunication across languages and cultures: the colonial interlocutors probably regularly misunderstood (and then, misrepresented) one another, and some documents were preserved only in translation.

In addition, the documents preserved in the archives do not provide a comprehensive view of life in the British settlement. What was communicated between government officials reflected government concerns, preoccupations, and worries, not the multitudinous other aspects of life in the region. When things were going to plan, they went unspoken. For example, we know from offhand mentions now and again that debt servitude was a central aspect of employer-employee relations in the British settlement. However, it did not become a matter for investigation and elaboration by the lieutenant governor until it was seen as problematic—when, in the late 1860s, British Honduran employers characterized the wage advance system (which led to indebted servitude) as a system exploited by the workers and British officials perceived it as threatening the colony's safety. Moreover, decisions about what to preserve would have been influenced by government interests and initiatives. Certain documents that would normally be expected to be archived are missing, indicating that some British officials may have engaged in deception regarding sensitive political matters.[28]

Moreover, the documents consulted for this book were warped by violence, abuse, and fear. (Since I needed to trace conflicts and alliances, I directed attention to documents with those foci.) Wherever violence, crime, and abuse are found, however, misinformation of various kinds follows. The documents are replete with strategic lies, idle threats, and rumors that proved false. People would lie to smear foes or to shield themselves from retaliation by political enemies, colonial officers, employers, landlords, and/or creditors. Idle threats provoked fear in order to ensure compliance. Rumors floated on the wind, electrified by a steady current of anxiety. As a lieutenant governor once remarked: "Allowances must necessarily be made for the difficulty of obtaining evidence at a village where nearly every one is directly or indirectly implicated, and in a district where each person is more or less controlled by fear."[29] Consequently, innumerable statements in these documents cannot be taken at face value, but instead, have to be read carefully and critically, looking for contradictions, evaluating the likelihood of certain events, and considering the motives of the authors and their sources.

Finally, I supplemented the historical documents with interviews of elders who had lived in the San Pedro region. After San Pedro was abandoned in the first part of the twentieth century, San Jose (Yalbac) became the largest Maya settlement in western British Honduras. After the wholesale eviction of San Jose residents in 1936 by the Belize Estate and Produce Company (a later manifestation of the British Honduras Company, which figures largely in this book), one group resettled in San Jose Palmar (south of Orange Walk) and another in Santa Familia (east of San Ignacio).[30] In these interviews, fourteen people who lived in San Jose prior to the 1936 eviction spoke about what they remembered of the village in the

1930s and what their relatives had told them about earlier decades. These interviews shed light on patterns of land tenure, production, consumption, labor, historical memory of Pacífico-Kruso'ob conflicts and debt servitude, and the powerful position of the company within the colony. The original goal of those interviews had been to supplement the information derived from archaeological and archival investigations—to fill in the gaps, under the assumption that some of what was true in the 1930s might also have been true in earlier periods. However, the elders from San Jose revealed a great deal of information about the relationship between the company, the colonial government, and the Maya residents in the 1930s, which should be developed at length in a separate work.

OVERVIEW OF THE BOOK

Chapter 1 offers historical background for understanding the competing land claims that would be central to the Pacífico-British conflict beginning in the 1850s. The chapter describes the flight of northern Maya to the Belize region during the colonial period, where they developed strategies of resistance to European rule. It also delineates the Anglo-Spanish territorial competition and the British commercial pursuit of logwood and mahogany that led woodcutters farther into the Belizean interior, leading to clashes with Indigenous inhabitants. Chapter 2 reviews the conditions north of the Hondo River (land alienation, taxation, and debt servitude) that triggered the Social War peasant uprising in 1847. It charts developments south of the river once the uprising was underway: the reliance of the rebels on British munitions, the importance to rebel leaders of land (and what they could leverage thereby), the flight southward of thousands of Yucatecan refugees, and the patterns of land monopolization and reliance upon indebted servitude that meant that peasant refugees in the British settlement experienced many of the same pressures as they had done in Yucatán prior to the war.

Chapter 3 discusses the fragmentation of the rebellion and the 1853 Pacífico-Yucatán peace treaty, which promised to the surrendering rebels some tax relief, emancipation of (some) indebted servants, and (apparently) use of lands within what is now northwestern Belize. It traces the deteriorating relations between the Pacíficos and the British as Pacífico leaders made demands for rent from British timber companies, backed by threats of force. It describes the secession from the Chichanhá Pacíficos of the San Pedro Maya and how they were welcomed into the British settlement as laborers and company tenants. Chapter 4 lays out how the Kruso'ob and Pacífico Maya competition over land intensified pressures on British Hondurans for open trade in munitions and for rent, and also led to occasional raids across the Hondo River related to that competition. It charts the processes of land consolidation and the rise of a company of overweening power: the British Honduras Company. The lieutenant governor of the newly formed colony of British Honduras—worried about invasion by both the Pacíficos centered at Chichanhá and the Kruso'ob—was grateful when the leader of the San Pedro Maya, Asunción Ek, proposed that he be given a position within the colonial government as essentially a frontier guardsman, police captain, and private security for the British Honduras Company.

Chapter 5 outlines the territorial anxieties, hyperlocal disputes, blunders, and misunderstandings that resulted in a British military march on San Pedro in 1866. The ethnic hierarchy of northern Yucatán was reproduced in the British settlement, as the most prominent subcontractors for the logging companies were wealthier Yucatecan refugees of Spanish descent who subsequently had positions of authority over Maya people as landlords and bosses; their actions contributed to a deterioration of relations between the Maya and the British. Frustrated by British munitions sales to their Kruso'ob enemies and frustrated by deceit and trickery on the part of the British Honduras Company, the Pacífico generals in southern Campeche (including Luciano Tzuc and Marcos Canul) employed ever more aggressive tactics, including armed raids on logging camps, large-scale theft, and kidnapping hostages for ransom. Precisely when Marcos Canul was rumored to be heading to San Pedro to use that as a base from whence to place forcible demands for rent at a series of British Honduran logging camps, a major dispute broke out at San Pedro between village residents and the company foreman. The foreman threatened to have San Pedro leaders arrested just when a company of West India regimental soldiers arrived to suss out whether the residents planned on conspiring with Canul against the logging companies. Confused, misunderstood, and pressured on several sides, Asunción Ek threw in his lot with Marcos Canul and the Battle of San Pedro ensued.

Chapter 6 overviews the further devolution of Maya-British relations in the colony, as British forces retaliated with a scorched earth campaign of the western villages and a demand for total surrender, including relinquishment of all Maya land claims within the purported limits of the colony. The San Pedro Maya were later allowed to return and rebuild their villages, but their rights were curtailed and official rhetoric turned increasingly racist. Pacífico and Kruso'ob leaders conducted raids into the British settlement to capture deserters and debtors, and to protect the integrity of their supposed border, British officials aided in their deportation, thereby reinforcing a cross-border dynamic of labor exploitation. The so-called "final Indian attack" in the colony took place in 1872 as Marcos Canul led an attack on Orange Walk. Canul was mortally wounded, and although Maya groups would continue to lay claim to the western region of

Belize for decades to come, the San Pedro Maya and Pacíficos never again took up arms against the British. From the colonial period through the nineteenth century, therefore, the region of Belize continued to be a place where Maya people fled to escape military conflict, oppressive taxes, debt burdens, and forced labor, including the military draft. This book is inspired by the people who experienced exploitation and violence—and ran away.

Imperial Rivalry and Maya Resistance in the Peninsula's Southeast

This book moves between local, regional, and international levels, illustrating the mutual impacts of people of Maya, British, Spanish, and African descent as they pursued safety, security, and prosperity while moving through a landscape colored by suspicion, competition, and eruptions of violence. While the second half of the nineteenth century is our focus, in order to understand people's claims to lands and their motivations and strategies, in this chapter, we look back at preceding eras to discern the patterns of movement, production, profit, and competition that molded the parameters within that people eventually navigated. While in the prehispanic period, various Maya groups had inhabited the region of Belize, and successive waves of Europeans invaded the land in pursuit of profits and territorial control. While Belize lacked the rich mineral resources that the Spaniards coveted, its forests possessed timber of immense value in European markets, thereby attracting British buccaneers and loggers. This chapter narrates the development of flight as a form of resistance to European invaders, the Spanish-Anglo imperial competition over territory, and the pursuit of mahogany that led the British to push farther into the forests of the interior. British penetration into lands claimed by Indigenous Maya, and also contested with independent Mexico and Guatemala, set up the conditions of instability and resentment that affected all of the residents within the supposed British limits once the Social War subsequently broke out in 1847.

https://doi.org/10.5876/9781646424634.c001

MOBILITY AND MAYA LEADERSHIP

The national borders dissecting the Yucatán peninsula now in the twenty-first century tend to obscure the longstanding patterns of movement within the region. While some foundational works established the village as the most basic social unit of Maya social life in the Spanish colonial period and the twentieth century,[1] movement across the land has also been critical for Maya survival and well-being throughout the centuries. The ability of Maya peasants to set up new households was long facilitated by practices of self-sufficiency and minimalism. As late as the twentieth century, Maya peasant households had relatively few material possessions, most of which could be fashioned by hand out of local materials. The relative ease with which Maya families could relocate was remarked upon by a British colonial administrator, Thomas Gann, who wrote: "His indispensable belongings consist of a hammock, a few calabashes and pots, a machete, and a cotton suit, all of which he can carry slung over his back in a macapal [net bag]; with his wife and dogs trotting behind him, he can leave his old home and seek pastures new with a light heart and untroubled mind, knowing that the bush will provide for all his needs."[2] Gann exaggerated somewhat, as he overlooked women's work, which entailed many heavy items that are not easily replaced, particularly grinding stones, tortilla griddles, and cooking pots. Moreover, setting up a new household is a significant undertaking, requiring knowledge of local resources and peaceful relations with new neighbors. Nevertheless, Gann's basic point about relative ease of movement linked to self-sufficiency and minimalism is sound.

The most basic element of Maya subsistence from prehispanic times into the twentieth century was milpa agriculture (Maya: *kool*): shifting, multi-cropping cultivation of different fields within a section of forest, which would be cleared using slash-and-burn techniques, followed by long periods of fallow and forest regrowth. Milpa agriculture was supplemented by hunting, fruit-tree cultivation, beekeeping, and fishing. While the Maya at various times adopted more intensive forms of cultivation, milpa provided both subsistence and the advantage of mobility. In fact, movement of residences was not uncommon for Maya peasant families. In milpa agriculture, cultivated fields must be rotated every couple of years, and out from a central parent village, over time, families may establish hamlets closer to their fields. Such hamlets can grow into a more sizable child settlement.[3]

Even prior to the Spanish invasion, Maya people had relocated from the northern part of the peninsula to what is now the northwest quadrant of Belize. The Yucatecan branch of the Mayan language family contains four, closely related languages: Yucatec, Itzá, Lacandon, and Mopan. The dynastic Itzá lineage had been centered at Chichén Itzá in northern Yucatán during the Post-Classic period.

Following political strife among various noble lineages in the fifteenth century (or earlier), the Itzá moved southward, established a center at Nojpeten (what is now Tayasal, on an island in Lake Petén Itzá, Guatemala),[4] and some also settled to the east in the region thereafter termed Ts'ul-winiko'ob (meaning "foreigners"; archaic spelling: Dzuluinicob). Ts'ul-winiko'ob extended roughly as far south as Stann Creek in the east, south and westward to encompass the full length of the New River (formerly, Ts'ulwiniko'ob River), the Belize River as far west as the Guatemalan border, and its political center was at Tipu (now, Negroman, on the Macal River). It also encompassed the Yalbac Hills region, which would later be the residential center of the San Pedro Maya.[5]

The relationship between leadership and territory must be clarified here. In an earlier work, Ralph Roys described the Yucatecan peninsula at

Figure 1.1. Maya woman grinding corn with mano and metate. Source: Frederick A. Ober, *Travels in Mexico and Life among the Mexicans* (San Francisco: J. Dewing, 1884), 125. Credit: Internet Archive.

the time of the Spanish invasion as subdivided into sixteen discrete, territorially based states (*kuchkabal*), each with its ruling lineage.[6] Thereafter, historians and anthropologists generally accepted that premise and merely sought to pinpoint more precisely the boundaries between such provinces. Following a close reading of Maya-language texts from the early colonial period, however, Sergio Quezada clarified that conquest-period Maya power was not based in territory, but rather in people. Patrilineally defined family units would be united under a local chief (*batab*). A *batab* might at times give allegiance to a lord among lords: the *jalach winik* (true man). However, allegiance to a *batab* or a *jalach winik* was not determined by territory, but rather by patron-client relationships that a leader would have to forge and maintain. The Maya word for a political subject, *kuchteel*, according to Quezada, is best translated as "vassal." Bonds of vassalage were not determined by residence and they could be broken. Family units dissatisfied with one *jalach winik* or *batab* could tie themselves to another one (sometimes through migration, but not necessarily so). Single settlements could be and were divided in allegiance to more than one *batab*.[7] Consequently, when we think about the region of Ts'ulwiniko'ob (or any region in the early colonial period), it is important not to assume uniformity or fixity of political allegiance within a geographical region. The personalistic, patron-client type of leadership may have lived on in settlements largely outside of Spanish reach, and this style of leadership would come to the fore again in the mid-nineteenth century.

FLIGHT AS RESISTANCE

By the mid-sixteenth century, another wave of refugees from the northern part of the peninsula had resettled in the Ts'ulwiniko'ob region: Maya people who were fleeing Spanish raids and the harsh conditions of colonialism. The disruptions and burdens of Spanish colonial rule were several. First, in a pattern known as *reducción* or *congregación* (a pattern employed throughout New Spain), natives living in settlements dispersed throughout a region were forcibly relocated to form a compact settlement (Maya: *kaj*; Spanish: *pueblo*) centered around the residence of the *batab* or *jalach winik*. This centralization would enable surveillance of the natives who were newly Christianized to ensure that they did not backslide into "idolatries" (worship of the old gods).[8] Second, native families had to pay a variety of taxes and tributes, in both cash and kind (to the tune of a staggering 72.5 *reales* per year for the average family). Native families were also assigned to *encomiendas*, in which they owed tribute (in cash or goods) and labor to a designated Spanish overlord (*encomendero*). Other civil taxes included the *comunidad* and *jolpatan* taxes. Church taxes included a head tax (*obvención mayor*) and the *doctrina*. Maya peasants also had to pay hefty fees for church services (*obvenciones menores*), including baptisms, confirmations, weddings, and burials. Colonial-period Maya were required to perform labor on public projects, which not infrequently included labor on the personal properties of Spanish townspeople and Catholic clergy.[9] Resisting these colonial burdens, throughout the three centuries of Spanish rule, Maya peasants continued to flee southward into the region that is now Belize.[10]

The northern Maya who resettled in the Belize region put up steady defenses against European depredations. Spanish attempts at settlement and colonization in the region were small-scale and sporadic.[11] Physical geography was perhaps their greatest obstacle. Modern-day Belize is a small country of 22,970 square kilometers. Bordering on the Caribbean Sea, with low average elevation and a hot, tropical climate, a tangle of rivers, streams, lagoons, and mangrove swamps carves out pockets of cohune ridges and thick hardwood forests. The extensive system of waterways is sustained by heavy rainfall and facilitated the transport of woodcutters' logs from the interior to the ports. However, those same physical conditions hinder overland navigation, and Europeans discovered that paths for horses and mules would be quickly overgrown by vegetation and washed out by rains, and wagons would sink in the mud, especially during the rainy season. One road to Bacalar, for example, became known as "Horse Bones" for its notoriously perilous mud traps.[12] Consequently, all the way through the early twentieth century, most long-distance transportation was conducted by water, specifically pitpan canoe. To escape from Spanish raiders, Maya inhabitants could, and did, move their settlements inland, deeper into the forests.

In the sixteenth and seventeenth centuries, therefore, Bacalar (founded 1544), in what is now southeastern Quintana Roo, was the southernmost Spanish settlement in the peninsula. Bacalar supposedly governed the Ts'ulwiniko'ob region, although it remained tiny and otherwise surrounded by Maya people who resisted Spanish systems of forced labor and taxation. The town was nearly obliterated by a Maya revolt in 1638 and successive attacks by pirates in 1642 and 1648, and Spanish attempts to impose *encomienda* obligations to the south of Bacalar were largely unsuccessful.[13]

While a mission (*visita*) church was established at Tipu (the Ts'ulwiniko'ob center) in the sixteenth century (making it the southernmost Spanish mission church in the province of Yucatán), the Franciscans did not maintain a steady presence there. Tipuans resisted *encomienda* requirements, they reinterpreted Christian teachings and symbols (to the clerics' horror), and they revolted against Spanish authority several times in the sixteenth and seventeenth centuries. Not only were Tipu and the Ts'ulwiniko'ob region comprised of refugees and descendants of refugees, therefore, but they also established a cultural stance of resistance to the Spanish. In turn, the southern forests would have served as a beacon of hope for northern Maya seeking autonomy and security.[14]

Throughout the sixteenth and seventeenth centuries, the Maya of the Ts'ulwiniko'ob region engaged in long-distance trade that also would have built a large social network—a sort of social investment that might be leveraged at a later time. Taking advantage of the extensive network of waterways, Ts'ulwiniko'ob Maya could travel from Tipu northward to Bacalar on the eastern coast; from Tipu, they were a short overland route from Lake Petén Itzá (in modern Guatemala). They traded cacao to the Itzá, as it did not grow well in the Petén region, but it was valued as currency. They also collected wild vanilla and grew annatto (a spice and source of red dye), both valuable trade goods. To Maya people in the north, they apparently traded honey, beeswax, and copal (used as an incense) in exchange for axes, machetes, cacao, and salt, which they then traded to the Itzá for cotton clothing.[15] The connections that the Ts'ulwiniko'ob, Itzá, and northern Maya made through this long-distance trade (and probably intermarriage) would have facilitated resettlement of Maya from one location to another across centuries.[16]

The Itzá kingdom at Nojpeten was the last remaining independent Maya kingdom when Spanish forces conquered it in 1697. In 1707, the military commander ordered that the remaining Tipuans be relocated to the new Spanish settlements in the Petén region, where their labor could be overseen and further "idolatries" curtailed. Already by this time, Spaniards and British loggers had been conducting slaving raids on Tipuan settlements.[17]

However, not all the Tipuans were removed to the Petén region, but some appear to have scattered to smaller, hidden settlements deeper in the forests, while others who were removed found their way back. As late as the 1920s, people living around the New River Lagoon identified themselves as descendants of refugees from Nojpeten. "Here in the fastnesses of the bush they lived undisturbed by either Spanish or British, till the middle of the nineteenth century," wrote Gann.[18] Those who fled from Nojpeten tended to do so in very small groups, often of five to twenty people. This rendered them more difficult to find, as they would be hunted down to be returned to the *reducción*, both by Spanish militiamen and by Nojpeten-area Maya leaders who could thereby demonstrate their fealty to the Christian religion. Perhaps because they could not return to areas in which they easily might be discovered, the small settlements these refugees ultimately formed were often multiethnic and polyglot, with speakers of different Yucatecan-family languages.[19] A map provides additional evidence that Tipuans returned to the Belize region from Nojpeten. The map, created in 1775 by Crown geographer Thomas Jefferys, shows a region called "Tipu" extending throughout what is today northwestern Belize and the northeastern Petén region, roughly from the New River Lagoon northward at least as far as Blue Creek (and Río Azul on the Guatemalan side).[20] Consequently, throughout the three centuries prior to the Social War, the northwestern quadrant of Belize was inhabited by Maya people who viewed it as a zone of refuge from and resistance against European colonialism.

THE SPANISH-ANGLO TERRITORIAL COMPETITION AND COMMERCIAL LOGGING

When the Spaniards were attempting to forcibly subdue the last independent Maya kingdom, British woodcutters already had begun harvesting timber in the region of Belize. Their extractive activities fed into the long-standing Anglo-Spanish international geopolitical competition. Understanding why and how the British gained a foothold in the region of Belize, which stretches of land they came to view as British territory, and the precarity of their claims is critical for understanding the subsequent conflicts with Maya people in the mid-nineteenth century.

The rivalry between England and Spain over valuable Caribbean resources had led to the Treaty of Madrid in 1667, in which both countries promised to suppress piracy. Consequently, British fortune seekers turned their efforts to cutting logwood. Or, in the more colorful language of a nineteenth-century journalist: "Earl Sandwich's Treaty of Madrid finally compelled the abandonment of privateering in these waters, and the crews naturally enough turned their cutlasses into machétes, and commenced to lop his Spanish Majesty's forest-trees on shore when they no longer were permitted to cut off with impunity his lieges' heads and limbs on the high seas."[21]

Logwood (*Haematoxylon campechianum*) was valued in Europe as a source of red and purple dyes, and British logwood cutters worked extensively in the Bay of Campeche area and in the northern part of the Yucatecan peninsula in the second half of the seventeenth century, during which time some may have made smaller logging trips along the Belize River.[22] Treaties aside, the early British logwood cutters were in essence still buccaneers, plying their trade surreptitiously on Spanish-claimed territory and shirking the law. They were "a most notorious lawless sett of Miscreants who are artful and cunning and who after having practiced every ill fly from different parts thither to avoid justice where they pursue their licentious conduct with impunity," opined Admiral Parry.[23] These buccaneers and also Miskito raiders (of mixed African and Indigenous descent from the Mosquito Coast) often looted Maya settlements and kidnapped people into slavery—the men sometimes sold to slavers in Jamaica and the women and children forced to work as household slaves and concubines.[24]

Logwood thrives in wet soils and grows wild in thick stands along the coast and inland rivers. Therefore, in the seventeenth and first half of the eighteenth centuries, the Baymen (as they called themselves, after the Bay of Honduras) could and did remain close to the coast and inland rivers to transport the timber, at a distance from the Maya who increasingly concentrated deeper in the forests of the interior. The first permanent British settlement was at the coastal island of St. George's Caye, established in 1716.[25] Enslaved Miskito people and other enslaved Africans and African-descended people (often brought in from Jamaica) were put to work in the British settlement at least by 1724, in logging and as domestic servants.[26] Soon thereafter, in 1729, Bacalar was repopulated, but as a Spanish military outpost and fort from which to launch attacks on the British loggers.[27] The Spanish tried multiple times throughout the eighteenth century to remove the Baymen from the region, and did so successfully five times.[28]

Imperial competition over the region then intensified in the second half of the eighteenth century. The price of logwood had dipped sharply following the Seven Years' War (1756–1763) between Great Britain and Spain. At the same time, the durable mahogany wood, with its red, glossy sheen had become preferred in furniture making and shipbuilding in Britain and its colonies in North America. While Jamaican mahogany was considered of the highest quality, excessive logging had greatly reduced Jamaica's supply, leading British loggers and entrepreneurs to search elsewhere for this valuable commodity. The forests of the Bay of Honduras abounded with the majestic trees (*Swietenia macrophylla*).[29]

At the conclusion of the Seven Years' War, the Treaty of Paris (1763) reasserted Spanish dominion over the Bay of Honduras and required that all British military fortifications had to be demolished. (This will prove highly significant a century later). As a concession, British subjects were granted usufruct rights to extract logwood for export. However, the treaty did not specify the exact limits within which the British would be permitted to work beyond the vaguely worded "the Bay of Honduras."[30] In addition, much to the dismay of the Baymen, the treaty did not permit mahogany extraction. Nevertheless, the crews routinely flouted the treaty and shipped boatloads of mahogany to importers in Britain as a "mahogany gold rush" in the Bay of Honduras ensued.[31]

The Anglo-Spanish rivalry did not end there. In 1779 (during the American Revolution, in which Spain backed France against Britain), Spanish forces destroyed the British settlement at St. George's Caye and all the logging camps. At the end of the war, the Treaty of Versailles (1783) reaffirmed Spanish sovereignty in the Bay of Honduras, and again awarded usufruct logwood logging rights to Britain, this time within the somewhat more precisely defined limits of the region between the Hondo and Belize Rivers.[32] At this point, British loggers and the Miskito and other African people they had enslaved returned to the region and established a settlement at the mouth of the Belize River. The first superintendent of the settlement was assigned in 1784, and he answered to the governor stationed in Jamaica. The town they named Belize (now Belize City) was thereafter the political center of and the largest town within the settlement.[33]

The language of the 1783 treaty was problematic from the start, laying the basis for future conflict. The full description of the territory and the map accompanying the treaty expose a poor understanding of the region's geography, rendering the exact limits difficult to determine from the documents alone. Nevertheless, boundary markers were laid down at key locations, as approved and attested to by the Governor of Yucatán and British officers.[34] Equally problematic from the perspective of the Baymen mahogany cutters, the treaty of 1783 precluded rights to harvest mahogany. Undeterred, however, they continued their illicit work.[35]

Figure 1.2. "A Map of part of Yucatan, or of that part of the Eastern Shore within the Bay of Honduras allotted to Great Britain for the cutting of logwood, in consequence of the Convention signed with Spain on the 14th July, 1786. By a Bay-man," William Faden, 1787, CO 700 British Honduras 12/1. Credit: National Archives (UK).

Pressured by the woodcutters, Britain resumed negotiations with Spain. Three years later, an agreement was reached that would carry immense consequences for the Maya inhabitants of the western Belize region. The resulting 1786 Convention of London reaffirmed the 1783 limits for British timber harvesting and added rights to extract timber in the region between the Belize and Sibun Rivers (to the south). On the map that was created to accompany the 1786 treaty, sometimes referred to as "the Bay-Man Map" (figure 1.2), the darker-shaded region in the black-and-white reproduction (pink in the original) represents the British timber limits as established in the 1783 treaty, which were as follows. The northern boundary followed the Hondo River westward from Chetumal Bay to the eastern edge of Albion Island (near the modern-day settlement of Pucté). From that point, the boundary followed along the southern edge of the island (and slightly past that along a stream), then angled in a southeasterly direction over land, intersecting with the New River around Eight Mile Creek and Backlanding, and then stretched eastward to connect a series of lagoons, and finally angled southeast along Black Creek to its confluence with the Belize River (near the modern-day settlement of May Pen). The southern boundary of the 1783 area then followed the Belize River (then called Old River) to meet the coast at the town of Belize.[36] In 1784, four crosses were erected as boundary markers at each of those points that marked the western boundary. Denoted in the key as "Crosses erected by the Spaniards to fix the Boundaries," they are too tiny to view reproduced here, but are visible in the original. The new timber region apportioned to Great Britain in the 1786 treaty is marked by lighter shading in this reproduction of the map (yellow in the original). In 1787, new markers were erected, presumably again at the locations of those Old Spanish Crosses.[37]

The region that is of central importance in this work—specifically the region inhabited by the San Pedro Maya—lies to the west of the British use-rights region as defined by the 1783 and 1786 treaties (see figure 1.3). The Pacífico people who knew about the earlier Spanish-British treaties would have (rightly) concluded that the British had no treaty-based claim to those lands. Consequently, that region—shaded with stippling dots on the map—comprises the lands that were contested between the Chichanhá/Icaiché Pacíficos and British Honduras throughout the mid-to-late nineteenth century.

In 1798, the Spanish made one final attempt to remove the Baymen from the peninsula. However, at the Battle of St. George's Caye, the Baymen and their enslaved Africans and African-descended soldiers prevailed. The British thereafter heralded this victory as the moment when Britain secured sovereignty over the region by virtue of military conquest. In other words, from the British perspective, the 1783 and 1786 treaties were now moot. The colony's handbook for 1888–1889 declared that the Battle of St. George's Caye "freed the hardy Baymen from Spanish attacks for ever, and on that day [the colony's] limits were then and there determined, no longer resting on treaty boundaries with Spain, nor its existence for the future a mere tolerated occupation for special purposes, but by the right of undoubted conquest."[38] However, the battle did not result in any treaty that would have indicated such a stipulation by Spain. In fact, the Treaty of Amiens (1802) following the War of the Second Coalition committed the British to restoring to Spain all lands that it had occupied during the war, which would have included the Belize region.[39] The Baymen, consequently, remained vulnerable to removal.

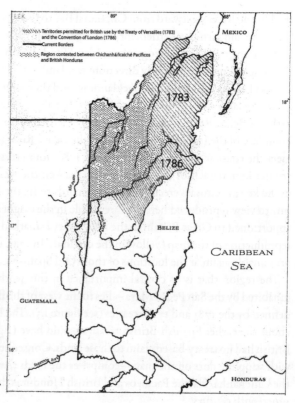

Figure 1.3. Region contested between the Chichanhá/Icaiché Pacíficos and British Honduras, mid-to-late nineteenth century. Credit: Emily Kray.

WOODCUTTERS IN THE WESTERN REGION AND THE QUESTION OF PROPERTY

British thirst for timber propelled the woodcutters farther inland. After the Spanish had ousted the British loggers from Campeche in the early eighteenth century, the loggers increasingly concentrated their work within treaty-defined limits, extracting more timber along the Belize, Hondo, and New Rivers, in what is now central, northern, and western Belize.[40] Within the timber economy of the eighteenth century, enslaved Africans and African-descended people were the primary source of labor, and by 1779, enslaved people composed 86 percent of the enumerated population in the British settlement.[41] In 1779, most of the British and "Creole" (of African or mixed African descent, with the exception of the Garifuna) people clustered in the town of Belize, at the terminus of the Belize River, except for the logging crews as they headed out for a season, leaving their families in town. The region to the west of the timber treaty limits remained largely unknown to the British officials, and they made no attempt to govern it.

The woodcutters, however, plied their trade far beyond treaty limits. Plant biology played a role in this unfolding scenario, as growth patterns of the mahogany tree set parameters for its harvesting. Called "giants of the forests," mahogany trees grow to a towering height of 100–200 feet and several feet in diameter, each tree producing up to four tons of wood. However, the trees are widely dispersed, as they grow either singly or in a small cluster (at an average of one tree per two and half acres). Moreover, the trees are slow-growing, and once harvested, it takes more than thirty years for a replacement tree to mature to a harvestable size. Consequently, mahogany zones are quickly depleted and commercial loggers want to be able to work across large areas of land. In addition, whereas logwood prefers the damp soils along waterways, mahogany grows best in dryer soils. These facts of plant biology led Baymen loggers to increasingly move farther upriver and deeper into the forests. As we shall see, many gangs violated these terms, working on the "wrong side" of the rivers;[42] in many cases, such illicit commercial work sparked diplomatic disputes.

By the early nineteenth century, about three-quarters of British Honduran settlers were living and working outside of the treaty-defined limits. As for the northwestern and western regions, mahogany crews were already working near the New River Lagoon by the 1780s, if not much earlier.[43] Although the Crown did not assert British sovereignty in the Belize region before international audiences, British officials and settlers were already taking action that carried that implication. Specifically, they began to treat land as private property, which assumes territorial sovereignty. Proclamations emerging out of three Public Meetings would come to be known as the "location laws," and they all assumed private ownership of land. A 1765 meeting established a mechanism by which a logwood cutter could claim the territory in which he alone could extract wood; this was referred to as his "work," and was sometimes referred to as his "property." A meeting in 1784 clarified that these works could be transferred by purchase (and in theory land can only be sold and purchased if it is first owned). Then, a meeting in 1787 established the mechanism by which a mahogany work could be acquired, noting again that mahogany works could be purchased, and that the titles and transfers would be publicly recorded. These logwood and mahogany works were called "locations" and were essentially treated as private property, and as such, they implied British sovereignty without stating it outright. However, concerned that the settlers were taking too many liberties, Earl Bathhurst declared in 1817 that in the British settlement no lands should be occupied without the express prior written consent of the superintendent. In other words, the Crown had ultimate control over the land within the settlement, and any titles, sales, and purchases of land required the Crown's approval (through its local representative, the superintendent). Superintendent George Arthur confirmed later that year that any land claims needed to be backed by a superintendent-approved title. All other lands in effect became Crown Lands.[44] This division of the land into either private property or Crown Land would be highly significant for the Maya in the 1860s.

The situation for the British in the Bay of Honduras became decidedly more fraught after the wars for independence in Central America. Would the new republics of Mexico and Guatemala recognize British use rights in the region or perhaps even British sovereignty, or would they move to dislodge the British? Faced with such uncertainty, Great Britain entered into negotiations with Mexico, and the resulting Treaty of Amity, Commerce, and Navigation (1826) reaffirmed British use rights to the same region, stipulating: "The subjects of His Britannic Majesty, shall, on no account or pretext whatsoever, be disturbed or molested in the peaceable possession and exercise of whatever rights, privileges, and immunities they have at any time enjoyed within the limits described and laid down in [the 1786] Convention."[45] However, the 1826 treaty was perfectly silent as to the issue of sovereignty: it neither asserted British sovereignty nor relinquished it to Mexico. Moreover, the boundary between the British settlement and Mexico remained vague and therefore problematic. While the 1783 treaty described the supposed boundary and while boundary markers were laid in 1784, no precise survey had been conducted and the boundary's delineation was disputed.[46] Furthermore, the newly formed Republic of Guatemala did not recognize British claims in the region at all, instead asserting that it had inherited all of Spain's possessions in the region.[47]

Despite these diplomatic predicaments, British officials in the town of Belize in the 1830s saw an opportunity. A global demand for mahogany was booming, stimulated by the expansion of railway systems and the suitability of durable mahogany for railway ties.[48] As Spain no longer had a foothold in Central America, British officials envisioned claiming dominion over the territory its settlers inhabited, asserting political sovereignty and gaining unfettered use of the land. Most worrisome to the British officials, in September 1834, the Commander in Chief of the Troops of Central America announced that the Guatemalan government had granted him the use of lands, the eastern boundary of which would be a line from the Hondo River down to the point at which the Black Creek empties into the Belize River (essentially, the same line as that of the 1783 and 1786 treaties).[49] The officials decided to make a formal declaration of the limits of the British settlement. Accordingly, in November, Superintendent Francis Cockburn and his Council concluded that the British settlers enjoyed "undisturbed possession" of the region bordered by the Hondo River on the north, the Sarstoon River to the south, and on the west, a line heading straight northward and southward from Garbutt's Falls on the Belize River. This was the region that the British began to imagine as British Honduran territory.[50] We know that the British were not the only occupants in the region, but that maintaining that fiction was crucial for British officials. Where the settlers were living mattered, because while Britain could not make a claim to sovereignty based on prior possession based in law (*uti possidetis juris*), it could try to make it based on de facto possession (*uti possidetis de facto*).[51] These were aspirational borders, of course, since no international treaties recognized such sovereignty.[52] For the next sixty years, British Honduran foreign policy would be driven by the desire to secure sovereignty in the region and the physical security and financial prosperity thereby promised.[53] As we shall see, time and again, the uncertainty of British claims in the region created an existential anxiety that shaped British actions toward the Indigenous people and neighbors to the north and west throughout the nineteenth century.

Three years after that council meeting, in 1837, intent as he was upon securing the largest possible territorial claim for Britain, Superintendent Alexander MacDonald set out on a three-day, upstream exploration of the Hondo River and the Blue Creek in a pitpan canoe. He concluded that the Blue Creek was the largest tributary of the Hondo River, and that, therefore, it was the true source, upon which territorial claims might be rested. "The depth of water, the extent of its course, the breadth, all leave no doubt on the subject," he opined.[54] All of the major tributaries of the Hondo River (Blue Creek, Río Bravo, and Booth's River) lay to the west of the Anglo-Spanish treaty-defined limits; consequently, which of the tributaries was the true source of the Hondo would not have mattered if those limits were to be strictly honored. However, Superintendent MacDonald may have reasoned that any future agreement with Mexico about a border would likely begin with the Spanish treaty limits and might expand outward from there. He may have reasoned, therefore, that it would be to British advantage if Blue Creek were established as the Hondo's true source to the west, as that would place the greatest extent of territory within British limits. Thus began the geopolitical obsession with Blue Creek.

Having concluded that the Blue Creek marked the northern limit of the British region, in that same year (1837), Superintendent MacDonald distributed grants to timber companies to work lands denoted as "Crown lands" far to the west and to the south of the prior Anglo-Spanish treaty limits, including in the region that would be claimed by the Pacíficos and San Pedro Maya. These grants extended in the west even as far as Blue Creek. (In some cases, the lands were already being worked by logging crews and the grants merely recognized the locations *ex post facto*.)[55] Particularly relevant is the fact that George Hyde's logging crews were working as far west as the Río Bravo in the late 1830s.[56] In addition, at least as early as the 1830s, mahogany crews were working along Labouring Creek (in the Yalbac Hills region, near San Pedro).[57] The fact that Superintendent MacDonald issued these grants outside of the Anglo-Spanish treaty limits set up the conditions for the clashes of the 1860s and 1870s.

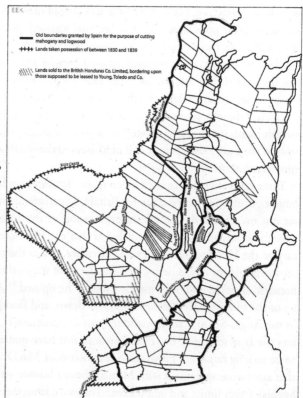

Figure 1.4. Mahogany works and trespasses, with parcels drawn, 1858. A modified transcription of "Plan of Part of the British Settlement of Honduras between Rio Hondo and Sibun drawn by Robert Hume, sworn surveyor, Belize, April 1858, copied by Edward P. Usher, sworn surveyor, Belize, December 1859, with boundaries colored in accordance with other plans," CO 700 British Honduras n° 20. Credit: Emily Kray.

A map illustrating the crux of the conflict was drawn by sworn surveyor Robert Hume in 1858 (see figure 1.4). The map delineates the boundaries of the British settlement as established in the 1786 Convention of London (thick, black line), as well as an area labeled "Lands taken possession of between 1830 and 1839" (outer edge marked with cross-hatching). The entirety of the 1783 and 1786 usufruct regions are divided into private parcels. In addition, emboldened by Superintendent MacDonald's grants, woodcutters had claimed private parcels extending far to the west of the treaty limits, as far north as the Blue Creek, encompassing almost all of what is now western Belize (including the entirety of the Río Bravo and Booth's River regions), and even into what is now northeastern Guatemala. These new lands roughly doubled the size of British use. North of the Sibun River, the only significant chunk of land that was not claimed privately (and was therefore considered Crown land) is a triangle on the western edge, where the towns of San Ignacio, Succotz, and Benque Viejo are now located, but the lands were then rented by

Messrs. Young, Toledo & Co. The map also shows the expansive area claimed in 1858 by the British Honduras Company, which figures largely in this work.[58]

MAYA INHABITANTS OF THE WESTERN REGION

We have seen that what is now northwestern Belize had never been effectively conquered by the Spanish. Even as late as the beginning of the nineteenth century, the Indigenous inhabitants carried out their lives largely free of colonial interference. In an important line that is revisited in chapter 5, a mahogany company agent would later state that: "the English Logwood cutters settled as high as the Bravo although the Indians were the possessors as they never would permit the Spaniards to take possession either before or since the Independence of Mexico."[59] The Indigenous inhabitants maintained a studied distance from European intruders, cultivating "their small plantations, on which they raised corn, beans, tobacco and cotton, hunting the bush for game and wild honey, and the streams and lagoons for fish and fresh-water turtle, never coming in contact with the logwood and mahogany cutters, . . . and retiring ever deeper and deeper into the fastnesses of the forest."[60] They deliberately hid their settlements in thick forest, discoverable only through narrow, nearly overgrown and winding trails.[61]

In the 1830s and 1840s, the Indigenous inhabitants of the western Belize region included speakers of Yucatec Maya, and probably also some Lacandon, Itzá, and Chol Maya speakers.[62] Most of the British descriptions do not provide enough detail to discern the linguistic or cultural identity of the people. Several accounts refer to "wild Indians" (or in Spanish: *indios bravos*), and it is not always clear whether the reference is to a particular cultural group or whether "wild" was a label that the British applied to "Indians" liberally, regardless of cultural identity. In many instances, the British writer clearly used "wild" to essentially mean "subsistence cultivator" (as opposed to wage laborer) or to mean "resident in an autonomous native community" (as opposed to a European town). One linguistic clue to the ethnic diversity is that the village of San Pedro was sometimes referred to in mid-nineteenth century British documents as San Pedro Siris, and "Ceris" was the former name of the village.[63] "Siris" stands out because an *r* sound is not found in the Yucatec nor Itzá Maya languages, but it is in the other two languages in the Yucatecan branch: Lacandon and Mopan (the *r* in those cases representing a flap sound).

Evidence of Lacandon and (Yucatec) Maya occupation is provided, along with the most vivid detail of contemporary Maya life, in a travel account by a First West India Regiment major in 1852. Setting out from the mahogany camp at Qualm Hill (on the Río Bravo) and led by Yucatec-Maya speaking guides from Chichanhá (north of the Hondo), the major's party visited a group identified as *indios bravos*.

The party appears to have traveled between the Río Bravo and Booth's River to the Yalbac Hills region, perhaps as far as Yalbac Creek. Material culture items would suggest the inhabitants were Lacandon Maya—items including poisoned hunting darts, ceramic god pots, a single tunic garment worn by men, bows and arrows, and a large sexagonal house with a conical roof. The *indios bravos* could understand the (Yucatec) Maya spoken to them. The facts that the Maya guides from Chichanhá were familiar with the region and that their language was understood affirms long-standing (Yucatec) Maya use of the region.[64]

OFFICIAL IGNORANCE

British accounts, however, for a long time denied or seriously downplayed the presence of those native inhabitants of the western region. The political advantages of such a narrative are clear. If the British were going to establish sovereignty on the basis of possession (*uti possidetis de facto*), they needed to spin a tale of *terra nullius*—that the land was essentially vacant when they encountered it. Major Sir John Alder Burdon, who served as Governor-General of British Honduras from 1925 to 1932, was up to the task. In the "Historical Note" introduction to his three-volume *Archives of British Honduras*, he penned a line of lasting impact: "There is no record of any indigenous Indian population and no reason to believe that any such existed except far in the interior. There are traces of extensive Maya Indian occupation—temples, wells, foundations, cultivation terraces—all over the Colony, wherever the land is suitable for agriculture. But this occupation was long before British Settlement."[65] This was a fallacious assessment, and is in fact belied by many documents in his own compilation. Nevertheless, his introduction was reprinted in official reports of the colony for decades. It became the standard narrative—the origin myth of British Honduras. This *terra nullius* declaration was repeated by missionary-turned-historian Stephen Caiger, who wrote that the "enterprise of [Great Britain's] subjects rescued a desolate coast from the savage dominion of nature."[66] British assurance in the role of colonizers therefore rested upon both a fallacious history and an ethnocentric self-appraisal as masters of civilization, ready to put the land to good use.

The land was not vacant when the British arrived, and yet the archival sources tell us very little about the Maya inhabitants of the western region between the time that the Tipuans were ordered to be relocated (in 1707) and the mid-nineteenth century. Several reasons account for the paucity of written records. First, the native Maya population throughout the peninsula had suffered catastrophic decline due to a combination of European and Miskito raids, forced relocation, disruption of food production and supply networks, and exposure to Old World diseases (smallpox, measles, influenza, typhus, yellow fever, cholera, and others) to which the natives had no immunity.[67] Once malaria was introduced into the coastal and inland swampy areas, it became endemic, as it continues to be in the twenty-first century. Diseases spread even to places where no Europeans set foot.

Second, as regards Spanish documentary sources, since Spanish colonization efforts had essentially failed in the region south of the Hondo River, Spanish administrators and missionaries concentrated their activities in the northern part of the peninsula. There was essentially a hiatus in Spanish Catholic evangelization efforts in what is now Belize between 1707 and 1851, at which time a Jesuit mission was established.[68] Reflecting what he called "cartographic ethnocentrism," Restall suggested that Spanish maps even marked the region of Belize as "depopulated" (*despoblado*) largely because it was unconquered, not because there were no people there.[69] Reported absences of people in one generation would be taken as fact by the subsequent generation of administrators, who would therefore direct their attention elsewhere. Finally, after 1727, Bacalar's purpose as a military outpost was to remove the British rather than to govern native inhabitants. The Spaniards would have reported little about inhabitants of the region in question because they rarely ventured there.

As to the paucity of British accounts, the Baymen of the eighteenth century kept very few records at all. Their task was resource extraction rather than governance or saving souls. There were no British-sponsored Catholic missions to the Maya until after 1851.[70] In addition, until 1763, the Baymen woodcutters were essentially working illegally on Spanish soil, so they would not have wanted to draw attention to their presence. This would have been particularly the case for those involved in other illegal activities such as slave raiding and looting. As for those who did have violent confrontations with local Maya, they would have handled those situations on their own rather than reporting them to British officials, knowing that, since they were on Spanish-claimed land, any incident that drew in British military forces would subsequently bring down a Spanish attack on their locations. Then, after 1763, the Treaty of Paris permitted British logwood extraction within specified limits, but it also prohibited any British military fortifications, and thus there would have been few British military records of confrontations with the Maya. Again, since the British were focused on logwood, which grows along waterways, they would likely have avoided contact with the Maya, who were, it seems, intent on keeping themselves hidden from European intruders.

CONFLICTS WITH THE TIMBER CREWS

It was not until after 1786, when the first British superintendent was seated in Belize and he had to make regular reports to the governor in Jamaica, that there are more written accounts of British interactions with local Maya; again, though, they remained rare. British loggers were by that time extracting more mahogany, which again, prefers dry soils, grows very slowly, and at very low density, pushing the loggers farther upriver and deeper into the forests, which would have put them into more frequent contact with the Maya inhabitants. By this time, however, relationships between the Maya and the British loggers were decidedly antagonistic. A certain degree of hostility is understandable, given the history of raiding, colonial tax and tribute obligations, enslavement, and other types of forced labor. However, because the relations were already tense, that gave the British few opportunities to learn anything about the Maya.

British woodcutters reported several attacks by "wild Indians" on their logging works between 1788 and 1848.[71] In 1811, in his book-length account, which purported to be a comprehensive description of the British settlement, Captain George Henderson dedicated a mere paragraph to the *Bravos* (the wild ones), stating that they were "numerous" and "wander[ed] over an immense extent of country," but they were "little known" and "the habitations of these people have never been traced." Showing that British-Maya relations were already mutually hostile by then, he said they would emerge from their "recesses in the woods" to loot British Honduran settlements, and if resistance were put up, they would commit "the most sanguinary murders." Several times British forces had been sent in pursuit of the "ferocious" raiders.[72]

The causes of the conflicts between the Indigenous people and the woodcutters may have been several, but the most basic reason was probably the discordance of milpa farming and mahogany extraction as types of land use. Milpa cultivation entails controlled felling and burning of forest vegetation. Yucatecan farmers in the contemporary period, for example, will clear and plant a field, cultivate it for two to three years, then let it lay fallow for a period of about fifteen years, while moving on to clear and plant a new field.[73] From the perspective of woodcutters, the felling and burning of vegetation would have threatened their profits. Some negotiations had taken place, as in 1859, when the British superintendent reported about "other tribes of Indians within our borders . . . who have learnt to respect the mahogany tree in their clearing operations so there is peace between them and our woodsmen."[74]

At the same time, mahogany harvesting threatened Maya survival. Prior to the introduction of mechanized vehicles, once an enormous mahogany tree was felled and cut into logs, the mahogany crews used large teams of cattle to haul the heavy logs to rivers and streams, from whence they would float them down to ports for overseas export. As we shall see, in their extensive hauling and grazing activities, the cattle would at times destroy the Mayas' milpas. Cattle in fact had threatened Maya farming since the earliest days of Spanish colonization, and in northern Yucatán in the eighteenth century, the cause of the majority of Maya-Spanish land disputes was the destruction of milpa crops by cattle. Following in the Iberian ranching tradition, Spaniards' cattle were allowed to roam and forage freely, and milpa crops would have been very tempting for them. In theory, stone fences might have kept them out of the fields. However, since milpa plots are used only temporarily, the labor required to build a stone fence would have been prohibitive.[75] In the Belize region, the threat posed by woodcutters' cattle was substantial. For example, as we will see in chapter 5, at the Qualm Hill camp in 1866, the workers used 175 head of cattle. The resulting clashes between the Maya and the woodcutters were both predictable and disastrous.

Clashes with the woodcutters culminated in an episode in 1837 in which apparently large numbers of Maya were forced to leave the Río Bravo region when George Hyde's crews worked there. Three decades later, in 1865, John Hodge, the agent of the company that subsequently absorbed George Hyde's lands, reported that, in 1837, the Indigenous inhabitants "readily yielded when notice was given by [Superintendent] Col. MacDonald" and "all the Indians left their plantations peaceably."[76] There is considerable doubt that they left willingly. Hodge was not an eyewitness to these events and was not even living in the Belize region at the time. Further, as we shall in chapter 5, Hodge's suggestion that their exodus was peaceable was a self-interested statement (because at the time he was in serious trouble with the lieutenant governor for having created a grave conflict with the Icaiché Maya) and he essentially needed to show that the company was not to blame. The fact that Colonel MacDonald gave them "notice" to leave shows that they left under duress. Moreover, as is now obvious, even if some were forced out of the Río Bravo region, other Maya people continued to live elsewhere in the western region, and some who were forced out may well have returned.[77]

Finally, in March 1848, less than a year after the Social War began, British mahogany workers encountered hostile "Indians" in the New River region. A group attacked mahogany works owned by Messrs. James Hyde & Co. at Hill Bank (on the southern tip of New River Lagoon), firing arrows at workers in the house. The next day, they were spotted at the Hyde & Co. bank on Irish Creek (which extends westward from New River Lagoon).[78] Note that these two locations (Hill Bank and Irish Creek) lay to the west of the British usufruct logging limits as established by treaty, into the region where the native inhabitants had previously enjoyed relative freedom from intrusion. These attacks again show the strained relations between western Belize Maya and the timber companies, all the way up until the time period that is the focus of this work.

Finally, the timing of the forced exodus of people from the Río Bravo region (1837) is significant—it being just a decade prior to the outbreak of the Social War.

If those western region inhabitants had simply moved north of Blue Creek, into the region that is now southern Campeche, those still alive a decade or two later would well remember the land and would even still consider it "home." How they envisioned that land is one of the central questions of this investigation.

As for the British, in the 1830s, when they looked at the Hondo River, they saw promise and opportunity: the possibility of British sovereignty and unfettered use of the land's bountiful resources. They wanted to push back the river to the furthest extent possible to reach out and grasp what was in their view. By 1848, however, they would see the river quite differently, imagining it as a hard barrier to keep out several forms of danger.

To the South of the Uprising

British Munitions, Refuge, and New Landlords (1847–1850)

War is weapons and wounds. It is also footpaths through the forest, the machetes that blaze them, and the rains that wash them out. It is ports, banks along a stream to pull up a canoe, horse tack, saddlebags, medical supplies, ink and paper, and lightweight foods that resist spoiling. It is military leaders, enlisted soldiers, conscripted ones, scouts, flag bearers, drummers, porters, tax collectors, livestock rustlers, spies, deserters, kidnapping victims, prisoners of war, traitors, and common criminals. It is translators, scribes, messengers, encrypted communications, interrogators, witnesses, liars, passport agents, religious advisors, and negotiators. It is marketplaces, merchants, supply lines, blockades, ramparts, and escape routes. It is traps, poison, prison cells, ransom demands, ropes, blindfolds, and chains. It is victory parties, the spoils of war, hasty burials, and scavengers.

War is legion. The things of war come from many places and they go to many places. War sprawls and has little patience for borders. But if it is everywhere, it is also nowhere. It inheres in moments of violence: the raid, the blow of the machete, the siege. It fades when people pull away, retreat, or decline to engage.

While in the first half of the nineteenth century, the Maya inhabitants of the western Belize region largely kept their distance from the British, the parameters of their interactions changed dramatically once the Social War uprising was underway. In this chapter, attention to the material realities of access to food, natural resources, the organization of labor, physical safety, and weaponry clarifies how patterns of flight, amity, and apprehension developed along the Hondo River

https://doi.org/10.5876/9781646424634.c002

during the first three years of the war. We will see how, despite an official British stance of neutrality, British settlers and officials were pulled into the conflict and the Social War was regional in scope almost immediately. British Honduran merchants sold munitions to the rebel fighters, and British timber companies were pressed for rent and timber fees which served as war financing. Although the monopolization of land and reliance on indebted servitude were major factors that had triggered the northern uprising, when thousands of Yucatecans fled into the British-claimed region as refugees, they encountered similar, dispiriting conditions of land and labor. The presence of Spanish-descended Yucatecans on the "British side" of the Hondo River led to attacks back and forth across the river, stimulating British efforts to fortify the region. Understanding the experiences of Maya Yucatecans leading up to the war and the financial designs and evolving political goals of the British south of the Hondo River will help us understand the subsequent alliance of the San Pedro Maya and the British as well as the alliance's critical vulnerabilities.

On the eve of the war, the British still clustered primarily in the town of Belize, and they did not assert administrative control over the Indigenous villages in the interior, nor did they include them in census counts. The 1835 census of the British settlement enumerated 222 Whites, 670 Coloured, 467 Free Black, and 1184 Slaves, for a total of 2,543.[1] By 1845, just prior to the war and following emancipation in the British empire, the (enumerated) population had tripled to 9,809 inhabitants.[2]

PEASANT GRIEVANCES AND UPRISING IN EASTERN YUCATÁN

The Yucatecan Social War was complex in origin and manifestation, but it consisted initially of a series of uprisings of (primarily) Maya people against (primarily) Spanish-descended Yucatecans in what is now eastern Yucatán state. Other scholars have thoroughly documented the uprising and those details are not belabored here. However, we should briefly reflect on the conditions that ignited the rebellion, since those conditions also stimulated flight southward across the Hondo River and affected how Yucatecans (of Maya and Spanish descent) living south of the river would interact with one another and with British landlords and employers. Similar patterns of the monopolization of land, indebted servitude, and forced labor would continue to spark conflict in new locations, time and again. The taxes, debt burdens, exploitative labor conditions, and competition over land that fueled Maya peasant anger in 1847 derived from colonial period arrangements and new arrangements that followed upon Mexico's independence from Spain in 1821.

Taxes and Indebted Labor

We have seen how the array of Spanish government and Catholic church taxes, tributes, fees, and forced labor systems frequently led to long-term, intractable personal and community indebtedness among the Maya throughout the colonial period in Yucatán. Even after the *encomiendas* went into decline and Maya peasants were thereby relieved of the *encomienda* tribute obligation, an annual civil head tax took its place. The burdens were heaviest during times of epidemic disease or plague, when mortality rates increased, yet a village's tax burden remained fixed. We have seen that Maya peasants would sometimes escape heavy debts by fleeing into the Belize region, but in other instances, peasants would go to live on a Spanish-owned cattle ranch (*estancia*), where the tax burdens levied on "Indian" villages did not apply. On the *estancia*, they would live as tenant farmers and be allowed to work their own milpas, but they would typically owe one day of work a week to the owner. That day was often Mondays (*lunes*), and they became known as *luneros*.[3]

In the second half of the eighteenth century, however, more Yucatecans of Spanish descent turned to commercial cultivation, on estates known as *haciendas*, of products for the regional markets (such as corn, cotton, sugar, and rice). Workers for these haciendas also were frequently recruited from among Maya villagers seeking debt relief. The conditions of work, however, were decidedly worse. By the late eighteenth century, hacienda tenants more frequently worked full-time in agriculture. Moreover, *hacendados* (hacienda owners) used deceptive tactics to ensnare laborers, such as giving them advances on wages, which kept them indebted and therefore tied to the estates as servants (*criados*). Some *hacendados* took advantage of the tribute system and paid the tribute of their tenant farmers in advance; this would trap *luneros* in debt and debt servitude.[4] What is more, in 1786, the colonial government required that *hacendados* pay the church tribute owed by their *luneros*. The *hacendados*, unwilling to shoulder this burden exclusively, added it to the workers' debts. This new regulation effectively ensured that all hacienda tenants would become indebted servants, tied to the estates. So widespread had the pattern of indebted workers living on estates (*peones acasillados*) become, that in 1800, more than half of Maya peasants in the northwestern region (around Mérida) were resident workers on haciendas, and even in the less-populated eastern region, roughly 25 percent of peasants were resident hacienda workers.[5]

Indebted servants did not necessarily live on the estate, and an employer in fact profited more if they resided elsewhere. In the 1840s, American traveler John Lloyd Stephens compared the Yucatecan system of servitude, in which they were "in debt to their masters and their bodies mortgaged" favorably to the system of slavery in Louisiana. In the latter, he observed, planters had to make an initial capital investment in the purchase of slaves and thereafter interest on any debt, plus the costs of food, clothing, and shelter. In Yucatán, Stephens noted, there was no initial investment nor maintenance expenses, and the Indians' wages (about a *real* per day) were less than the interest due on the purchase of a slave. Indian servants were subject to flogging by the majordomo, and Stephens lamented the debased state to which they had been reduced. "Originally portioned out as slaves," he wrote, "the Indians remain as servants. Veneration for masters is the first lesson they learn."[6]

Independence from Spain brought little relief to Maya peasants in Yucatán. They continued to shoulder a heavy burden of assorted civil and church taxes and fees. All residents had to pay an annual civil head tax of one peso. All the colonial-period church taxes and fees initially carried over without disruption. In a new manifestation of the colonial-period trick, a landowner would often pay the church taxes (*obvenciones*) of a group of peasants directly to the priest. He would then seek out a local judge who would subsequently require the workers to repay the debt by way of forced labor on the landowner's estate. This tax-debt-labor trap gave flexibility to the landowners; they did not need to rely solely on their tenants, but could be ensured of labor for different projects, as the need arose.[7]

Just as in the colonial period, peasant resistance to the tax burden was immense. "Between 1800 and 1847, taxes generated more invective and spilled more ink than all other peasant grievances combined," according to Terry Rugeley. Peasant hatred of taxes and demands for tax relief increased in the decades just prior to the 1847 uprising. The (short-lived) liberal Spanish Cortes constitution of 1812 reduced colonial powers of taxation and forced labor, and a decree later that year forbade racial difference from being used as the basis for differential treatment under the law. While these reforms were scuttled in the return to monarchy in 1814, nevertheless, those considered Indians in the Spanish colonies held tight to the promise of tax relief. Many Maya peasants simply stopped paying the church *obvenciones*. A series of revolts in the peninsula, including separatist strikes for independence from Mexico, all obliged leaders to promise tax relief if they wanted to recruit peasant fighters (without whom they stood no chance of winning).[8]

Relief from taxes was the clarion call of the day. And yet, throughout the first few decades prior to the 1847 uprising, the system of taxation grew more complicated and oppressive. The myriad military campaigns had to be financed by taxes. In 1834, the church tithes were abolished by the Yucatecan government. However, priests simply made up for the lost revenues by hiking the fees for church services (*obvenciones menores*), such as fees for baptisms, weddings, and burials, and by introducing other fees.[9] In the meantime, the consequences of mounting debt had grown more severe. In 1843 (four years prior to the uprising), a Yucatecan law indicated that it would be illegal for an employer to hire an indebted worker without first paying his debt in full. Local officials were also required to apprehend absconders and return them to the employer to whom they were indebted.[10] The legislative, executive, and judiciary functions of government therefore encoded and enforced the systemic tax-debt-labor trap.

LAND ALIENATION

The process by which Maya communities lost control over lands was set in motion in the colonial period. As mentioned in chapter 1, a key element of Spanish colonial rule was the *reducción* of Maya peasants living in dispersed hamlets into compact villages centered around the residence of the *batab* or *jalach winik*. The *batab* became responsible for the allocation of house and milpa lots. As Quezada discussed, *reducción* triggered the transformation of Maya leadership in the northern part of the peninsula from personalistic (based in patron-client relationships) to territorial.[11] During the colonial period, however, the tribute system contributed to the alienation of land. Assigned the task of collecting and delivering village tribute amounts, a *batab* could generate revenue for the village by renting out village lands.[12] In cases of dire need (such as in times of epidemics, plagues, and crop loss), a *batab* would sell community lands; this would relieve an immediate crisis, but weaken the villagers' long-term welfare and security.[13] In piecemeal fashion, private landowners expanded their estates by buying village lands.[14] With communal lands in many areas greatly reduced, even though Spain's 1812 liberal constitution freed indebted servants, those newly freed who did not have communal lands to return to often ended up simply working on other haciendas.[15]

Subsequently, in the aftermath of Mexican independence, a series of laws enabled the expansion of landed estates and radically reduced the extent of lands available to Maya peasants for milpa cultivation. First, in 1825, Yucatán's state constitution specified that *terrenos baldíos* constituted public property. *Terrenos baldíos* literally means "empty lands," but those labeled as such could simply have been recently cultivated milpa lands that were merely laying fallow to be reused later. However, now labeled as public property, they could be purchased by private owners. Then, in 1833, a law stipulated that *cofradía* lands were *terrenos baldíos* and could be sold to private buyers; *cofradías* were Catholic brotherhoods, and in colonial Maya villages, cultivation of those lands supported fiesta expenses and community charities. With growing global demand for sugar in the 1820s and 1830s, Yucatecan hacienda owners, particularly in the east (around Valladolid and Tihosuco), were eager to expand their estates. The alienation of lands exploded following the revolt for Yucatecan independence from Mexico led by Santiago Imán in 1839. Subsequently, in 1841, a new law stipulated that community land reserves (*ejidos*) could be no larger than one square league in size, and anything beyond that was *terreno baldío* and therefore subject to purchase. Finally, in 1842, the president of the newly independent

Republic of Yucatán, struggling to hold on to power, offered *baldío* lands as rewards to military recruits and as compensation to anyone to whom the republic owed money. As a result, between 1841 and 1847 alone, 460,000 hectares of *terrenos baldíos* moved into private ownership.[16]

Sugar yielded higher profits than any of the other commercial crops or ranches at the time, and more Spanish-descended entrepreneurs relocated to the eastern region to take advantage of the newly expropriated lands. However, the rhythms of work on a sugar estate required far more discipline (faster output, longer hours, and more exertion) than was true for any of the other commercial crops or the cattle estates up to that point. The sugar estates therefore came to resemble plantations with a need for an orderly and strictly disciplined workforce. New "vagrancy" laws ensured that those deemed "not employed" (which could have included milpa farmers during a less busy time of the agricultural cycle) could be pressed by a magistrate into work for an employer. Thereafter, a new steep agricultural tax levied in 1844 had the effect of pushing even more Maya peasants off their lands and into commercial agricultural labor.[17] Given the low wage rates, their debts ballooned and more workers ultimately became tied to an employer.

So common was the pattern of indebted labor in the 1840s that it was used by all manner of Yucatecan employers, not only owners of larger estates. In southern Campeche, John Lloyd Stephens was surprised to find a community of men who appeared to do nothing all day but gamble. He learned the "secret" of their life of leisure:

> Each man had several outstanding loans of four or five dollars made to Indians, or he had sold agua ardiente [*aguardiente*, a potent rum] or some other trifling commodity, which created an indebtedness. This made the Indian a criado, or servant, and mortgaged his labour to the creditor or master, by the use of which, in milpas or tobacco plantations, the latter lived. By small occasional supplies of cocoa or spirit they keep alive the indebtedness; and as they keep the accounts themselves, the poor Indians, in their ignorance and simplicity, are ground to the earth to support lazy and profligate masters.[18]

Another American traveler described the Maya as essentially feudal vassals. "They are always in debt, and are consequently at the mercy of their creditors," wrote B. M. Norman in 1842. "They have not even as much liberty as the most abject vassal of the middle ages . . . [and] they are literally degraded to the position of serfs," he added.[19] Not only were workers trapped in debt service, but so were their children. Children would be held as collateral to ensure the repayment of a parent's debt; if it remained unpaid, the debt passed to the child, and the obligations of debt servitude were passed down through the generations.[20]

ESCLAVITUD

Exploitation on its own will not generate armed rebellion. What makes the difference between an individual worker raising a fist against their employer and a group revolt is coordinated action. And that requires talk—from whispers in the cane fields to notes passed in the market to secret meetings under the cover of darkness. Peasants have to tell one another their stories of exploitation and abuse. They have to share them with siblings, their neighbors, their in-laws, *compadres* (fictive kin related through godparenthood), and children. They have to develop shorthand ways of talking about such abuse.

Maya peasants began to use a Spanish word—*esclavitud* (slavery)—to describe and critique the condition of indebted servitude. At least by the late eighteenth century, Maya hacienda workers were characterizing indebted servitude as *esclavitud.*[21]

A genre of story emerged and coalesced: A tale of the time of slavery. The phrase "epoch of slavery" (*época de esclavitud*) is often used by historians to refer to the presidency of Porfirio Díaz (1876–1911), in which henequen plantations swallowed up Yucatán's northwest and relied overwhelmingly on indebted Maya servants. However, Maya oral histories of an "epoch of slavery" push the epoch back in time and describe the 1847 uprising as a rebellion against those forms of labor exploitation and the loss of freedoms.

These stories refer to and describe an "epoch of slavery" with remarkable similarities. Since these stories have been recounted across a wide region—from as far as the Valladolid region in the north, to southern Quintana Roo, and as far south as western Belize—and since they were recorded over a very long period of time (from as early as 1971 and as recently as 2005), this suggests a discourse that was frequently repeated, passed from one community to another, and passed on from generation to generation. In 1971, a descendant of rebel leader Crescencio Poot living in Felipe Carrillo Puerto recounted to Victoria Reifler Bricker a lengthy account called "The Epoch of Slavery," which began: "The beginning of that war / What you call the caste war. . . . / They were people / Of the epoch of slavery. . . . / People were tired of being slaves. / They never ate, / Nor was there time to bathe, / Nor even to sleep."[22]

On only the third day of Paul Sullivan's 1978 fieldwork research in Tuzik, Quintana Roo (near Chan Santa Cruz)—the timing being an indication of the salience of the concept—someone asked him if he thought the Epoch of Slavery would come again. Residents traced the origins of the Social War to "slavery," by which they meant the forced labor resulting from insuperable debts. "Their descriptions of the workaday life of the slave," Sullivan wrote, "vary little from one telling to the next, always dwelling upon the long hours of work and precious few hours of sleep; days, invariably begun before sunrise . . . tasks that followed . . . whippings administered." They could never work their way out of slavery because the master would charge them for everything they consumed.[23]

Accounts of *esclavitud* employ similar patterns and cadences. During my 1994 fieldwork in Dzitnup (near Valladolid, Yucatán), Lucía Tamay Cocom—unsolicited—recounted stories of *esclavitud*, in which: "You have to buy things, but you don't have money. So you have to take on a debt. You don't have food. Sometimes you don't have clothes, just a *pik* (petticoat). At four in the morning, you are already awake and grinding corn. You have to draw water. Whatever they say, you have to do it. If not, you will get hit." Similarly, in Michael Hesson's fieldwork near Cobá, Quintana Roo, in the 1990s and in Betania, Quintana Roo—in the heart of former Kruso'ob territory—in the 2000s, Maya villagers recounted abuses of the "epoch of slavery."[24]

I was not completely surprised, then, when people who had lived in San Jose Yalbac (in what is now Belize) in the 1930s, recounted stories about how their grandparents and in-laws had fled Yucatán because of the conditions of *esclavitud*. They used similar phrases—like a memorized litany of complaints—recounted in a couplet cadence, so that it became clear that these were stories that had been communicated with purpose—the purpose being that the lesson should not be forgotten.[25] The recounting of these tales across a wide region and spanning decades demonstrates that Maya peasants throughout the peninsula developed a genre of stories about the horrors of *esclavitud* that they communicated to their descendants who then preserved these historical memories throughout their continual recounting. They developed a critical consciousness of exploitation and a discursive mechanism for drumming up collective action.

TO THE SOUTH OF THE UPRISING

The 1847 uprising took place in a string of pueblos in the eastern region south of Valladolid, where the sugar boom had taken hold and where a solid stream of goods was crossing the Hondo River in both directions in trade with the British. The British purchased food and rum from Yucatecans, and guns, gunpowder, and British manufactured goods circulated from Belize to Bacalar, Tihosuco, and beyond.[26] Amid the ongoing centralist-federalist partisan fight, on July 26, 1847, the *batab* of Chichimilá, Manuel Antonio Ay, was assassinated on suspicion of treason. Centralist Antonio Trujeque had already been engaged in a partisan struggle with two other eastern *batabo'ob* (*batab*, plural), Jacinto Pat (of Tihosuco) and Cecilio Chi (of Tepich). Trujeque seized upon apparent evidence of a rebel conspiracy between Ay, Chi, Pat, and Bonifacio Novelo (a mestizo from Valladolid). On July 28, Trujeque's troops marched on Tepich, then Chi, Pat, Novelo, and

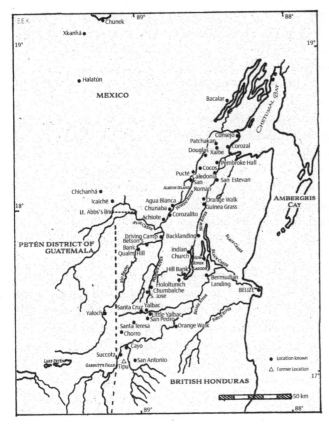

Figure 2.1. The British Honduran region, 1850s–1860s. Credit: Emily Kray.

their recruits retaliated, thus setting off a cycle of conflict. At the time, it was not clear whether this uprising was a continuation of the centralist-federalist conflict or something else entirely. However, almost immediately, Yucatecan officials and officers of Spanish descent began to treat the conflict as a race war, making mass arrests of Maya *alcaldes* (village commissioners) throughout the region, treating all "Indians" as suspect, declaring martial law, and calling up all non-Indian males to military duty. These actions, coordinated around a theory of racial hatred, in fact helped bring about the ethnic conflict they had imagined. Uprisings in villages throughout central and eastern Yucatán took place through the fall and winter.[27]

At this point in the narrative, our vantage point shifts southward to the Hondo River and beyond. Initially, British officials in the town of Belize hardly took notice of the conflict north of the river. By December 1847, however, the war had become a matter of international diplomacy for the British. Cognizant of the steady stream of guns and powder moving northward from Belize to Bacalar and beyond, the

Yucatecan governor urged Superintendent Fancourt to prohibit sales of munitions to the "Indians," and instead to allow the Yucatecan army to purchase them.[28] The next month, warning that Maya rebels were poised to attack the town of Bacalar, the Yucatecan comandante at the fort requested British military aid. Fancourt established a neutral position, however, writing to the Yucatecan governor that he could neither supply munitions to them nor prevent the flow of gunpowder northward. The rebels ultimately captured the town—an important win for them, given the security offered by the fort and the strategic location close to British Honduran arms merchants. As a gesture of goodwill, the superintendent announced that any "Spaniards" who wanted safe refuge from the war could settle in the region of Punta Consejo, south of the river.[29] Those Yucatecan refugees who arrived following the siege at Bacalar—at the time, mostly Spanish-descended Yucatecans, but also some Maya—would become the core of the new town of Corozal.

Throughout the spring of 1848, Bay of Honduras settlers expressed concern that the rebels would cross into the British settlement in pursuit of the Yucatecan refugees living south of the river. Worry was an appropriate reaction, as the British settlement was nearly defenseless. The 1786 treaty with Spain had forbidden the construction of defensive fortifications, the stationing of troops, and stockpiling of military weaponry in the timber-harvesting region.[30] The garrison in Belize housed less than one hundred soldiers, and the closest additional imperial troops were West India regimental soldiers stationed in Jamaica, who could only be deployed by order of the governor (in Jamaica) or his superior.[31] Ten thousand Maya fighters were occupying Bacalar and much of the town had been burnt in the attack. The British Secretary of State for War and the Colonies urged the governor in Jamaica to maintain a strict position of neutrality, but as a precaution, the governor dispatched regimental troops to protect the woodcutters on the Hondo. The position of neutrality became more difficult to sustain, however, as the fighting reached the water's edge.[32]

GESTURES OF AMITY

Less than a year after the war began, the fighting was widely dispersed, with skirmishes throughout western, central, eastern, and southern Yucatán. However, the rebel alliance began to fracture, and one group of rebel fighters sought a peaceful resolution. The peace negotiations that ensued would establish a pattern for Maya-British relations in the decades to come, including expectations about recognition of Maya political autonomy and the regalia of office. In April 1848, one of the main rebel leaders, Jacinto Pat (a *batab* and the owner of a sugar estate in Tihosuco) brokered a peace treaty with representatives of the Yucatecan forces at Tzucacab, and the treaty was signed and ratified by Governor Miguel Barbachano.[33]

The text of the Treaty of Tzucacab reveals the primary concerns of those who had taken up arms: taxes, fees, debts, and access to land. The first three articles simply reaffirmed governmental decrees issued within the prior year: the *contribución personal* (civil head tax) was to remain abolished forevermore; fees for baptisms and weddings would be greatly reduced; and peasants could plant on community lands and *terrenos baldíos* without paying rent. More importantly, Article 3 stated no more community lands would be alienated. Article 7 was perhaps the greatest achievement of the negotiations: "All of the indebted servants would have their debts forgiven" (although newly acquired debts might be repaid with labor). Two other articles bear the imprint of Jacinto Pat's personal ambitions: one reaffirmed that *aguardiente* distillers (which would have included Pat) would not need government permits, and another declared that Pat himself would be the "governor of all of captains of the Indians of the pueblos of Yucatan."[34]

Jacinto Pat was given a flag bearing his title and a silver-headed staff of office. The ink had barely dried on the treaty, though, when another rebel leader, Cecilio Chi, sent fifteen hundred troops to destroy the treaty, along with Pat's flag and staff of office. Pat escaped the fray, but the treaty and its promises were thereby nullified. Fighting resumed, but the rebel alliance had been shaken and Pat remained a target of suspicion by other rebel leaders.[35]

As it turns out, tens of thousands of Maya people shared Jacinto Pat's desire for an end to the fighting. Several times, the Corregidor of the Petén district in Guatemala wrote to Pat, inviting Maya people from Yucatán to resettle safely in his district. As early as 1847, Maya people had been doing so—not as a large wave, but in small groups, sometimes as single families headed by widows. By 1867, an estimated ten thousand had resettled in the Petén.[36]

As for the other Maya rebel leaders, however, they quickly demonstrated an understanding that their success depended upon business transactions with British Hondurans, as well as good diplomatic relations with British officials who would facilitate such trade. Control over land was critical, not only as a place where people could live and work their fields safely, but also because land could be used as leverage to meet other ends. Those giants of the forest—the towering mahogany trees whose durable, resplendent wood fetched a high price on international markets—were quickly identified as a critical resource for war financing. Maya rebels asserted ownership over lands seized in battle and the mahogany thereupon. As seen in the opening passage of this book, in May 1848, the rebel comandante at Bacalar informed the superintendent at Belize that any mahogany extracted from "our Indian lands" that had been seized in battle would need to be paid for, at a cost of two pesos per log. The comandante asked that the superintendent pressure any people who extracted timber from their lands and hauled it southward across the river to render payment.[37] An early example of Maya-British diplomacy, the letter reveals the critical importance of the rebel-British unofficial alliance.

The friendly gestures of the Maya rebels proved to be persuasive. Seeing that the rebel leaders were "anxious to be on friendly terms with us," Superintendent Fancourt assured the governor that they posed no threat to the British.[38] Meanwhile, the economic contributions of the estimated one thousand Yucatecan refugees, clustered around what was to become the town of Corozal, were busily farming corn and beans for local consumption, while the practices of sugarcane production they brought with them—and the rum derived from that—would become prime economic generators in the British settlement.[39] In the friendliest of tones, Comandante General (General, or Commander-in-Chief) Cecilio Chi invited the British to come to the port at the Bay of Ascension and "other towns belonging to the liberating government" to trade freely. Chi's primary objective came into view, however, as he requested from Fancourt a license to purchase gunpowder, which was in fact denied.[40] As long as the rebels aimed to engage the Yucatecan forces in battle, trade with British merchants was the quickest means to an end.

SKIRMISHES ACROSS THE HONDO

Fancourt's favorable view of the rebels was short-lived. Word reached him that "jealousies exist among them" and that the rebel commander at Bacalar (Juan Pablo Cocom) had been assassinated by a rival leader. Despite Fancourt's requests, the British troops were withdrawn. Adding to the heightened state of fear, unidentified groups of "Indians" were spotted crossing the river to steal cattle belonging to Yucatecan settlers, and a Yucatecan sloop of war was spotted off the coast.[41]

The Hondo River became, to borrow Restall's phrasing, not an obstacle but a bridge—an "avenue of human movement."[42] Diverse groups of people would cross the river opportunistically, in both directions, taking advantage of the ability to hide, knowing that complainants might not be able to pursue them freely, find them easily, or exact retribution. However, this opportunistic border hopping sometimes had broader, international consequences, as more powerful groups were pulled into the quarrel. Already in 1848, removing mahogany to the safety of the "other side" of the river (in either direction) was a very common practice; it fomented international disputes, ultimately feeding back into Social War tensions. In one early such incident, in September 1848, a group of "refugee Spaniards" absconded into the British settlement with more than twenty-five hundred mahogany logs from the northern side of the Hondo River. Comandante General Venancio Pec again insisted that those logs belonged to the rebels as the just spoils of war ("in the lands that belong to us as a consequence of possession by victorious troops"), and again requested the superintendent's help in pressing the thieves to submit payment.[43] A British settler, Edward Rhys, had been assigned by rebel leaders as an agent to collect the mahogany fees. Rhys had fought in battle alongside the rebels and already established himself as a go-between in Maya-British relations (and he will later play a key role in relations with the San Pedro Maya). One of the "refugee Spaniards" reportedly took the logs under the order of Young, Toledo & Co., and as we shall see, the company's repeated such actions would create severe consequences for the British in their relationships with the Maya and the Yucatecan government.[44]

The Hondo River became a sort of battleground in the war, as Maya rebels to the north and Yucateco refugees living in the British settlement crossed the river to raid, only to return to the safety of "their" side. Fearing that such raids by Yucatecos living south of the river would invite retaliatory attacks within the British settlement, the superintendent warned that any such raiding would result in deportation.[45] Ignoring the warning, in December, a large group of Yucatecan refugees crossed the Hondo and attacked the rebels at Payo Obispo (now, Chetumal) and also set up a blockade at Chac Creek, resulting in the loss of lives and property and the commission of "many atrocities." The new rebel comandante at Bacalar, José María Tzuc, warned the superintendent not to allow such depredations to continue, for if they should, the rebels would chase the perpetrators back into the British settlement.[46] Increasingly, the British settlers were finding themselves squeezed in a conflict not of their choosing.

THE TRADE IN MUNITIONS AND FAILED PEACE NEGOTIATIONS

This unfettered trade in munitions from the British settlement to the rebels had turned into a serious international problem for the British. Of critical importance was Article XIV of the 1786 Convention of London treaty between Spain and Britain, which indicated that "His *Britannick* Majesty, on His part, will strictly prohibit all His subjects from furnishing Arms, or Warlike Stores, to the *Indians* in general, situated upon the Frontiers of the *Spanish* possessions."[47] Were British officials violating this treaty by allowing British subjects to sell weapons to the Indians? It mattered, clearly, whether that treaty, which had been brokered with Spain, still pertained in the post-independence period.

Fancourt recognized that the munitions trade might backfire on the British, and yet he could do little to stop it. A witness spotted a British vessel carrying three thousand muskets and three hundred arrobas of gunpowder dock at Isla Mujeres in the northeastern corner of the peninsula (obviously intended for rebel buyers).[48] Among those detained in the Yucatecan blockade at Chac Creek were some "Englishmen" traders heading to Bacalar with munitions on board.[49] Townspeople in Campeche commonly believed that the British were encouraging the Maya rebels by trading guns and powder to them. Reportedly, British merchants had even opened a store in Bacalar just to sell munitions to the rebels. Such trade was denounced as being in violation of the 1786 treaty with Spain, and what was worse, these munitions were traded in exchange for goods that had been stolen from Yucatecan citizens in rebel raids.[50] The British were clearly squeezed in this conflict between the Yucatecans and the Maya rebels—any gesture of support for one side was taken as an act of treachery by the other.

Meanwhile, the British Foreign Office was consumed with the legal question about whether the 1786 treaty with Spain pertained now that Mexico had gained independence, and Lennox Conyngham reasoned that it did not, even while recognizing that Mexico might nevertheless expect that it should be honored.[51] After Mexican soldiers, searching boats along the Hondo, discovered that a boat operated by Florencio Vega, a "Spanish" Yucatecan living in the British settlement, was laden with munitions, Mexico issued a formal complaint with the Secretary of State for War and the Colonies.[52] Fancourt acceded to orders from Jamaica and London that he should aim to prevent the sale of munitions to anyone involved in the war, although, as per his orders, he would not explicitly "acknowledge any claim on the part of Mexico founded on the Treaty with Spain of 1786."[53] Curiously, the official compilation of the *Archives of British Honduras* by Governor Burdon in the 1930s does not include the full text of the treaty as signed and ratified in 1786; the reprint includes only up through Article VIII plus the final declaration, thereby omitting the Article XIV prohibition against selling arms to Indians.[54] Did someone want that provision to disappear from official memory?

Complicating matters further, other British settlers had inserted themselves more directly into the Yucatecan conflict. They proposed the creation of an autonomous Indian region—a homeland, in essence. In January 1849, Baptist missionary Reverend John Kingdom and Edward Rhys suggested to Comandante General Jacinto Pat that the lands of Yucatán should be divided, with one part reserved for the Indians in which they could govern themselves, and Pat welcomed that solution. Kingdom, Rhys, and other Brits living in Bacalar offered that the British might mediate in peace negotiations,[55] and Comandante General Cecilio Chi and Comandante Venancio Pec then requested the superintendent's help in negotiating the separation of the peninsula between whites (*blancos*) and Indians (*yndios*).[56]

Undoubtedly hoping to be seen as a trustworthy negotiator, the superintendent assured Mexico's Minister for Foreign Affairs that he was making every effort to prevent the sale of munitions to the rebels.[57] Peace negotiations were imperiled, however, as captured Maya rebels were being sold into indentured servitude in Cuba. When Fancourt inquired if that were true, Yucatecan Colonel Cetina protested that the rebels were essentially just being banished, but remained "free men," each with their own labor contract. The British Consul in Cuba confirmed they were sent as contracted laborers, not slaves,[58] but to Maya peasants, this must have seemed like dishonest hairsplitting. Fancourt promised Jacinto Pat that in his role as mediator, he would push for an end to the practice.[59] The fighting bore on, as Yucatecan forces recaptured Bacalar in May 1849, but immediately thereafter, rebel Comandante José María Tzuc, now based at the southern Yucatecan town of Chichanhá, raised a replenished force of four thousand fighters and launched another siege on Bacalar.[60]

Peace negotiations began to break down in the fall of 1849. Reflecting British concern about the northern border, two new magistrates were assigned (at Santa Helena and Douglas); Fancourt ordered them to search all vessels on the Hondo River for munitions, and he dispatched spies to watch the river. Another British boat, this one belonging to a foreman for Messrs. Vaughan Christie & Co., was discovered transporting a commissioner of Jacinto Pat's, plus gunpowder and lead.[61] Before this smuggling infraction could be resolved, however, Jacinto Pat was denounced by his officers, Venancio Pec and Florentino Chan, for abusing his men with labor drafts, flogging, and levying a head tax to purchase gunpowder; Pat was assassinated by Pec's men.[62] Thereafter, representing the rebels, Pec and Chan advised Fancourt that they did not trust the Yucatecans to honor the peace and that they would accept nothing less than total independence from Yucatán.[63]

The failures of the British to curtail the munitions trade further stymied the peace negotiations, as the British lost all credibility with Mexico. Merchants from the British settlement had continued to transport weapons and gunpowder to the rebels, primarily through the Bay of Ascension, and some overland, through Chichanhá. (Chichanhá by this time had critical strategic importance—as a key thoroughfare for the munitions trade as well as a rebel base.) Two of Austin Cox's ships were seen at the Bay of Ascension, allegedly to purchase salt and turtles, but they in fact carried munitions from New Orleans.[64] The capture of the boat carrying munitions for Jacinto Pat had been interpreted by the Mexican Minister of Foreign Affairs as proof that the British merchants "protect and encourage the atrocious war waged by the indigenous race in Yucatan."[65] British claims to neutrality were essentially meaningless so long as the munitions trade continued.

LORDS OF THE LAND

The assassination of Jacinto Pat by one of his own generals requires further reflection. Recall that Cecilio Chi had previously sent an army to attack Pat's soldiers after Pat's first attempt to declare a truce. Similarly, Juan Pablo Cocom (comandante at

Bacalar) had been killed by a rival rebel leader. Assassinations of Maya rebel leaders by political rivals turned out to be extraordinarily common. As regards the Kruso'ob Maya in particular (the subgroup that will emerge in 1850), Gabbert noted that throughout the war, those leaders were more likely to be assassinated by rival leaders than to die by any other cause, including death at the hands of the enemy. Gabbert situated these assassinations within the context of a Kruso'ob cultural style of leadership. He described it as a "personalistic" style, in which leadership is not guaranteed by any institutionalized laws or norms, but it is instead secured by the personal characteristics of the individual—essentially, how well they are able to convince others to follow them. This kind of patron-client leadership is particularly brittle, because it depends upon the leader's ability to meet the people's expectations; failing that, a rival leader may emerge from within the group and force the first one out.[66] A British magistrate who visited the new rebel comandante at Bacalar in 1848 sensed the vulnerability of the Maya leadership structure to challenges from below, noting that "the authority of the Chiefs is not always respected, in fact the Indians appear to be runaway schoolboys who try to do the most of their momentary liberty."[67]

We will see this kind of personalistic leadership among the Pacíficos, as well. The relationships between leaders and followers were brittle, and even though the frequency of assassinations of rival leaders was lower among the Pacíficos than among the Kruso'ob, nevertheless, leaders who failed to meet their followers' expectations were readily usurped and pushed aside. We have seen (in chapter 1) how a personalistic style of leadership was characteristic of Maya leaders in the Post-Classic period and was replaced by leadership based in territory as a consequence of Spanish colonial policies (including *reducción* around the *batab*'s residence and allocating fixed territory to communities under a *batab*'s leadership). It may be that a personalistic (patron-client) style of leadership lived on within regions less fully under Spanish control, such as in the southern half of the peninsula.

What we see emerging in the mid-nineteenth century, however, is a hybrid form of leadership. Maya leadership in the context of the Social War was personalistic in that it depended upon patron-client relations. It was also territorial in that—in the context of intense competition over land, processes of land alienation, and the need for war financing—a leader needed to have access to land to offer that to his followers. In a sort of feudal mode, these followers would be tenants who could then be depended upon for material contributions and military service. Venancio Pec, Marcos Canul, and Rafael Chan in fact called their followers "vassals" (*vasallos*).[68] Maya leaders in the mid-nineteenth century in essence needed to become lords of the land.

The fragility of personalistic leadership predictably generates those whom some would call "deserters." People could become disaffected with a leader for any number of reasons, including failure to provide protection, failure to secure resources for the group, or demonstrations of weakness before foes. Breaking away from the group to follow new leadership or to strike out in search of new terrain would be read by the abandoned leader as desertion. Since the power of a personalistic leader is completely dependent upon the number of followers, personalistic leaders might take steps to bring those deserters into the fold once again, through promises of rewards, or simply through armed force, as we shall see.

LANDED ESTATES, LAND TENURE, AND INDEBTED LABOR

A period of quiet descended upon the British settlement in 1850, as skirmishes along the Hondo dwindled. By then, about five thousand Yucatecans (of Maya and Spanish descent) had resettled in Punta Consejo, Sarteneja, and other villages in the region of Corozal, and the corn they grew was welcomed in the markets in Belize.[69] Some wealthier Yucatecans of Spanish descent were able to invest in small, landed estates and merchant businesses. Sugarcane and rum production were taking off, to such an extent that the British no longer needed to import rum to satisfy local demand.[70]

However, sugar production might have been the most labor-intensive of all the European colonial ventures. Cultivating the cane in the field is just the first step. The cane stalks are susceptible to rot (especially in the tropical climates in which it grows), and so the cane needs to be processed in the mill soon after it is harvested. Consequently, in the colonies, each sugar estate had its own processing center. First, the cane had to be crushed in a press to squeeze out the juice, and an enormous amount of force needed to be applied to push the mill wheel to crush the canes. While the first presses used in the Americas were human-powered (with teams of men pushing at a time), at this time in the Belize region teams of oxen were used. In this age prior to refrigeration and before the first steam-powered mills were introduced, the press had to be operated constantly, day and night. Then, once the juice was extracted, it would be boiled and condensed. The boiling houses would be steaming hot and entire crews were needed just to keep the fires going below the cauldrons. The products from the boiling house were crystallized sugar and molasses, the latter of which would be distilled into rum. All told, to process all the cane stalks before they rotted, during the harvest months, crews of laborers would be required to work in shifts around the clock.[71]

Where did the labor come from for these estates? Given that labor exploitation in large part provoked the Social War uprising, it is not surprising that the new settlers of Maya descent generally were not eager to become laborers once again. If enough land were available to them, Maya peasants could support their families through

subsistence techniques, including growing a variety of crops in their milpas, supplemented with hunting, fishing, some foraging, and raising smaller domesticated
animals such as chickens, turkeys, and pigs. They could fashion most of their material items from forest materials. In addition, they generally could purchase many of
the consumer items they wanted (such as cotton cloth and thread, metal tools and
utensils, medicines, and gold jewelry) through selling or bartering a surplus of their
subsistence products.[72] From a British perspective, this self-sufficiency was simple
laziness, as in the estimation of Robert Downer, Magistrate at Orange Walk:

> The aversion of the Indian to bind himself to a written contract is doubtless attrib-
> utable to natural laziness of disposition, and the great ease with which he can get
> a living, without, as he imagines, making a sacrifice of his liberty. . . . These people
> with few exceptions have their milpas, where they grow sufficient corn for their own
> consumption, and very little more for ordinary sale, or perhaps just enough to enable
> them from time to time, with the aid of the poultry yards, which all have to realize
> a little money. . . . Truly their love of independence and ease far surpasses anything
> I have ever witnessed in any other people. Those that seek for employment, or are
> prevailed upon to undertake it, are perhaps barely equal, numerically, to those that
> remain at home and squat in their houses, or lounge in their hammocks, the whole
> live long day.[73]

Would-be employers, therefore, needed to somehow entice the Maya to become
laborers. "Indian" workers were preferred over Creoles and "Caribs" (Garifuna),
according to a northern district magistrate, because they would work for lower
wages, complete their tasks well, they were "tractable and obedient," and "they will
attend [work] for weeks together, during the night, at the mill without murmur-
ing."[74] Their willingness to work in teams through the night would have been especially valued by sugarcane planters. Even if the new arrivals in the British settlement
wanted to sustain their families through cultivating their own milpas and had access
to land on which to do so, they still would have needed a way to feed themselves in
the interim until they could harvest their own crops. For those newly arrived settlers, therefore, work on landed estates would have been the easiest way to earn cash
or rations to feed their families. By both importing the knowledge of sugarcane
production and supplying thousands of people desperate for wages, the Social War
kickstarted the British Honduran sugar and rum industries.

Just as in Yucatán, however, the creation of debt was the primary means through
which employers in the British settlement secured a cheap and reliable workforce.
Debt was created in one of several ways. First, British laws regarding land tenure
worked to this effect, reaffirming Bolland's conclusion that, "in the British West
Indies . . . the control of each aspect [land and labor] was a means of further control

of the other." We have seen how, in the 1760s and 1770s, the so-called "Principal Inhabitants" among the British settlers in the Bay of Honduras passed location laws, in which they laid claim to tracts of land for timber extraction. Even though they could not legally own land within the context of presumed Spanish sovereignty, and locations extended rights of use only (not outright ownership), nonetheless, they treated these locations as private property. Consequently, within one year, four-fifths of the lands delimited by the 1786 treaty were claimed as "locations" by just twelve men.[75]

This monopolization of land in effect created a pool of tenant-workers. After the emancipation of the enslaved people in the British empire went into effect in 1834 and a four-year transition period of "apprenticeship" of newly freed people ended in 1838, the logging employers were deeply concerned with how they would recruit laborers. Control over the land was critical, for if the freed Creoles could not maintain a living as small farmers, they would be obliged to continue working on the logging crews. We have seen how, in 1817, the superintendent asserted Crown control over all the lands in the settlement, declaring that all location tickets need to be reviewed and approved by the superintendent, and that any lands not claimed as locations consisted of Crown Lands. (Since the northern half of the Belize region had already been almost completely claimed as timber locations, this meant that the remaining Crown Lands were concentrated mainly between the Belize and Sarstoon Rivers.) At the same time, the superintendent indicated that Crown Lands could be distributed by a Crown representative as usufruct "grants," and we have seen how Superintendent MacDonald extended large grants to timber companies in the western region in 1837. In 1838, coinciding with the end of the apprenticeship system, the superintendent indicated that Crown Lands would only be made available by sale, at a steep price of £1 per acre. This measure was designed explicitly to prevent freedmen from becoming subsistence cultivators, in effect steering them toward continuing to work as woodcutters, only now as wage laborers.[76] It worked: In 1855, Superintendent Stevenson confirmed that no Crown Land grants "for money have ever been made." Moreover, he noted that since 1818, lands initially apportioned as locations or grants had been treated essentially as private property by proprietors and the courts: "sold, mortgaged, settled, divided, and allowed to descend."[77]

Moreover, a mahogany boom between 1835–1847 depleted mahogany resources closer to the ports, driving woodcutters even farther up rivers and into the western region.[78] As figure 1.4 (in chapter 1) shows, almost the entire northern half of what is now Belize was, by the late 1830s, claimed by timber companies and other private estates. Consequently, Yucatecan refugees, whether of Spanish or Maya descent, would have encountered a dearth of unclaimed land upon which to erect houses or cultivate fields.

In fact, in 1848—coinciding with the first wave of Yucatecan refugees during the war—a single estate (Goshen Estate) encompassed 30,720 acres (48 square miles), including the entire Four Mile Lagoon (with its strategic location for transporting lumber to the seaport). It also included the 70 acres upon which the town of Corozal would be built and from which a new magistrate would govern, plus several other villages which gained their own names, such as Xaibe, Pembroke Hall, and Chulim.[79] Settlers owed the estate owner and manager $5 per year to lease a house lot, plus $8 to $9 per year to lease a 100-*mecate* lot of milpa land.[80] To pay their rent (and make any other purchases), tenants would have needed to either sell a surplus of their produce or perform some wage work. In addition, the size of the milpa lot, 100 *mecates*, bore significant implications. A *mecate* is a 20x20 meter square unit of land measurement (400 square meters). A Maya farmer typically plants 50 *mecates* for the family's subsistence, and another 50 *mecates* (for a total of 100 *mecates*) if he wants a surplus to sell (or has an especially large family).[81] A 100-*mecate* lot on the Goshen Estate, therefore, would have sustained a family for a two-year period, after which time the soil fertility would have been depleted. A family would then have needed to lease another plot, move to another location, or make heavy investments of time and capital in the form of soil amendments. The pressure to supplement milpa cultivation with wage work would have been strong.

Some landlords south of the Hondo River, especially wealthier Yucatecos, might have used the *lunero* type of arrangement common in Yucatán, in which tenants could tend their own milpas, in exchange for working one day per week for the landowner. Other landlords established sharecropping arrangements with their tenants. Such was the case at the Goshen Estate (now frequently and simply called Corozal), which was purchased in 1859 by a merchant from Liverpool, John Carmichael Sr. (who will play an outsize role in later events). To maximize the production of sugarcane and rum, Carmichael allowed tenants to plant their own milpas, provided that they also planted so much in sugarcane, which they would sell to their landlord at a fixed rate.[82]

Other agricultural laborers worked in exchange for a monthly wage. Workers were typically paid half in cash and half in goods. In one account, "Indian" laborers were given $8 per month plus rations of 12 quarts of corn, while in another, they would be given $11 per month or else $4 per month plus rations.[83] Even those who worked for wages would be given a little time off to work their own milpas.[84] By 1862, roughly two thousand agricultural laborers (Yucatecans, of Spanish and Maya descent) were working in the region of Corozal and Consejo alone.[85]

The advance system and the "truck" (company store) system were two other mechanisms typically used by employers on the agricultural estates in the northern districts that leveraged debt to ensure a reliable workforce from the late 1840s

onward. The advance and truck systems had historical precedents. Prior to emancipation in the British empire, a system of contract labor had been utilized by timber
employers to hire free Creoles, and following emancipation, this system absorbed
those newly freed, as well.[86] Workers of various ethnic backgrounds were subsequently hired under similar arrangements. Several descriptions of these conditions of work show remarkable continuity over time. Timber crew members were
employed with contracts of six to twelve months, and any who failed to complete
the terms of their contract would be subject to criminal punishment.[87] Advances
of wages were given, in part so that the men could leave some provisions with their
families while they went off to work in the forests. These advances on wages were
distributed right before the Christmas season, during which much would be spent
on festivities and alcohol. Consequently, the worker would begin the year in debt
to the employer, obligated to continue working at least until the debt was cleared.
The goods provided as part of the wages would be valued far above the typical retail
price.[88] On the agricultural estates, the "Indians" avoided signing written contracts.
Nevertheless, advances had to be given, according to one magistrate, because otherwise, the Indians were reluctant to work for wages.[89]

In addition, in the truck system, the employer would sell other items to the
worker, also at marked-up prices, further contributing to the workers' indebtedness.
(It was called the truck system because, as it was employed in the logging industry,
the goods would be transported to the camps and stored in the foreman's cart.)
The debt accumulated over time and rarely were debts paid in full.[90] The Northern
District Magistrate affirmed that the Indian workers, called *mozos* (servants), were
"without exception, always in debt to their Employers."[91] As Samuel Cockburn
(Magistrate at Belize) described these systems in the 1860s:

> At the Christmas season the laborer engages his services for the next ten or twelve
> months, and obtains three or four months' advance of wages, half in cash and half in
> goods. The goods are charged at rates enormously above the market price.... These
> he hands over to his mistress, and with the money he resorts to the liquor shop, and
> next morning he rises and finds himself penniless! ... The Indian finds himself ...
> bound to his ... master. Work, work, work is the order of the day, but the debt accu-
> mulates and there is no release.[92]

Just as in Yucatán, the indebted "servant" could be transferred from one employer
to another if the second one paid the debt on the servant's *papelito* (lit. "little
paper"; sum of accounts). However, if the estate were sold, indebted servants would
be transferred as part of the estate to the new owner.[93]

Alcohol played an insidious role in securing workers for estates. According to
a Northern District magistrate, half of the goods provided to laborers would be

"ardent spirits."[94] Alcohol as part of compensation for labor was common in the nineteenth century throughout the region. When the logging companies had relied on the labor of enslaved people, the workers' rations included one gill (five ounces) of rum per day, plus salt pork, flour, sugar, and tobacco.[95] In one example from Yucatán in 1822, workers who built a road (for transporting sugarcane) would earn "a daily bottle of *aguardiente* and a ration of corn and, upon completion, a 'barrel of the same liquor.'"[96] From the perspective of an estate owner, if the alcohol were produced on the estate itself, that would keep labor costs down. In addition, any resulting alcohol dependency would provide an incentive for the worker to remain on the job. Estate proprietors in fact often applied for licenses to manufacture and sell alcoholic beverages, according to one magistrate, "from a desire to increase their gains . . . [from their Indian employees who are] of a race much addicted to drinking."[97]

Just as debt stimulated flight in colonial-period and nineteenth-century Yucatán, so it did in the mid-nineteenth century south of the Hondo River. On the one hand, debt tied the laborer to the estate, but once the debt became unsustainable, workers would often run away, in search of another employer who might purchase their debt or in search of land for subsistence cultivation, even though escapees would be hunted down and punished.[98] The flight of indebted workers was very common in the northern British districts and was a frequent complaint of employers. In one episode, José Remigio Pérez, a worker from John Carmichael's estate in Corozal, had fled to San Pedro, where he was working on a British Honduras Company (BHC) crew. Carmichael (his "master") and a Mr. Sims came in pursuit of him. The BHC foreman asked Carmichael what Pérez owed him, to see if he might pay the debt and thereby retain his new worker. The debt being $32, the foreman could not pay, so Carmichael and Sims tied Pérez up and carried him back to the estate in Corozal.[99] As we shall see, debt evasion also had profound political consequences at this time.

A TALKING CROSS

In early 1850, as the northern district was settling into rhythms of commercial farming and milpa cultivation, it seemed as if the Maya rebellion to the north might be reaching a close. In January, the British Minister in Mexico wrote to Superintendent Fancourt that the Mexican government was pleased with his attempts to mediate the peace with the Maya rebels, and that they were prepared to offer them control of certain lands in perpetuity. By April, however, the rebellion's strength was waning, as large numbers of rebel fighters were deserting. Perhaps because of the weakened rebellion, the Mexican government dragged its feet in the negotiations. Fancourt rightfully worried that such stalling would destroy the rebels' faith in the sincerity of Mexican negotiators.[100]

Sure enough, Mexico's foot dragging in the peace negotiations backfired. The hiatus in fighting allowed for the emergence of a new religious sect that fused Christianity and militarism, and this religion ultimately injected new vigor into the rebellion. Sometime between May and October of 1850, one of the rebel leaders, José María Barrera, set up headquarters at a location that became known as Chan Santa Cruz (Little Holy Cross) in what is now the town of Felipe Carrillo Puerto in Quintana Roo. It was named for a cross found carved on a mahogany tree at the entrance to a *cenote* (a cavern leading to an underground river). Chan Santa Cruz (often simply called Santa Cruz) became both the rebel headquarters and the center for religious observances for the icon that became known as the Talking Cross. The Cross would issue communiqués to the rebel followers through an interpreter called Manuel Nauat. On March 23, 1851, Yucatecan soldiers entered Chan Santa Cruz, killed Nauat, and confiscated the Cross. However, a new Cross took its place later that year, and it communicated in writing through a person who signed the letters Juan de la Cruz (John of the Cross).[101] Later on, during nighttime services in the chapel, the Cross would issue a whistling sound, the meaning of which was interpreted by a trio of religious-military leaders stationed at Chan Santa Cruz. The communications were interpreted as the word of God, and most of the Cross's commands were military orders.[102] The followers of the Cross referred to themselves as Kruso'ob (the Crosses) or Krusilo'ob (the people of the Cross). While the vast majority of the Kruso'ob could be identified as ethnically Maya, others who would have been considered mestizo or Black also joined in the rebellion.[103]

Peering northward, officials in Belize in 1850 might have thought that the rebellion was dying down and they need not worry about being drawn into the conflict. With large numbers of rebels deserting and others suing for peace with the help of British mediators, they might have felt relatively safe. One thing they did not anticipate, however, was how people who had taken up arms against land alienation and debt servitude might feel upon encountering those same conditions in the place in which they expected to find refuge. They also did not foresee how peace treaties among two groups of Yucatecans would ignite a new conflict and pull the British directly into the center of it.

The Pacíficos del Sur and Battling Land Claims (1851–1857)

In 1851, British land claims around the Bay of Honduras remained tenuous, and the events of the next several years would only heighten British anxieties about their political position and commercial activities in the region. British officials would help negotiate a treaty of peace between the Yucatecan government and about half of the Maya rebels, and this treaty would strengthen Pacífico Maya claims to the northwest quadrant of what is now Belize. At the same time, administrators in Belize aimed to form an official colony of British Honduras and facilitate the extraction of mahogany from those lands. By 1857, a political rift at Chichanhá led to a large-scale movement of Pacífico Maya people into the western region of Belize, onto lands then claimed by a precursor to the British Honduras Company. The British superintendent aimed to incorporate these Pacífico migrants as mahogany laborers on lands they had good reason to consider their own, setting up the conditions for territorial conflicts with profound consequences across the region—for the Maya, the British, and Mexico, alike.

PLANS FOR A COLONY AND THE PROBLEM OF TRESPASSES

Within the first few years of the Social War, British officials and settlers in the Bay of Honduras had grown sufficiently concerned about their security to try to renegotiate their political standing by gaining recognition from other sovereign states. Britain first initiated negotiations with the United States. In April 1850, the

https://doi.org/10.5876/9781646424634.c003

resulting Clayton-Bulwer Treaty stipulated that neither party should "exercise any dominion [over] any part of Central America" (although the United States later stipulated that the treaty did not apply to "British Honduras").[1] The reference to "British Honduras" lent an official cast to a term that already had been used colloquially. British merchants and representatives of mahogany companies sent a petition to the governor urging that the question of British sovereignty in the region be settled with Spain once and for all and that the settlement become a formal British colony. The British government affirmed this goal, and in January 1851 at a Public Meeting in Belize, a committee was constituted to design a colony.[2]

However, any formalization of British governance in the region would shine a spotlight on illicit British logging. Again, no other countries recognized British sovereignty in Central America, nor were borders defined that would separate the aspirational colony of British Honduras from its Mexican and Guatemalan neighbors. There were the British timber harvesting limits as defined by earlier treaties with Spain, but the relevance of those treaty-defined limits in the post-independence period was uncertain. Mexico and Guatemala might insist that the British usufruct stipulations of the prior treaties should continue to be honored. As we have seen, British mahogany companies routinely extracted timber in lands outside of the treaty-defined limits, a pattern that predated the 1830s and that was reinforced by the Crown licenses granted by Superintendent MacDonald beginning in 1837. By the end of 1851, British officials wanted to engage in formal treaty negotiations with Mexico and Guatemala in order to expand the limits of the aspirational British settlement and establish legal claim to the resource-rich lands to the west and the south, in areas in which the logging companies had already been working. Again, they wanted to claim as far west as Garbutt's Falls on the Belize River, as far north as the Hondo River (with Blue Creek designated as its true source), and as far south as the Sarstoon River.

Recognizing the diplomatic sensitivity of the situation, in confidential communications, the new superintendent, P. E. Wodehouse, urged the governor that any border negotiations with Mexico and Guatemala should not reference earlier treaties because "our undeniable encroachments in some quarters, and probable encroachments in others" would expose treaty violations. New treaties, he said, should be based "upon the principles of possession and mutual convenience alone," that is, by customary use.[3] However, border agreements would necessitate careful surveying and marking of the borders. The lands through which those borders presumably would stretch were not well-known to British officials. Moreover, they would extend through lands inhabited by the Maya. As we shall see, these "undeniable encroachments" of British mahogany companies would only exacerbate tensions with Yucatecans and Maya groups over time.

THE PACÍFICOS DEL SUR

Meanwhile, in southwestern Yucatán, passion for the rebellion had waned. At the same time as the Kruso'ob rebels in the east were settling into a divinely inspired rebellion, in August 1851, Modesto Méndez, the Corregidor of Petén, and Juan de la Cruz Hoil, a Guatemalan priest, traveled north to Chichanhá to serve as mediators and help the rebels who were based there issue a declaration of peace. In this declaration, those at Chichanhá indicated their intention to surrender to Governor Miguel Barbachano in exchange for amnesty. The Maya centered at Chichanhá were subsequently considered the core group of Pacíficos del Sur (peaceful ones of the south) or the *sublevados pacíficos* (pacified rebels). Almost immediately, rebel leaders elsewhere asked Méndez for help in negotiating the peace, including José María Cocom in the Chenes region. Similarly, the following month, after a skirmish at the Bacalar garrison, when the rebels were driven out of the area, José María Tzuc (once again at Chichanhá) reached out to Méndez for help in negotiating a peace settlement. However, none of these declarations of peace resulted in formal treaties.[4]

Nevertheless, the mere declarations of peace triggered violent retribution. Angered by Chichanhá capitulation to the Yucatecan government, in September or October 1851, a force of four hundred Kruso'ob rebels seized Chichanhá, burned the town, and captured its leaders.[5] Two months later, on December 26, 1851, two Kruso'ob leaders led a second attack on Chichanhá, the stated reason being that the Chichanhá people, under the leadership of José María Tzuc, would not follow the commands of the Talking Cross. "The streets of Chichanhá ran with blood and corpses," it was said.[6] Several months later, in April 1852, Yucatecan forces attacked and reclaimed Chichanhá in favor of the Pacíficos, but by that time, much of the town had been destroyed by the Kruso'ob.[7]

It is worth considering why the Kruso'ob were so enraged by the Pacíficos that they attacked Chichanhá twice within a period of months. Why not, one wonders, just let go those who were no longer inclined to keep up the fight? A clue lies in the logic of personalistic leadership. Again, if the power of a leader derives from the number of followers, then desertion translates not only into a reduced fighting force, but also strikes a blow at the leader's reputation. The Pacíficos, by proposing a truce, additionally implied that Kruso'ob leaders were not worthy of their position. To save face with their remaining followers (and perhaps to send up a warning to any other potential defectors), Kruso'ob leaders needed to pursue and punish the deserters. Regardless, these attacks on Chichanhá created an irreparable rift between the two Maya groups. While the Chichanhá-region Maya had established peace with the Yucatecan government, they had gained a new set of enemies.

In 1853, the toll of the devastation was clear. The Yucatecan census enumerated 360,000 people, about 150,000 fewer than at the beginning of the rebellion. How many died, how many had fled to small, uncounted settlements, and how many had fled into what are now Belize and Guatemala, we will never know with certainty.[8] It is not surprising that many people throughout southern Yucatán would have tired of the death and destruction.

With the town of Chichanhá having been reclaimed for the Pacíficos, the Yucatecan comandante at Bacalar contacted José María Tzuc at Chichanhá with another proposal for peace. Once again, the British became involved in peace negotiations, as Tzuc asked Superintendent Wodehouse to mediate.[9] Tzuc and Andrés Zima (of Chancacab) met with representatives of the Yucatecan government in Belize in September, and the two Maya leaders had been appointed to represent many towns of the south and some from central Yucatán, including Kancabchen, Tixcacalcupul, Mesapich, Tipikal, Yakaldzul, Chikindzonot, Lochhá, Oxkutzcab, Macanche, Rancho Teul, Chichimilá, and Polyuc (see figure 0.1). Looked at another way, the Pacífico region was extensive, encompassing roughly half of what are now the states of Campeche and Yucatán.

The resulting 1853 Pacífico-Yucatán treaty stipulated that the towns would submit to the Yucatecan government, would provide four hundred troops to fight the remaining rebels, and would surrender their military muskets at the conclusion of the war. In return, they would receive amnesty and be permitted to return to their homes or else continue to reside in any newer settlements that had been established during the war. In addition, they were promised relief from many of the exploitative conditions that had inspired the rebellion. Residents in the Pacífico settlements would be exempted from the civil and religious head taxes. Forced terms of contract, which had frequently resulted in debt servitude, were constrained by the stipulations that: "No indigenous person will be compelled to perform unremunerated labor" and "No authority or private individual will be allowed to compel the Indians to receive a set amount in exchange for work." Finally, men were allowed to rescue their wives and children from debt servitude following upon this article: "An Indian who finds his wife or child in the custody of another person can reclaim them if proof [of relationship] be given, and they will be turned over immediately without any obligation to provide compensation." Those assenting to the treaty would sign a registry to that effect at Chichanhá, ensuring that Chichanhá would become the political center of the Pacífico region for some time.[10]

One very important piece of information was missing from the written text, which is what were to be the boundaries of Pacífico jurisdiction. Would the jurisdiction encompass solely those villages and towns of the signatories, or would it extend beyond that? This matter was discussed at the treaty negotiations in Belize. According to one account, it was agreed that permanent markers were to indicate the southern portion of Pacífico lands. The Belize River represented the southern limit, and the eastern boundary would seem to have corresponded with what was the western boundary of the British usufruct limits as established in the 1783 treaty with Spain (see figure 1.2). A little over thirteen years later (in 1867), two men who had accompanied José María Tzuc to Belize in 1853 told a priest dispatched by the British Honduran lieutenant governor: "That . . . they themselves had seen the marks of the boundaries placed, one at Punta Gorda on the New River, where Pancho [Francisco] Pat lived, and which still exists; and the other in Black Creek, which old Mr. Oscia caused to be taken up and thrown into the river." Regarding the southern boundary, they stated that "all the right bank of the river Belize belongs to the [Pacífico] Indians."[11] The wording is ambiguous, and the markers referenced may have been the boundary markers laid down following the signings of the 1783 and 1786 treaties, or they may have been new markers freshly laid in the same locations.

In 1867, the lieutenant governor (who had not been in the Belizean settlement in 1853) recognized the locations referred to by the Maya men as those of the "Old Spanish Crosses": the old treaty boundary markers, as indicated on the Bay-Man Map (figure 1.2). This 1853 territorial assignment may have been determined on the basis of prior use by the Maya; in addition, the Yucatecan officials may have considered these appropriate boundaries because, after all, those lands had never been allocated by Spain for British use.[12] (Again, the British treaty-defined western boundary extended southward from Albion Island, intersecting with the New River near Backlanding, then moving in a southeasterly direction to connect with Black Creek, and then the Belize River.) In other words, British officials were aware of the Pacífico claim to those lands and apparent official Yucatecan consent to that claim. In addition, having hosted the peace negotiations, the British could be seen as having conceded to that claim. At the very least, the Maya men participating in the 1853 negotiations had good reason to believe that the British acknowledged and would respect their claim. However, the fact that almost the entirety of the northwestern Belize region was claimed as the property of and worked extensively by British Honduran logging companies set up the conditions for clashes over the next half century.

At the time the 1853 Pacífico treaty was signed, roughly equal numbers of people were found in the Pacífico and the Kruso'ob rebel groups (about twenty to twenty-five thousand in each).[13] While the Pacíficos and Kruso'ob were already enemies by this time, when the Kruso'ob learned that this 1853 treaty committed the Pacíficos to fight alongside Yucatecan forces against the Kruso'ob, any animosity surely would have turned to rank hatred. Competition and armed conflict between Pacífico and Kruso'ob Maya thereafter became a new dimension of the Social War that had its own dynamic, and that conflict would affect the relations of each Maya group with the Yucatecans, the Mexican government, and the British.

Superintendent Wodehouse sent a copy of the 1853 Pacífico-Yucatán treaty to the British minister in Mexico, but he subsequently warned José María Tzuc that the Mexican federal government notified him that it would not recognize this treaty which had been made only at the state level.[14] Tzuc replied that he had negotiated the treaty "with truth and sincerity," and he expected it to be upheld.[15] Interestingly, the Pacíficos and the Yucatecan state government (and later, the Campechano state government) apparently generally observed the treaty agreements at least until 1895.[16] However, the fact that this treaty was recognized at the state but not at the federal level created a contradiction that would haunt the peninsula for decades to come.

"BRITISH HONDURAS" AND LAND OWNERSHIP

The threat posed by the Yucatecan Social War continued to stimulate the formalization of government in British Honduras. In 1854, Britain established a constitution for a government (although still not a "colony") called British Honduras, including a Legislative Assembly. Among other reasons for this change was the fact that the steady influx of settlers from Yucatán had led to the appointment of three district magistrates in the north (plus two in the south), requiring a more robust administrative and judicial system.[17]

British officials would not rest easy, however, until the boundary with Mexico could be resolved. In 1854, the new superintendent, William Stevenson, again urged the governor to survey and mark the western boundary, as British mahogany works continued to extend beyond the treaty-defined limits. "Some of the very best mahogany works are upon some of the encroachments," to the west and south, he explained, and large capital investments had been poured into them.[18] Pressured by the timber companies, Stevenson took the bold step of officially recognizing previously apportioned use-right "locations" and Crown "grants" as privately owned and titled lands.[19] Locations had ceased to be allotted in 1817, and no Crown grants had been assigned after 1839. Stevenson observed, however, that those locations and grants had been treated effectively as private property since 1818. In 1855, he passed an Act, asserting:

> whatever may have been their primary object and limit the gradual changes that
> have taken place have produced such corresponding increase of power over the soil
> itself, as to have invested the Locations and those claiming under them with absolute
> dominion over the located lands in like manner as if the sovereignty had always been

in the Crown of England, and the possessors had held under unconditional grants from the Crown. The lands have always and particularly within the last half or quarter of a century been dealt with as Estates in fee simple, and, as such, have been sold, mortgaged, settled, divided, and allowed to descend, without any idea of their being anything else than absolute ownership.

Through an "Act to Declare the Laws in Force," the Crown assented.[20] Consequently, even though British Honduras was not a formal colony, proprietors of lands that had been previously allocated as locations and grants could rest assured of the Crown's support for their land claims.

However, even with enhanced powers of self-government, British Honduran officials could not be assured of their physical safety. Immigration from Yucatán had continued; by 1855, roughly 14,000 Yucatecans had resettled in the northeastern corner of the British settlement, including in the town of Corozal. This wave of immigration more than doubled the size of the British settlement (the 1845 population of which had been 9,809).[21] The new settlers greatly increased the agricultural output of the settlement, but their interests and loyalties were not always clear.

Moreover, British Honduran munitions sales to the Kruso'ob rebels continued to fuel the cycle of conflict. This trade kept the rebellion alive, and it also provided the firepower for Kruso'ob attacks on the Pacíficos of the Chichanhá region. London's Foreign Office continued to pressure Superintendent Stevenson to suppress illicit munitions sales. Incredulously, Stevenson assured the governor that most of the sales of guns were to hunters. Few guns were sold across the Hondo, he said, and in any event, prevention of all such trade would be nearly impossible. Washing his hands of the matter, he concluded: "The only course is for the Yucatecan Government to establish their own preventative service in suspected places."[22]

TIMBER SUBCONTRACTORS AND LOGWOOD HARVESTING

Even while the raids and counterraids of the war continued, the necessities of daily living persisted, and by this time, Maya people had become thoroughly involved in commercial timber harvesting operations on both sides of the Hondo River. While in an earlier era enslaved and freed Africans and African-descended people were the primary laborers on logging crews, by the middle of the nineteenth century, the crews consisted of Creole, Garifuna, Maya, and mestizo workers. By 1858, in fact, the Maya had essentially taken over the declining logwood work.[23] Even the Chichanhá comandante himself had been working on a logwood crew run by a Maya subcontractor who worked for James Hyde & Co. in 1854.[24]

The British logging companies (for both mahogany and logwood) in the mid-nineteenth century regularly subcontracted their work to Spanish-descended

Yucatecans, people who in fact had experience overseeing Maya laborers. (An ability to communicate with them in the Maya or Spanish languages, as well, was undoubtedly an advantage.) The most prominent of these Yucateco bosses were people who will figure significantly in events to come: Florencio Vega at San Estevan (on the New River), Basilio Grajales at San Roman (on Albion Island, Hondo River), and Manuel Castillo at San Antonio (Hondo River). In fact, from the perspective of the company managers, these Yucatecos' strict discipline of Maya workers would have made them ideal subcontractors. For example, in 1850, Florencio Vega disciplined one of his Maya workers by putting him in "campaign stocks" for seven hours. (The man was placed on his back, his wrists were bound below his knees, and a gun was inserted between his arms and thighs.) Vega was prosecuted in Belize for this harsh punishment,[25] but after a month in jail, agents of the largest mahogany companies signed a petition for him to be released, demonstrating their early reliance on him as an effective manager.[26] One vivid example of how Maya people were persuaded to work in logging dates to a few years hence. In 1862, Francisco Pat (a Maya logging subcontractor who had an estate at Hololtunich near the New River Lagoon) was said to have prevented Maya settlers at Chumbalche (in the San Pedro Maya region) from entering their milpas to work their crops, doing so to force them to work for him.[27]

Although perhaps not ideal, it was possible for Maya families to combine timber harvesting and milpa cultivation. Milpa work is seasonal and different tasks can be assigned to different family members, allowing for one or more people in a family to venture out for other economic activities. In Maya milpa cultivation, fields are cleared in the spring (the dry season) and planted in April, just before the rains begin in early May, and crops are harvested in the fall. While the heavy work of clearing is typically done by adult or teenage males, women and children participate in the lighter tasks, such as weeding and harvesting. Consequently, even if adult or teenage males were away, the other family members could still have brought in the milpa harvest.

Regarding logwood in particular, the work did not require the coordinated action of large crews nor, necessarily, long-distance travel. Logwood trees are small in comparison with mahogany trees (rarely reaching fifty feet in height or two feet in width) and they grow in thick stands, often on the water's edge. Because the roots and the lower part of the tree are the valuable portions from which the dye is extracted, the trunks would be cut, then chopped into smaller segments that could be carried in a sling or basket on a man's back. These smaller logs would be loaded into pitpan canoes for transport downstream.[28] The logs would have been delivered to a foreman or subcontractor, who would see to their transport to ports and out to sea.

In addition, commercial farming and woodcutting were not mutually exclusive spheres of activity in the mid-nineteenth century. The three biggest timber subcontractors mentioned above (Vega, Grajales, and Castillo) all also had landed estates on which they charged rent from and employed tenants (of Maya and Spanish descent). Just as on the agricultural estates, the logwood subcontractors leveraged debt to ensure a supply of labor. They paid "Indian" workers "three dollars per ton with rations or four dollars [without]" for cutting the wood, and they would pay the mule drivers $10–$12/month plus rations. The subcontractors would hire Maya workers for an agreed upon number of months and provide advances on the work, of "up to $40 or $50," in cash and goods. While at logging camps, the workers could purchase other necessities from the company truck, at greatly marked-up prices. Once again, the wage advance and truck mechanisms of employment frequently resulted in debt servitude. "The Indian labourer is scarcely ever out of debt," affirmed the Orange Walk magistrate.[29] As was true in Yucatán and on the agricultural estates, the urge to abscond and escape one's debts would have been strong.

CHICHANHÁ-MAHOGANY COMPANY CLASHES ON BLUE CREEK

In 1856, competing land claims erupted into violence. A serious clash between the Chichanhá Maya and a British mahogany company broke out along Blue Creek. The conflict exposed the various competing financial and military interests in the region and revealed some of the deception and extortion that actors in the region would use in advancing their interests. It also showed how very localized, small-scale disputes in the frontier region could escalate, spin out, and take the form of an international diplomatic episode. In this 1856 Blue Creek incident, the specific stretch of land in question was north of Blue Creek, in a region that Britain recognized as Mexico's sovereign territory.

By way of background, a British Honduran company, Young, Toledo & Co. (YTC), had been given use contracts in 1851 and 1852 by the Mexican government to extract mahogany from stretches of land north of Blue Creek for a period of fifteen years. The company had prepaid the Mexican government for those contracts. However, the Pacíficos based in Chichanhá identified those lands as part of their domain. The Yucatecan government might have been inclined to support the Chichanhá claim, given that it continued to rely upon the Comandante General at Chichanhá to serve as military commander in that region and thereby serve as a check against the Kruso'ob rebels. In addition, Maya crews were busy harvesting logwood in that same stretch of land.

The specific dispute began with numerous acts of harm by YTC workers inflicted upon Pacífico residents. Luciano Tzuc now enters the picture. Luciano Tzuc had become Comandante General at Chichanhá following the death of his father, José María Tzuc, and he at one time had worked for a British logging company.[30] YTC workers had, Tzuc charged, stolen personal property and milpa produce, whipped workers, caused the destruction of milpas by allowing their cattle to roam, occupied people's houses, and had been interfering with the work of the Maya logwood cutters. In one episode, the crew leader, Charley, "took from one Comrade Caba a Demijohn of Aniseed and then beat him." Tzuc also reminded Toledo that the contract allowed YTC to harvest only mahogany, but the crews had been taking cedar and sapodilla, as well. Tzuc threatened that if the depredations did not cease, he would force an end to the mahogany work: "for if your Agent knows how to inflict stripes, I can also inflict them ... and I also know how to use [musket] Balls."[31]

Depredations by the mahogany crews continued unabated, so Tzuc upped his demands. In September, Tzuc and his men—now armed—occupied the mahogany works at Blue Creek Bank. They seized and held captive the company agent (Stephen Panting) and demanded restitution for 1,416 mahogany logs taken from the northern side of the river. Payment equivalent to $5,600 ($4/log) was to be made in the form of $2,000 cash, 25 flint guns, gunpowder, and shot, or else the entire "bank" (the mahogany works) would be set on fire. Tzuc asserted his authority over the region on the basis of the 1853 Pacífico treaty, reminding Toledo: "Because you know very well that according to the arrangements made in Belize—Bacalar was only to exercise authority as far as Pucté [roughly halfway between Bacalar and Chichanhá, at the eastern edge of Albion Island] & that I was to have command over all the land from Cacao [six kilometers to the west of Pucté] to Blue Creek."[32] Since Pucté was the westernmost point of the British timber extraction region according to the 1783 and 1786 treaties with Spain, Tzuc's understanding that Bacalar's comandante's territory extended as far west as Pucté (and that this was "according to the arrangements made in Belize") provides further confirmation of the notion that the 1853 Pacífico-Yucatán treaty negotiations assured the Pacíficos that they would control the lands to the west of the British timber extraction region (see figure 1.3).

With his agent and his logging works held hostage, Toledo sought the assistance of Superintendent Stevenson in Belize. However, from the superintendent's perspective, this was not just a landlord-tenant dispute, but an unfortunate incident that exposed and further imperiled the already weak position of British interests in the region. British officials could not send a military party to rescue the company agent and remove the occupying Pacíficos because the YTC workers were on land that Britain recognized as Mexico's. Stevenson, writing to the governor in Jamaica, called the "unexpected and most extortionate demand ... absurd." All that he could do was plead to the governor to resolve the dispute with the chargé d'affaires in Mexico and to resolve the larger border issue, as well.[33] As Stevenson saw it, Tzuc had no basis for a claim. While Tzuc might have felt that he could charge rent on lands assigned to the Pacíficos based on the 1853 Pacífico-Yucatán treaty, such an arrangement would have been superseded by the prepaid use contracts, Stevenson argued. Moreover, the 1853 treaty was never ratified by the Mexican government. "The sooner they teach Zuc his proper position and rights . . . the better it will be for all parties concerned," he wrote.[34] Up until this incident, none of the British superintendents had expressed such harsh criticism of any of the Pacíficos; this incident in particular soured Stevenson on Tzuc. Following negotiations mediated by Mexico's Vice Consul, the dispute concluded without loss of life. The occupation ended after about two weeks, the company agent was released, and the company paid Tzuc $600, promising another $200 in rent annually.[35]

Following this incident, Stevenson set about to review the legal situation and, in concert with the Colonial Office in London, determine a strategy to protect British financial interests in the region. In his office in Belize, he reviewed a copy of the 1853 Pacífico treaty, and the fumbling, defensive manner in which he wrote about it to the governor reveals that he recognized that the treaty was damaging for British interests. He conceded that the treaty did refer to land rights and that "the former chiefs and their Tribe" were used to harvesting logwood in the region in which YTC had been working, although he doubted that the lands discussed at that "immature convention" would have included that section. Since the treaty had not been ratified, it was immaterial, he protested, and "even if it had been ratified, there would still have remained the duty of assigning, by means of Commissioners, the 'lands' proposed to be left in their possession." (Stevenson apparently did not know about the 1853 affirmation of boundary markers, at least not at the time of this dispatch.) He raised the possibility that even though the Mexican government had not ratified the treaty, it was possible that the Yucatecan government had been silent about that fact in their communications with Pacífico leaders, which might have given the Pacíficos the impression that the treaty was valid.[36] Regardless of its validity, Stevenson recognized that its existence was problematic for British logging enterprises in the frontier zone. In fact, while such a document normally would have been archived both in the official colonial records in the Belize Archives and Records Service and in the Colonial Office documents in the National Archives (UK), Dumond could not locate a copy in those files. He discovered a copy only as an enclosure in a dispatch to the Foreign Office.[37] Did someone try to make this inconvenient treaty go away?

Precisely during the Chichanhá occupation at Blue Creek—while Stevenson was undoubtedly distracted—he received an entreaty from another Pacífico leader who begged him to put an end to the sale of munitions to the eastern rebels by Yucatecos who lived on the British side of the Hondo. Pablo Encalada, stationed at Xlich, wrote of "the very injuries" that had been inflicted upon the Pacífico people for three years already by the Kruso'ob using such gunpowder. These munitions enabled them to "surprise towns and take away the lives of men, old men, women and children and also merchants." These smugglers (Pedro Briscéño, Pascual Ojeda, and José María Trejo), moreover, regularly stole the trade goods and profits of Pacífico merchants that were being transported along the river. Encalada begged the superintendent to stop these "rogues and smugglers."[38] Stated differently, Pacíficos had begun to identify residents and officials in the British settlement as complicit in the Kruso'ob attacks upon them. Stevenson shrugged off these concerns.

The 1856 incident at Blue Creek reveals several important dimensions of Pacífico-British relations at the time. First, Luciano Tzuc probably felt his claim to those lands around the Hondo River on behalf of the Pacíficos was solid, given: continuous Maya occupation of the region, references in the text of the 1853 Pacífico-Yucatán treaty to land rights; the boundary markers that had been affirmed at the time; and the fact that Chichanhá-region people had long been engaged in cutting logwood in the region.

Second, Tzuc would have concluded that even if the Chichanhá Pacífico land claim could not be settled beyond doubt, it was strong enough to be taken seriously. The capitulation of YTC and the British superintendent to Tzuc's demands showed him that the British recognized that Indigenous claims were worthy of consideration. Tzuc would have seen that no land claims in the region were set in stone. After all, Britain had never been recognized as a sovereign power in the region; Spain had never granted Britain usufruct rights to the lands in question; the Spaniards had never effectively controlled the region; the Mexican government just a few years prior had been considering creating an autonomous region for the Maya rebels; Yucatán had rejoined the Mexican federation only in 1848 following seven years of independence; and the Yucatecan army relied on its Pacífico allies in the Social War. Tzuc might have reasoned that the Pacíficos—just as much as any other political group in the region—stood a fighting chance, and they had the most points in their favor.

Third, the capitulation by the company and the British superintendent told Tzuc that, when dealing with the British, threats, armed occupations, and kidnapping were effective means to an end.

Fourth, the British officials were hard negotiators with the Pacíficos, giving little credit to Maya grievances and using deceptive measures, including downplaying inconvenient treaty documents.

Fifth, since Tzuc knew some details of the company's use contracts with the Mexican government, someone within the government apparently provided him with that information, probably hoping for a Pacífico-British confrontation. This is one example of a pattern in which Maya groups would sometimes be deployed as proxies in larger international boundary disputes.

Sixth, the incident began—not as a fight over mahogany or rent payments—but with complaints about mahogany crew depredations on Maya fields, homes, personal property, and personal safety. In other words, the dispute was multifaceted. When threats to Maya security and livelihood went unaddressed, the conflict escalated, pitting Maya and Mexican officials against British ones.

Seventh, the officials in Belize bore some responsibility for creating the conflict. The unfettered flow of munitions from British Honduran merchants to the Kruso'ob since the beginning of the war, and even after the Pacíficos made peace with Yucatán, had enabled the Kruso'ob to successfully attack Pacífico people and settlements repeatedly for five years already by that point. Resentment of British Hondurans for Pacífico losses of lives and property surely contributed to the conflict at Blue Creek. These seven dimensions of the conflict foreshadow others on the horizon.

The 1856 Blue Creek incident then triggered a careful review by British officials of all documentation regarding treaties and logging contracts in the northern region. In a secret dispatch to the governor, the superintendent revealed that he knew that a 1783 treaty boundary marker was placed on a different tributary of the Hondo than the Blue Creek, as he wrote that the Spanish commissioners placed a mark on the "wrong tributary," not the Blue Creek, "which is supposed to be the true Hondo."[39] Stevenson also secretly urged the Colonial Office to resolve the boundary problem because the land grants allotted by Superintendent MacDonald beyond the 1783 treaty limits were doubly problematic since they had been issued following the 1826 treaty with Mexico. "These authorized Trespasses are very extensive, & embrace by far the most valuable Mahogany Country in the Settlement," he regretted.[40] These illicit, but valuable, trespasses made the boundary dispute even more pressing from the British perspective—and made Tzuc's threats even more vexatious.

"WILD INDIANS HAVE INVADED, THOUGH PEACEFULLY"

While Luciano Tzuc initially might have seen the Young, Toledo & Co.'s payment of rent to the Chichanhá as a success, the Blue Creek incident gained him enemies among the British and among his own people, as well. A major disagreement broke out at Chichanhá over the distribution of the funds paid by YTC. Tzuc was deposed as Comandante General of the Pacíficos and he "now wander[ed] about harmlessly within the [British] settlement."[41] Tzuc "was in disgrace" among the Chichanhá because of the Blue Creek incident, and he "would in all probability have been killed by the Indians, had he not taken timely refuge on our side of the river," opined the Crown Surveyor.[42] This was by no means the first time that peasants at

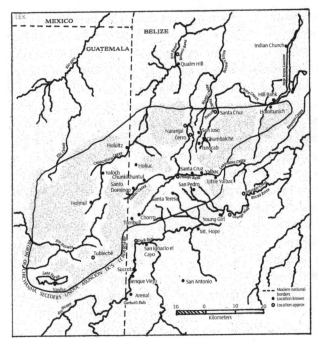

Figure 3.1. The British Honduran western frontier, 1857–1867. Adapted from Grant D. Jones, "Levels of Settlement Alliance among the San Pedro Maya of Western Belize and Eastern Petén, 1857–1936," in *Anthropology and History in Yucatán*, ed. Grant D. Jones (Austin: University of Texas Press, 1977), 142. Credit: Emily Kray.

Chichanhá revolted against their leader. In 1801, for example, the *alcalde* and one of his aides were stabbed to death by local residents, and in 1819, Chichanhá residents as a group sued their *batab* for collecting too much in taxes (while simultaneously suing the local judge for illegally pressing some into forced labor).[43] All of these incidents reflect the fragility of personalistic leadership. An ineffective, greedy, or tyrannical leader would be ousted, by one means or another.

In the case of the Blue Creek incident, however, so severe was their disappointment with Luciano Tzuc that hundreds (and perhaps thousands) of the Pacífico residents in the Chichanhá area crossed Blue Creek and resettled in the Booth's River region (see figure 3.1). (This is one part of the group of people who would come to be known as the San Pedro Maya.) In this migration, they sought both freedom from Luciano Tzuc and also protection from Kruso'ob attacks.[44]

Who were these migrants from the Chichanhá region? Some likely had resided in the Pacífico region north of the Hondo River prior to the war, others may have settled there from other parts of Yucatán more directly involved in the Social War fighting, and others were likely deserters from the Yucatecan armed forces.[45] In addition, many may have lived in what is now northern Belize in prior decades, were displaced by the British woodcutters in the 1830s, and were simply returning to lands they considered home. These various groups would have been intertwined by marriage and *compadrazgo* (godparenthood) relationships over time. In crossing the Hondo River, these migrants were following a centuries-old pattern of rejecting economic and political conditions in Yucatán and striking out in search of a better life. Regardless of the specific origins of individuals, a sense of the land as a (collective) homeland would have been reinforced by the 1853 Pacífico-Yucatán treaty.

The presence of these new arrivals came to British attention when, in May 1857, the new superintendent, Frederick Seymour, made a visit to the region, probably with an eye to shoring up defenses following the 1856 Blue Creek incident. Seymour wrote to the governor that on this trip "some [other] Indian residents of British Honduras" told him that perhaps three thousand "Indians of another tribe, the Chichenhas," had crossed the Hondo southward, were living in the Booth's River region on or near the extensive timber works owned by Messrs. Hyde, Hodge & Co., and "they are employed in burning & otherwise destroying bush & mahogany trees with a view to the cultivation of the soil." They did not all arrive in 1857, since they had been "often seen by the laborers at remoter mahogany works."[46] Many of these new settlers might have entered in prior years, in smaller groups (as had been the case for migrants to the Petén region, who entered in small groups beginning in 1847[47]), but were only now coming to the attention of a new superintendent, for whom that region was now of particular concern.

"Wild Indians have invaded, though peacefully," Seymour wrote, conveying his trepidation. With primary concern for the mahogany, he determined that they should not be allowed to destroy the trees, but those concerns aside, he saw them as potential laborers and therefore a boon to the settlement. John Hodge now enters the picture. A London merchant, John Hodge had been the agent for Messrs. Hyde, Hodge & Co. since 1848,[48] and he takes an outsize role in events to follow. Seymour dispatched John Hodge to "order them to cease from destruction of valuable timber . . . and endeavor to persuade them to accept work & wages in the interior." In addition, Hodge would allow them to live on company lands.[49] The fact that the company agent was dispatched as an official representative of the British government also shows the perfect alignment of official and commercial interests at the time. The Chichanhá migrants might have wondered, however, by just what right these British men claimed to own these vast stretches of lands and impose upon them restrictions about where and how they could live.

"WE NEED BUSH PEOPLE"

At the time, mahogany employers were sorely in need of workers, and these arrivals from the Chichanhá region came at an opportune moment. Mahogany harvesting was a massive operation that transformed the forested landscape and a single "work" required the support of probably hundreds of people. A mahogany operation needed not just a village, but a network of villages. The task of felling the trees began in late August and would be finished by February (because mahogany wood that was felled between February and August would be dryer and more likely to split). The logs would need to be hauled to the bank along a river or stream in March and April, because the thick mud of the rainy season (May through August) prevented effective hauling.[50]

Describing mahogany harvesting in his 1858 annual report, Seymour called it "the very hardest work" in the West Indies. The size and magnificence of the trees were almost beyond comprehension. The bank, on the water's edge, was the center where the foreman lived, the stores were kept, and the logs were stacked until ready to be sent downstream. The harvesting work extended for miles in all directions. Again, the growth pattern of the mahogany tree shaped the parameters for its harvesting. Since the trees are dispersed widely (growing singly or in a small cluster, at an average of one tree per two and a half acres), each tree needed its own road. A network of roads therefore radiated out from the bank to the individual trees. For each long road, forest vegetation needed to be cleared and the ground leveled enough for the large wagons ("trucks") to haul the logs and transport water and supplies. A single tree might generate four tons of wood. The trees were not cut into small logs at the site where they were felled, but the bark would be removed, the logs squared and loaded onto the wagons. None of the work was completed with the help of machinery, but the individual logs—all massive in size—would be loaded onto the wagons with tackles and levers. Each wagon would be pulled by a "set" of oxen, meaning six pairs or more. Pulling the wagons in the heat of the day would have been too much for the animals to bear, so the work was done at night. Seymour described the scene: "Men bearing pine torches, precede and accompany each log, and it forms rather a striking scene as the several noisy and brilliant processions converging from the dense parts of the forest, meet on the common high road to the Bank along which the teams when united sometimes stretch for half a mile." Once at the bank of the river or stream, the logs would be lashed together into rafts for floating downstream.[51]

Laborers were needed for each step in this process. Supplemental tasks included transporting provisions from stores to fields (by mule or wagon), and men and women alike would have gathered fodder (especially breadnut leaves) for company livestock (including oxen, horses, and mules). Other tasks would have fallen exclusively to women, including the arduous chore of hauling water for the company livestock and crew members, cooking, and washing clothes.[52]

Even though mahogany harvesting and milpa cultivation often worked against one another (since the timber crews' oxen trampled agricultural fields and since

Figure 3.2. "Cutting & Trucking Mahogany in Honduras." Source: Chaloner & Fleming, *The Mahogany Tree: Its Botanical Character, Qualities and Uses . . . in the West Indies and Central America* (Liverpool: Rockliff and Son, 1850), frontispiece. Credit: The New York Botanical Garden, the LuEsther T. Mertz Library.

milpa farmers might damage mahogany trees when clearing their fields), the timber industry also needed local peasants. While Seymour envisioned the Pacífico migrants as woodcutters, their unique contribution to the timber industry was revealed when he wrote, "We want bush people in order to line [the roads] with farms and plantations."[53] The Pacífico Maya farmers, he imagined, could produce food for the woodcutting crews. The Pacífico settlers, however, ended up doing far more work for the mahogany companies than just growing food—and far more compromising work, at that.

TIMBER COMPANY TENANTS

Many (perhaps all) of the new migrants from the Chichanhá region who were discovered in the Booth's River region and who were invited by Messrs. Hyde, Hodge & Co. to settle, cultivate their fields, and join the mahogany crews appear to have settled in villages in the San Pedro Maya region in the Yalbac Hills district (see figure 3.2, above). They maintained connections with a group of Maya-speaking villages across what is now the Guatemalan border. San Pedro, at least, was a preexisting settlement.[54] In two short years (by 1859), Messrs. Hyde, Hodge & Co. would become reorganized as the British Honduras Company (BHC), a company of central importance in events to follow.

As was the case for the Maya peasants drawn into agricultural labor in the northeast of the putative British settlement, land consolidation ensured that many settlers in the Booth's River and Labouring Creek regions would have been compelled to perform at least some work for the logging companies, even if only on a part-time basis for shorter periods of time throughout the year. The years 1858 to 1861 were a time of rapid consolidation of land ownership (as we will see in the next chapter), and by 1859, the entire region encompassing the Río Bravo and Booth's River was claimed by the BHC. That same year, San Pedro, to the south of Labouring Creek, may have been situated on Crown Lands leased to Young, Toledo & Co.[55] Regardless, as we shall see, between 1860 and 1868, all relevant actors behaved as if San Pedro lay on lands claimed by the BHC.

The timber companies charged their tenants rent on both house and milpa lots. The new Chichanhá Maya migrants on BHC lands probably paid rates similar to those of BHC tenants in the northern district: $3–$8 dollars/year for a house lot, plus $2/year for garden plots, and an additional amount for each child.[56] Working for the company in some capacity would have been the easiest way to earn money for those rent payments, as was the case for San Jose residents in the 1930s.[57] Other tenants may have been required to provide some labor for the landlord in lieu of payment, as was common on Yucatecan haciendas, while others might have been required to hand over a share of their production (whether crops or domesticated animals), as was the case at Carmichael's Goshen estate. Those who were BHC tenants in the 1930s recounted felling trees, gathering breadnut leaves for company livestock, clearing roads and paths, removing the tree bark, and squaring the logs.

Seymour wanted "bush people" to grow food on company "plantations" to feed the logging crews. The milpa foods that the Chichanhá migrants cultivated would have been the same ones as were cultivated in San Jose in the 1930s: corn (*ixi'im*), black beans (*bu'ul* and *sama'*), lima beans (*tíib*), black-eyed peas (Spanish: *espelón*; Maya: *x-pelon*), yams (*makal*), elephant ear root (*kukut makal*), sweet potatoes (*íis*), cassava (*ts'íin*), tomatoes (*p'áak*), chilies of various types (*iik*), squash (*k'úum*), cushaw (*x-ka'*), and rice (some for household consumption and some as feed for domesticated animals). They would have raised hogs (*k'eek'en*), chickens (*káax*), turkeys (*úulum*), and ducks (Spanish: *pato*) for both household consumption and local sale, and a smaller number of families would have raised horses (*tsíimin*) and cattle (*wakax*).

The forests provided generously. From their own house and garden plots and from the forest the Pacífico migrants would have gathered the same variety of fruit as did San Jose villagers a few decades later, including avocado (*on*), mango, nance (*sakpaj*), sweet oranges (*chujuk pak'aal*), Seville oranges (*suuts pak'aal*), hog plums (*abal*), honeyberry (*wayam*), sapodilla (*ya'*), four types of bananas (*ja'as*), macaw palm (*tuk'*), coconut, tamarind, mamey, and pineapple. From the forest, they would have collected honey (*kab*), cohune nuts (Spanish: *corozo*), and shelf mushrooms (*xikinche'*). They would have hunted a variety of animal species, including ocellated turkey (*kutz*), collared peccary (*kitam*; also called *k'eek'en k'áax*), tapir (*tsiimin k'áax*), deer (*kej*), Great curassow (*k'anbul*), agouti (*tsub*), paca (*jaleb*), armadillo (*wech*), pheasant (Spanish: *faisán*), dove (*mukuy*), coati (*chi'ik*), parrot (*t'úut*), crested guan (*kox*), and kinkajou (Spanish: *mico*). Fish from local streams and rivers would have supplemented the diet, whether eaten fresh or dried.[58]

Those Maya who had left the Chichanhá region, whether to escape the violence of the war and/or oppressive labor conditions, taxes, and debt peonage, would have been dismayed to discover that south of the Hondo River, they were not free to settle where they wanted or to live simply through subsistence techniques of farming, hunting, fishing, and gathering foods. They had new landlords who used the land as leverage to secure labor and income. They had suffered through years of war to finally win real, concrete rights and concessions in the 1853 Pacífico-Yucatán treaty: protected village lands, reduced taxes, and the right to rescue wives and children from debt bondage. By migrating southward, had they unwittingly forfeited those rights?

Although the Maya of the northern and western districts were drawn into the British colonial economy as tenants and workers, other British institutions had little impact on their lives in the 1850s. For example, they had little contact with Christian clerics and there were no public schools. Seymour lamented the "moral & spiritual conditions" of the northwestern region, wherein lived "many Indians of the Chichenja & other wild Maya tribes who shirk observations, & do not apply for licence to roam through the forests," because there was only one minister for all the ten to twelve thousand people in the northern districts, not including the "Indians."[59] In practical terms, the lack of religious and educational institutions meant that for the Maya in the western region at this time, nearly all of the contacts they had with British Hondurans were with logging company agents, subcontractors, and workers.

KRUSO'OB RENT DEMANDS

For his part, Superintendent Seymour eyed the Chichanhá-region migrants from the perspective of security. He did not fear them but worried that the Kruso'ob, who had "followed closely on the footsteps of the fugitives," would launch raids across the Hondo River. At that time, Seymour had more than one reason to fear the Kruso'ob. Just as Luciano Tzuc had done the prior year, Kruso'ob rebels had been issuing demands for rent from Young, Toledo & Co. (YTC) on lands north of the Hondo River to which they laid claim. Similarly, they backed their demands with threats of force, as armed groups of Kruso'ob fighters twice that year crossed the Hondo. In one instance, roughly fifty armed men approached the logging works at Douglas, beating drums and shouting loudly; only when the manager raised the Union Jack flag did they retreat. On a second occasion, three boats of armed men crossed to Punta Consejo to settle a dispute.[60] The Kruso'ob demanded that YTC give them thirty arrobas each of shot and gunpowder, or else $300; Toledo's crew capitulated and paid the $300.[61] The company then had to shut down all of its work north of the river because the manager and crews refused to work under threat of attack, and the proprietors also wanted to avoid further confrontations.[62] British settlers were alarmed that now two sets of armed Maya groups were making extortionist demands.

In this context, Seymour was surely assessing whether the new "refugees" (as he called them) from the Chichanhá region would be peaceful or troublesome. Easing his worries, however, with Feliciano Yah as the new comandante at Chichanhá, those at Chichanhá had become "our professed friends," he wrote to the governor.[63] Furthermore, Chichanhá had become subordinated to the command of Pacífico Comandante General Pablo Encalada at Lochhá,[64] and Luciano Tzuc disappeared from official British communications for a few years.

As 1857 bore on, however, repeated threats from the Kruso'ob led Superintendent Seymour to shore up military defenses. Since the extortionist demands had worked to the favor of both Luciano Tzuc and the Kruso'ob, Seymour wondered just how many more Indian raids and demands would follow. Since the Mexican government could not subdue the rebels, they certainly could not be counted on to restrain Kruso'ob aggressions against the British settlement, Seymour lamented to the governor. Neither could the Mexican government be pressed on the issue, given the sensitivity of the boundary dispute. There were rumors of an imminent Kruso'ob raid on British mahogany works and Seymour was disquieted by the pitiful state of the British defenses. Creating a militia of woodcutters for frontier defense was out of the question, however, as "the laborers care but little for their masters' interests, and could not be induced to make a stand against the Indians."[65] The Kruso'ob attack on YTC, which had been more violent than Tzuc's 1856 attack, revealed a sense of impunity.[66] Having been at war for so long, Seymour suspected, the Kruso'ob had "no occupations but plunder & the chase."[67]

Would Corozal be targeted for attacks? The town had grown and become more prosperous, as the Yucatecan settlers had built a chapel and school, sugarcane and rum production were booming, and the town boasted a steam-powered cane processor.[68] Six Yucatecans were charged with conspiring to burn the town in July 1857, and while they were released due to lack of evidence, nevertheless residents were on edge.[69] In November, Kruso'ob fighters who had sacked and pillaged the Yucatecan town of Tekax (and left "1800 corpses of murdered Spaniards in the ruins of the Town") were fleeing toward the Hondo River. Laden with booty as they were, "rough & drunken scenes . . . will follow the disposal of the booty," Seymour fretted.[70]

Might one native group be pitted against another so that neither would attack the British? wondered the Crown Surveyor. Some Yucatecans living south of the Hondo had been smuggling gunpowder in demijohns along the river, and at Douglas, they traded the powder to the Kruso'ob in exchange for liquor stolen in Tekax. Surely worried that the Kruso'ob would use munitions secured from British Honduran traders to attack Pacífico settlements, Pacífico Comandante Pablo Encalada (from Lochhá) went to Chichanhá to assemble five hundred troops to prevent the Kruso'ob from reaching the Hondo River. Rather than intervening to stop the trade in powder—the Crown Surveyor suggested—the British should allow "the Chichanja Indians [to] act as our frontier guard." Divide-and-conquer began to emerge as a defensive strategy.[71]

Within the first decade of the Social War, therefore, the aspirational British settlement had been radically transformed. The population had more than doubled in size and transformed in composition, and large-scale sugarcane and rum production were underway in the northeast, made possible by Maya and mestizo workers who tried to cultivate their own fields on the side. In the northwest, hundreds and perhaps thousands of Chichanhá-region Pacíficos had resettled on lands claimed as property by British Honduran logging companies. British officials and employers imagined them as useful logging workers and tenants, and many became just that, often working under Yucatecan subcontractors.

The British had maintained friendly relations with the Kruso'ob Maya, including a brisk trade in munitions. These munitions were put to use in attacks against the Pacíficos, whom the Kruso'ob now saw as deserters and turncoats. Yet relations between the Pacíficos and the British were frangible, continually eroded by those very munitions sales to the Kruso'ob and also by depredations on Pacífico personal property and resources inflicted by British Honduran logging crews. The British were in no position to defend themselves militarily from a possible Pacífico attack, since certain lands in question were on what the British recognized as Mexican sovereign land and since the Pacíficos had the backing of the Yucatecan government. At the end of 1857, with Luciano Tzuc deposed, the superintendent in Belize worried slightly less about the Chichanhá-region Pacíficos, but with the Kruso'ob now issuing extortionist rent demands on Young, Toledo & Co., Seymour's watchful eye remained fixed on the north. He asked the governor for latitude to make military decisions as they arose with respect to the "wild districts [to the north] . . . where all now appears to anomaly & confusion."[72]

He probably should have been paying closer attention to the Pacífico migrants in the western region who were now being treated like indebted tenants on lands they had reason to call their own.

4

"We Find the Indians Very Useful" (1858–1863)

Over the next several years, the uncertain boundary between the British settle-ment and Mexico, and the Social War conflicts to the north—especially the clashes between the Kruso'ob and the Pacíficos—continued to undermine British Honduran security, leading to a frantic search for alliances in the region. Friends one day would be belligerent the next, as competition over resources and the shuffle of alliances led groups to continually reassess their strategies. The Kruso'ob rebels would keep up their fight with Yucatecan and federal Mexican armies. On another front, the Kruso'ob and Pacíficos battled for control over lands, upon which they could collect rent payments from both logging companies and agricultural tenants. Sums thereby accrued maintained soldiers who then would be readied for the next round of fighting.

The Kruso'ob for the most part would maintain friendly relations with the British Hondurans, who were their primary supplier of munitions. However, both Pacífico and Kruso'ob leaders would use threats and violence to extort rent payments from British mahogany crews and to meet other military and financial goals. Following two dramatic episodes, British officials increasingly came to view the Kruso'ob as unreliable allies, under the thrall of superstition and inflamed by drink. Within the context of possible invasions of the British settlement from either the north or the northwest, Asunción Ek, leading the San Pedro Maya, initiated an alliance with British Honduran officials. A convergence of interests would lead to a happy arrangement, at least for a time. This chapter shows how sprawling conflicts across

https://doi.org/10.5876/9781646424634.c004

the region, motivated by multiple and sometimes conflicting goals of sovereignty, security, profit, and personal power—all complicated by a riverine landscape and uncertain borders—led to multiple, unhappy surprises.

KRUSO'OB OCCUPATION OF BACALAR

By the beginning of 1858, the Kruso'ob had grown a mighty army that betrayed no fear of British action. In one incident in February, a force of about fifteen hundred well-armed Kruso'ob soldiers crossed the Hondo River to trade "Horses, Mules, Poultry, Hammocks, and various other articles" for gunpowder, alarming Captain William Anderson of the Second West India Regiment. Among them was Venancio Puc, the Kruso'ob leader who was known as the Patron of the Cross, who brought with him the Talking Cross, "which they consulted on all occasions of importance." At Douglas, Puc apologized to the YTC foreman for the aggression of the prior year, expressing a desire for good relations with the British. Nevertheless, said Anderson, the mahogany workers worried about their family members left at home and unprotected.[1]

Superintendent Seymour wrote the governor about the impossible bind in which he found himself. Mexican troops were continuing to inspect all boats on the Hondo for gunpowder, permitting no more than two arrobas of powder to be transported at a time. These inspections did nothing more than put the British at risk of attack from the Kruso'ob, Seymour felt, since the Kruso'ob had made clear that their friendly relations with the British depended on the steady supply of gunpowder. "It is not a pleasant state of affairs to have large bodies of wild Indians penetrating into the heart of our territory to carry off barrels of gunpowder by the score," he added.[2]

A few days later, however, a series of events unfolded that would shock British sensibilities and imperil the unofficial alliance with the Kruso'ob. The powder that the Kruso'ob had just purchased found immediate use, and British subjects were among its victims. Kruso'ob fighters captured Bacalar (for the second time) on February 21 and seized forty prisoners for ransom, including two "Englishmen" and many women and children. The magistrate at Corozal attributed native violence to the influence of alcohol, in what would become a standard trope in official British communications. "The Indians departed ... from their universal practice of indiscriminate slaughter," he wrote, "owing it is believed, to an absence of a sufficient quantity of spirits ... but the fate of the captured is extremely precarious; for should their captors procure the means of indulging their passion for drink, the consequent excitement, would doubtless lead to a universal massacre."[3]

Letters delivered to the superintendent from captives in and refugees from Bacalar contained "horrible details of Indian barbarities" and implored him to negotiate with Venancio Puc for the prisoners' release. The Cross demanded $4,000 in ransom per prisoner plus gunpowder. Seymour dispatched Captain Anderson and his WIR soldiers to Bacalar on a hostage rescue mission. With Anderson went James Hume Blake, the magistrate and owner of the estate that encompassed Corozal; Hume carried ransom money, but no gunpowder, ratcheting up the precarity of the meeting. Seymour's account of the rescue mission related many sensory details that heighten the sense of fear and foreboding. These sentiments directed subsequent policy, and therefore the account is worth quoting at length. He wrote:

> The main road parallel to the lake [lagoon] had been cleared & there were no human corpses in it, but even there the air was impregnated with the smell which came from the side streets where bodies, stark naked, male & female, in every stage of decomposition were being devoured by the dogs and "John Crows" (turkey buzzards). From the different degrees of decay it was evident that there had been successive massacres in detail. That many had been murdered when incapable of resistance the marks of rope round the arms shewed.

Once Captain Anderson's party reached Bacalar, Seymour's letter was translated into Spanish, then Maya, and read to the Cross. Since Blake had brought no gunpowder, Venancio Puc was displeased. Translating for the Cross, Puc complained of British treachery, having heard that the British had supplied gunpowder to Pacífico leader Luciano Tzuc (although Seymour denied this) and had given both gunpowder and refuge to Manuel Perdomo, the former Yucatecan comandante at Bacalar, who had fled to Corozal.[4]

The rescue party was made to attend a religious service that night in the chapel. The prisoners were brought out (about forty women and between twelve and fourteen men) and the Cross was consulted about which ones should be handed over to the regimental soldiers. The Cross demanded a higher ransom: $7,000 per prisoner. Blake said that he could provide it, although he did not have the full sum on hand. The Cross extended a final offer: It would hand over the prisoners if the British turned over the former Yucatecan comandante at Bacalar (Perdomo). Thereafter, four or five women were marched away, and then: "little girls 8 in number were separated from their mothers & the only scene of violence which had been witnessed yet was in the struggle & frantic screams of these little wretches, adjured by one of the women not to make such a noise or they would be killed with their mothers." A male prisoner and some thirty-five women were herded off toward a group of trees, and

> soon the butchery seemed to begin. Shrieks were heard, but in 10 minutes all was quiet again. Shortly afterwards the troops returned. The Indians always strip the clothing from themselves & victims during these massacres so there was no blood on

their shirts next day. All had relapsed with silence when fresh female screaming of the most violent description arose near the fort where one woman—it is conjectured the Consul's young sister in law who was not seen in front of the Santa Cruz—was ardently being cut down like tree stems with the Indian machete.

Later, Puc arrived, assuring the British that they should not be afraid. The Kruso'ob soliders had merely done to the "Spaniards" what the Spaniards did to their prisoners. Final details conveyed the terror of the rescue party as, "in the early morning all was quiet. The Indians washing their machetes in the lake." The John Crows had collected near the "clump of trees from whence the shrieks had proceeded at midnight."[5]

The massacre of prisoners in front of the British troops convinced Seymour that the Kruso'ob were indifferent to British opinion. A Kruso'ob attack on Corozal seemed highly plausible. The presence of five thousand Yucateco refugees in the town, including two former Yucatecan officers (Perdomo and Mariano Trejo), made it a prime target. Meanwhile, Perdomo had been escalating the conflict by trying to convince other Yucatecan refugees in the British settlement to retake Bacalar. With an estimated sixteen hundred Kruso'ob soldiers stationed at Bacalar, Seymour realized that the British would be crushed in an invasion. Angered by the vulnerable situation in which the British had been placed by Perdomo and other Yucatecan refugees, Seymour issued a neutrality proclamation. No residents of the British settlement should take part in or aid or abet any party in the Social War, or else they would face deportation. Bitterly, he complained to the governor about whether they were "to continue to receive the offscourings of the populations of neighbouring countries—including some of the greatest ruffians that the world can produce." The superintendent begged the governor to send additional troops to Corozal, a warship to dock at Belize, and a gunboat for the Hondo (which he thought was deep enough for a gunboat to be able to travel all the way up to Blue Creek). British soldiers set up a base at Cocos while the Kruso'ob maintained a camp across the river at Pucté. At Cocos, soldiers were to monitor all riverine traffic and prevent the sale of munitions to all "Indians," regardless of military affiliation.[6]

Seymour was exasperated by the menacing stance of the Kruso'ob and by the apparent unwillingness of the perhaps ten thousand Yucatecan refugees living south of the Hondo River to participate in their defense. He knew British efforts in securing their aspirational borders would be seen by the Kruso'ob as providing shelter to their enemies. However, efforts to recruit a militia in Corozal had once again failed. "The inhabitants of Corosal are always alternating between a state of presumptuous confidence and one of almost insane panic," Seymour griped to the governor. These people are "absolutely & entirely helpless for their own defense," he moaned.[7]

At the same time, Seymour evinced paranoia about multiple threats from the north, reporting to the governor that he had near-certain proof that the Chichanhá attack led by Luciano Tzuc in 1856 had been fomented by the Yucatecan government.[8] This suspicion that the Chichanhá were goaded into aggressive action against the British by Yucatecans would linger, with significant consequences, as we shall see. Seymour became convinced that one particular Yucatecan official had egged on Tzuc: Mariano Trejo, one of the former Yucatecan comandantes at Bacalar who was living in Corozal as a refugee. Because Tzuc had, in 1856, referred to an obscure stipulation in YTC's contract with the Mexican government about the type of allowable construction, Seymour concluded that he must have been informed by a government insider, and he surmised that it was Trejo.[9] If it were true that a Yucatecan official urged a Maya leader to stage an armed occupation of a British mahogany camp, that action would force a confrontation between Britain and Mexico. It would represent yet another instance in which native and colonial financial interests—within the context of both a border dispute and a regional war—complicated and inflamed international tensions.

LAND CONSOLIDATION AND THE BRITISH HONDURAS COMPANY

Ultimately, a Kruso'ob invasion of Corozal did not come to pass. The year 1859 brought a measure of political stability, but also severe economic crisis, to British Honduras. In a critical political development, the southern and western borders of the settlement were thought to have been fixed by a convention with Guatemala on April 30. The southern border of British Honduras was to be the Sarstoon River, stretching from the Bay of Honduras to Gracias a Dios Falls. The western border would extend northward from those falls to Garbutt's Falls on the Belize River and from there "due north until it strikes the Mexican frontier." The treaty turned out to be problematic, since Article VII could be interpreted to imply Guatemalan acceptance of British sovereignty in British Honduras, although the Guatemalan government explicitly rejected that.[10] Additionally problematic, while the treaty indicated that the northernmost point of the western line would be "the Mexican fronter," where that lay had yet to be determined. The northern line continued to unsettle British Honduran officials, and army barracks were under construction at Corozal. Seymour, however, was increasingly resentful about having to protect the town, writing: "The population . . . is totally alien and no persons can be more unfitted for self government than the Mexican and Central American Spaniards."[11]

At the same time, the 1850s to 1870s was a period of rapid and extraordinary consolidation of land ownership in British Honduras. A series of laws passed between 1855 and 1858 reclassified the old locations as privately owned and titled lands. However, the mahogany boom of the 1840s was followed by a mahogany depression in the 1850s, as companies that had expanded quickly to take advantage of the high prices found themselves saddled with debt once the price dipped in the 1850s. Those companies that consisted of a partnership between a local settler family and Britain-based merchants gained access to capital that enabled them to stay afloat and also to buy up lands put up for sale by companies under stress. Some companies were already formed as partnerships, and other partnerships were quickly forged.[12] Paul Sullivan situated this mahogany depression within the context of the larger, global financial panic of 1857–1858. Fueled by a variety of interrelated factors, a collapse in investor confidence led banks to call in loans and freeze lines of credit. On an international scale, debtor companies found themselves in crisis, with timber companies in British Honduras among them.[13]

Within this context, some British capitalists were hesitant to invest more in British Honduras until they could feel assured that any new land purchases would have secure titles. Consequently, the Honduras Land Titles Act was drafted in London in 1858, with the stated purpose being to "render land marketable even where the title could not be conclusively established"—in other words, to enable sales of lands that had no title or an inconclusive one. The bill was introduced at the urging of a company that would be formally registered in 1859 as the British Honduras Company (BHC), a new manifestation of the older partnership between James Hyde (of one of the oldest settler families) and John Hodge (a British merchant). James Hyde had been one of the largest landowners in the settlement, claiming ownership of more than one million acres (equivalent to one-fifth of the area of modern Belize), and his holdings represented one-half of all of the privately owned land. When the London house of Hyde, Hodge & Co. went under in 1858, so did its British Honduran partner, James Hyde & Co. Hyde's land was purchased by a group of Hyde, Hodge & Co. creditors at auction in June 1859, and the group then registered as the British Honduras Company (BHC). The Honduras Land Titles Act was finalized in 1861, and the BHC (which would change its name in 1875 to the Belize Estate and Produce Company), as the largest landowner by far, would become the single greatest political and economic power in British Honduras,[14] with enormous significance for the Pacíficos in the western region, as we shall see. Of immediate significance for the Pacíficos who were resettling in the northwestern districts was the fact that nearly all of the land was claimed as private property. There was almost no place for the settlers to live without becoming squatters or tenants on lands claimed as private property by logging companies or landed estates.

MAYA-MAHOGANY CREW CLASHES AT SAN PEDRO

In April 1860, we get our first up-close view of life in the village of San Pedro in the official colonial records—in the context of a dramatic manhunt to capture fugitive murderers. At this time, two mahogany companies were working extensively in the Yalbac Hills region, and tensions had flared between the local Maya and the companies. (YTC's bank was on the "left" side of the Hope River and that of the Honduras Land Company [British Honduras Company] was on the "right.") Seymour had gone on a leave of absence, and Thomas Price was the new acting superintendent. Price was newly arrived in the settlement and thus his understanding of local social relations was both weak and ethnocentric.

The precipitating event that brought Price to San Pedro, he reported, was that four "wild Indians" had killed two "tame" ones far in the north, near Four Mile Lagoon (which empties into the Hondo River, near its mouth at Chetumal Bay), and they fled to their homes in the Yalbac district. The demand for mahogany had driven the woodcutters into this more remote region inhabited by "wild Indians," Price explained, but the woodcutters did not always respect the property and milpas of the local residents, which had generated significant conflict. In contrast, there were some "tame" Indians who had "attached themselves to mahogany gangs." Price thought that the murders were the result of the resentment by the wild Indians of the tame ones for their involvement with the mahogany crews.[15]

Price joined a manhunt with troops of the Second West India Regiment in pursuit of the suspects. Demonstrating the difficulty of travel at that time, the search party set out from Belize, traveled five days westward in a flat-bottomed boat on the Belize River, disembarked at Hogsty, then traveled another day over land to Yalbac (on the Hope River, which connects with the New River then northward to the Four Mile Lagoon). The difficulty of travel to the region helps explain why it was so unfamiliar to officials based in Belize; Seymour in fact had never visited the region. The search party learned that the suspects had been taken prisoner and sent by Don Juan Can, the "chief" of Santa Cruz (near Great Yalbac), to "their own people" at Chichanhá instead of to Belize for trial. Given this, and the fact that Don Juan Can spoke "only Maya," it would seem that Can was part of the 1857 exodus and that, despite prior disagreements with Luciano Tzuc, relations with Chichanhá (now under new leadership) had been renewed (at least by some). Can cooperated with the search party and promised to send future prisoners to Belize. We see the ethnic diversity of the region (as well as Price's flair for the dramatic) as Price ordered all of the residents of Great Yalbac, Lower Yalbac, and Santa Cruz brought together, and he addressed the assembly of "the mahogany gangs, Spaniards, Indians, Caribs or Creoles . . . with a guard of honor in attendance, the Union Jack flying before my quarters and myself in official dress . . . [before] this gathering of mixed Savages and civilized beings."[16]

Meanwhile, regarding a wholly separate conflict, G. W. Hulse (a foreman work-ing for John Hodge of the BHC) informed the superintendent that one "Indian," Lauriano Narváez, had set fire to one of Hulse's houses and had fled to San Pedro, where Narváez lived. While the motive for the arson is unclear—Narváez might have been a disgruntled employee or otherwise angered by company depredations—the act of arson was another indication of growing tensions between the Maya and the mahogany companies in the region. The "tame Indians of Santa Cruz" joined with the search party and surrounded San Pedro, but Narváez had fled.[17] The willing-ness of the Maya of Santa Cruz to assist the British in capturing a fugitive from San Pedro points to some political division within the San Pedro area, but it also fore-shadows the arrangement that the San Pedro headman will make with the British in two years' time.

KRUSO'OB AND CHICHANHÁ COMPETITION OVER LAND

The year 1860 was a tumultuous one for all groups in the region. In January, nearly three thousand Yucatecan forces marched on Chan Santa Cruz—and they marched straight into a trap. The Kruso'ob soldiers had left the town, allowing the Yucatecan soldiers to capture it handily. Once the Yucatecan soldiers were settled in and rest-ing easily, the Kruso'ob surrounded the town, recaptured it and seized nearly two thousand guns, plus gunpowder, horses, the mule train, and other supplies. Only about six hundred Yucatecan soldiers survived the rout. This Kruso'ob victory enhanced their military might tremendously.[18]

In early February, the newly fortified Kruso'ob rebels were once again demand-ing payments of rent from the Young, Toledo & Co. timber company under threat of force, and they had raised their prices. What seemed even more ominous from Seymour's perspective was that Kruso'ob and Chichanhá leaders were competing over rent payments on the same stretches of land on the northern side of the Hondo. The prior month, an estimated five hundred Kruso'ob men had advanced on the northern side of the Hondo to "inspect" the work of YTC. Because of the 1856 Blue Creek incident, YTC had already ceased nearly all woodcutting operations on the northern side of the Hondo (despite having contracts to do so), except that it was still harvesting logs from both sides of the river at Blue Creek. The company's build-ings were on the northern side and the company was paying rent to several parties: to "each successive de facto possesser of the soil," including the Mexican government, plus $200/year to the Chichanhá Pacíficos and $300/year to the Kruso'ob.[19]

Assuredly emboldened by the Kruso'ob's enhanced military strength, Venancio Puc sought to consolidate Kruso'ob gains and seize additional assets. In May 1860, about three thousand of his men gathered at Agua Blanca on the Hondo River to collect rent.[20] At Agua Blanca, Puc issued an unprecedented demand of $4,000 from YTC for payment of mahogany extracted over several years. Fearing an armed attack, the company entered negotiations, ultimately agreeing to pay $900 per year going forward.[21]

Therefore, while the initial disagreement between the Kruso'ob and the Pacíficos was about whether they should maintain the rebellion, the conflict had long since morphed. By this point, in addition to the motive of revenge, another critical motivation for their armed conflict was control over lands upon which they could charge rent from the logging companies and other tenants. The political disagreement had become in part a competition over resources. They had come to view lands as territories, in the sense of lands seized by conquest and with borders jealously guarded, and also as leverage, upon which to charge rent.

That same month (May 1860), a smaller group of Kruso'ob men crossed the Hondo, where they kidnapped a Maya debtor who owed rent for cultivation of lands "on the Spanish side." They also commandeered three boats, including two controlled by a BHC foreman.[22] In other words, the Pacíficos and Kruso'ob Maya were competing over lands in order to collect rent not just from logging companies, but also from peasant farmers. The significance of this will soon come into view.

Competition between the Kruso'ob and the Pacíficos at Chichanhá over rent payments soon came to a head. Already by this time, some people were using lands on the northern side of the Hondo River (on the supposed Mexican side), but then residing south of the river (in the supposed British settlement) to avoid paying rent. In June 1860, Asunción Ek—an important figure in later developments—explained to Northern District Magistrate Edmund Burke that he had filed a lawsuit in Belize against seven such debtors. Ek identified himself as "General" of the "General Command of Chichanja," that the lands in question were within the district under his command, as had been settled by "usage treaties [which] were entered into in the year 1854."[23] Such annual dues were routinely paid and they supported the Chichanhá troops and garrison, he explained.[24] Looked at another way, the presence of British commercial enterprises in the region sustained and extended the Social War conflicts through providing military financing indirectly in the form of rent payments. The Chichanhá Pacíficos and the Kruso'ob were, to a certain degree, fighting over land so that they could continue to fight over land. The conflict had become a self-sustaining system.

Ek's letter also reveals his political ambitions and the jockeying among Maya leaders for supremacy. While Dumond concluded that "Ek does not seem to have ever been the actual commander at Chichanhá,"[25] this letter shows that he was at least gunning for that position. First on Ek's list of indebted tenants was Andrés Zima, who, with the "greatest impudence" refused to pay rent for his estate at Chunaba.

Zima had been one of the two Maya signers of the 1853 Pacífico-Yucatán treaty and had become Comandante General at Chichanhá following the death of José María Tzuc in 1854. Zima was apparently pushed out by Luciano Tzuc less than two years later, at which point Zima settled south of the Hondo, but maintained his estate north of the river (presumably with tenant-workers of his own) and he became somewhat wealthy.[26] Ek's attempt to use the British bureaucratic legal system to squeeze rent from a political rival shows his acumen and willingness to accept help from any quarter in pursuit of his goals.

Political strategy aside, Ek's letter—a request by a Pacífico commander to a British official for help in collecting rent that would fortify Pacífico military strength—might have been the precipitating factor in a devastating attack launched upon Chichanhá by Kruso'ob fighters the following week. If the Kruso'ob thought that British officials would aid their Pacífico enemies in their land dispute, it could not have been tolerated. About four hundred Kruso'ob men marched on Chichanhá on June 12. They burned the town, killed leaders, looted, and captured women and children to force them to carry the stolen provisions back to Bacalar. Along the way, at Ramonal, the Kruso'ob fighters killed most of their captives, who were too tired to keep up on the trek.[27] Survivors from Chichanhá subsequently dispersed across the region.

The following month, another curious letter was written about a rumor. If the rumor were true, it would provide a very important clue to how Maya groups in the region envisioned the land. If false, it would be one example of what would prove to be a pattern: letters filled with strategic lies, often written by shady intermediaries who took advantage of the chaos and violence of the war. The letter was written in July 1860 by Basilio Grajales, a Yucatecan of Spanish descent who had fled the violence of the northern rebellion and taken up residence in San Roman on Albion Island in the Hondo River (an island claimed for Britain). In San Roman, Grajales was the proprietor of a landed estate and was a subcontractor for logging companies, harvesting logwood and mahogany from both sides of the river.[28] Grajales wrote to the Mexican consul in Belize, warning him that "the Indians have risen" in Chichanhá and that they were headed to the Belize River "to destroy eleven Banks of the English." Since those woodcutting works were understood by them to have been on the "Spanish Border," and since the British had paid rent to the Kruso'ob, they should do so to the Pacíficos, as well.[29]

If this plan were true, it would be the first known instance of Pacíficos making rent demands that far south. If those eleven logging banks on the Belize River lay to the west of Black Creek, they would have been within the area that the Chichanhá Maya could claim in accordance with the 1853 Pacífico-Yucatán treaty. Alternatively, this plan might indicate what Grajales suggested: simply that those of Chichanhá felt that the British should pay them rent as they paid the Kruso'ob. Finally, it might indicate that they felt there was no harm in trying to extract rent by threat of force. After all, Luciano Tzuc had done so successfully in 1856 and Kruso'ob leaders were routinely doing the same.

At the same time, however, there are reasons to doubt the veracity of this letter. First, it seems unlikely that Chichanhá men would have told their plans to Grajales. Second, Grajales probably already had a tense relationship with the Chichanhá Pacíficos. Since his logging crews harvested wood on both sides of the Hondo River, he was probably routinely pressured to pay rent to the Chichanhá on lands they claimed north of the river. Grajales might have written this letter to the Mexican consul to damage Chichanhá relations with both the Mexican government and the British mahogany companies. As we shall see, four years hence, he was clearly aligned with the Kruso'ob.[30] He took advantage of his liminal position as a Yucateco living on a British-claimed island in a borderlands river to court favor with competing groups, even playing both sides off the middle, exaggerating and prevaricating along the way.

Ultimately, we do not know if Chichanhá leaders planned to attack British mahogany works on the Belize River in 1860; we do know that no such attacks were made. With their town destroyed and survivors scattered, the Chichanhá Pacíficos disappeared from official colonial records for a short while. Surely, however, once the Mexican consul communicated the content of Grajales's letter to British officials, they would have steeled for potential attacks on the mahogany banks.

The possibility of an attack from the Chichanhá region made the border issue all that much more urgent for officials in Belize. The small British settlement could ill withstand simultaneous attacks by Kruso'ob and Pacífico fighters. Survey work on the western border with Guatemala had been underway, directed by Major Wray. Young, Toledo & Co. were concerned that the survey work would reveal that the Río Bravo, rather than the Blue Creek, was the "true Hondo," and that the company would therefore lose access to mahogany on lands that it had long worked.[31] Indeed, if the Río Bravo were discovered to be the westernmost branch of the Hondo, the British use-rights area would be reduced by about one hundred thousand acres, and the party that stood to lose the most was YTC.[32] In addition, both the British Honduras Company and YTC knew that a line straight northward from Garbutt's Falls would destabilize their claim to lands west of that line that they had previously purchased, and they requested that the survey work should be halted. Ultimately, Seymour capitulated to these powerful companies, and agreed that no further survey work or border negotiations with Guatemala or Mexico should be pursued at that time because an agreement with one country would create problems with the other, and in any case, would stir up trouble with the Pacíficos and the Kruso'ob. In 1861, therefore, the survey work came to a halt.[33]

THE PLUMRIDGE-TWIGGE CEASE-AND-DESIST COMMISSION

The 1861 Census of British Honduras revealed enormous changes in the composition and distribution of the population in the settlement. The Northern District population had ballooned in size since the war's beginning. Out of a total recorded population for the British settlement of 25,635 people, more than half (13,547) lived in the Northern District. Yet within the district, only 2,883 lived along the Hondo, while 10,664 lived along the New River, showing the significant expansion of logging and agriculture in that region.[34] In addition to the timber banks, there were several large estates in the New River region, including at San Estevan and Orange Walk,[35] many of which provided food and other items for the timber crews.

The beginning of 1861 was marked by yet another rough display of Kruso'ob force. In late February, Kruso'ob rebels crossed the Hondo at Albion Island (claimed as BHC property) to seize seven cattle that, according to the superintendent, were either stolen by the Chichanhá or belonged to the Chichanhá, and either way, were bothersome to the rebels. Price was offended by this invasion of British lands (as he saw it) and also by the rebels' behavior. They "intimidated the inhabitants," "remained the whole afternoon on our side," and carried away the cattle. Once on the other side of the river, "they made a great row after the manner of such people, & sent their musket bullets flying over our people's heads."[36]

These various raids into British territory and shows of force by the Kruso'ob precipitated the Plumridge-Twigge expedition, which was a dramatic turning point in British-Kruso'ob relations, as British officials were shocked, offended, and plainly scared by Kruso'ob leadership. In late March, Price sent two lieutenants, James J. Plumridge (Third West India Regiment) and John Thomas Twigge (of the Royal Engineers), to communicate to Venancio Puc that the Kruso'ob should desist from crossing to the British side while armed and making such displays of force. The Kruso'ob needed to offer restitution for the cattle seized from the British settlement, and if they did not, British troops would be sent against them. A letter from Price to that effect was dispatched in advance of the commission. The commission's interpreter was José María Trejo—a merchant whom we have already seen operating as a Kruso'ob-friendly munitions smuggler. After the commission reached Bacalar, it was a four-day journey to Chan Santa Cruz along a narrow path through thick, scrub forest.[37]

Outside the village, the commission was met by a group of soldiers who seized them, held them in a guard room for hours, and then marched them to the church at midnight, where they were ordered to kneel before the Talking Cross. They could hear a "shrill voice" (representing the Cross) coming from behind a curtain, demanding to know what they wanted, and rejecting the demands of the superintendent's letter as "insulting." "If the English want to fight, let them come in thousands if they like," said the voice. The Cross ordered that a thousand arrobas of powder be delivered to Chan Santa Cruz and then the members of the commission were returned to the guard room.[38]

The next morning, the lieutenants were taken before Venancio Puc, who was quite drunk and belligerent. Puc "forced a tablespoonful of Cayenne pepper into Mr. Twigg's mouth and compelled him to drink a glass of aniseed afterwards. He made Mr. Plumridge swallow aniseed until he vomited," reported Trejo (the interpreter). Puc threatened: "Are they angry? Tell me? For if they are I will have them chopped to pieces at once." The lieutenants were detained for three more days and were repeatedly called before Puc, who was apparently on a binge. In those meetings, Puc "hauled and pulled them about, slapped them on the head, gave them aniseed, made them kiss him and hug him up, and made them dance and sing," reported Trejo. Finally, the officers were released with a reminder to send the gunpowder.[39]

Superintendent Price was shocked by what he saw as depravity, superstition, and complete indifference to British opinion. Venancio Puc was too erratic and violent to be trusted, he concluded. The governor was alarmed enough by Price's account to promise to send a warship for the Hondo River. Price ordered a cessation of all trade with Yucatán, including munitions (a "Powder Proclamation"). Rumors circulated that the Kruso'ob were planning an attack on the British, and Kruso'ob spies were said to be prowling about Corozal.[40] Eighty soldiers of the Third West India Regiment were sent to guard the town, woefully insufficient to protect the district against the estimated eight to ten thousand Kruso'ob fighters. Corozal residents were fleeing in great numbers. Even the Northern District Magistrate fretted to the superintendent that an invasion seemed likely:

> I remember that a large body of armed men, bloodthirsty ignorant, and uncivilized
> in the extreme, are subject to the sole and irresponsible control, of a wretch not less
> signalized by habits of excessive intemperance, than by acts of the most sanguinary
> cruelty, who almost daily, mercilessly hews in pieces the unfortunate captives whom
> chance or the fate of war places in his power, that this monster is believed by his
> barbarous dupes, to derive his authority from heaven—a delusion supported by
> pretended dialogues with their deity,—a wooden cross,—of which he is the guardian
> and with which he alone holds converse, and that by these means he rules the savage
> multitude with a sway the most despotic, his every command being promptly and
> hesitatingly obeyed as the will of heaven. . . . What I once considered as exceedingly
> problematical, I am now of opinion may occur at any moment.[41]

Martial law was declared, and two hundred reinforcements were sent in from Belize. In the end, however, no such raid came to pass.

Later that year, the Secretary of State for the Colonies chastised Price for having taken too much of an antagonistic position with respect to the Kruso'ob. He ordered Price to enforce the powder proclamation and put a halt to all trade in munitions with Yucatán, but Price lamented that stopping all trade was beyond his powers of control. British officials could only admonish traders not to sell munitions to the Indians.[42] Predictably, the powder proclamation had had little effect, as ships laden with gunpowder docked directly at Ascension Bay.[43] In late 1861, Price was removed from his position and Frederick Seymour returned as superintendent at Belize.

CHICHANHÁ, DIVIDED

During the months in which Price's attention had been fixed on the Kruso'ob to the north, Chichanhá society—emerging from the ashes of the smoldering town—experienced a new crisis of leadership. After the town had been burned by the Kruso'ob in June 1860, Chichanhá people had fled as far east as Pucté and as far south as Yalbac (in the San Pedro region).[44] Town leaders had been killed in the attack, creating an opening for new ones to emerge. Into the vacuum stepped José Ulúac and his deputy comandante, Luciano Tzuc, the mastermind of the 1856 occupation of the Blue Creek mahogany works. Tzuc had "wandered long about this Colony, a drunken outcast, living on the charity of the mahogany gangs," according to Seymour, but now he was back with a vengeance. In November 1861, Ulúac and Tzuc had grand visions of defeating the Kruso'ob at Bacalar and rebuilding their political center at Chichanhá. Ulúac announced his plan to the soon-to-be governor of the soon-to-be state of Campeche, Pablo García. García approved and supplied arms to the Pacíficos for the attack against "our common enemy."[45] According to Seymour, Campeche officials went so far as to press the Chichanhá to make Tzuc their leader, knowing Tzuc's reputation for bravery.[46] This alliance between Tzuc at (the newly repopulated) Chichanhá and the Campechano governor would later prove seriously troublesome for British Honduras.

However, not all of the Chichanhá-region survivors wanted to keep up the fight with the Kruso'ob. Asunción Ek put himself forward as the leader for those who opposed the renewed militarism. We have seen that on June 6, 1860, Ek identified himself as "General" representing the "General Command at Chichanja" in a letter to the Northern District Magistrate.[47] It may have been that at the time of the mid-June 1860 attack on Chichanhá, there was already a struggle over leadership, with different people laying claims to the title of Comandante General, and Ek may have been recognized as such within one group. It is equally possible, of course, that in his 1860 letter, Ek was puffing himself up to appear to be a person of consequence in his communications with the British official. Whatever may have been the case in 1860, by late 1861, Ek took decisive action as a general, leading half of the Chichanhá people southward. While Tzuc and Ulúac were gearing up to attack the Kruso'ob and retake Chichanhá, according to Seymour: "A division hereupon takes place, and nearly one half, it is computed, of the whole force, accompanied by women & children, under the guidance of Asuncion Ek march southward & settle in the territory of Guatemala and of British Honduras."[48] The Yalbac Hills region would have been a soft spot to land, already populated with Maya-speaking people, at least some of whom were aligned with Chichanhá.[49] Asunción Ek settled at San Pedro, and his authority was recognized in villages in western Belize and into the Petén region in Guatemala.[50]

While these villages have come to be known as those of the "San Pedro Maya," that label might imply more homogeneity than was the case. They were mixed ethnically and apparently also with regard to region of origin and political leanings, as Seymour described: "Both the great tribes of Santa Cruz and Chichanha are represented and many half breed Spaniards are mixed with them."[51] The region therefore continued to offer refuge to diverse people from across the region. Given that diversity, however, just how well would an alliance hold?

"CONVEY SOME AUTHORITY ON ME OVER EVILDOERS"

All of the planning and campaigning by officials in Belize came to fruition, and in February 1862, British Honduras became a British colony, headed by a lieutenant governor instead of a superintendent. In August, Frederick Seymour, with his new title, wrote to the governor in Jamaica that he wanted to take a less defensive posture vis-à-vis the Kruso'ob than had Price. He remained apprehensive of them, however, saying that they were not intimidated by threats nor by patient civility. He thought the internecine dispute between the Chichanhá Pacíficos and the Kruso'ob would work to the advantage of the British Hondurans, since the "Chichanha Indians, who, though themselves not friendly to us, shield our Western frontier from the aggressions of the tribes of Santa Cruz." Despite his misgivings, he decided to honor the request of the mahogany companies to cease enforcing the powder proclamation, as Messrs. Young, Toledo & Co. indicated that the slightest hint of hostility (such as the powder proclamation gave) discouraged Indians from signing up as laborers on the mahogany crews, consequently leaving the companies without workers on Blue Creek. The pressure exerted by the timber companies in this regard demonstrates both their heavy reliance on Maya workers at that time, as well as their financial interest in maintaining the peace. In essence, for these financial and political interests, Seymour was willing to scuttle the powder proclamation even though it would inevitably put more guns into circulation, extend the Social War, and anger Mexican officials, with which British Honduras still had an intensely vulnerable position with respect to a border. "Our frontier lies everywhere open to attack," he wrote to the governor, reiterating his plea for a standing military force in the colony.[52]

While José Ulúac and Luciano Tzuc at Chichanhá were busy making alliances with Campeche, Asunción Ek, now living in San Pedro in the Yalbac Hills region (see figure 3.2), initiated an alliance with British Honduras and the British Honduras Company. The BHC, now extracting mahogany extensively throughout the Yalbac district, was receiving rent demands, under threat of violence, from multiple directions. In May 1862, José Lino Lara, who had once served in the Kruso'ob forces, was the headman at Chumbalche (within the supposed "San Pedro Maya" region). Lara apparently had conspired with others to plunder and set fire to the BHC works at Yalbac and Irish Creek because the company would not pay rent on "Spanish" lands. However, the conspiracy was discovered, Lara allegedly murdered the person who threatened to expose the conspiracy, and then Lara and his coconspirators fled to the Petén district.[53] While in Guatemala, Lara somehow convinced the Corregidor of Petén to give him an official title as commissioner with the task of taking a census among the villages in the Holmul district in Guatemala, villages populated at least in part with (Yucatec) Maya people who had been part of the Ek-led migration southward.[54] Following the Corregidor's orders, Lara and two of his deputies began appointing *alcaldes*, levying poll taxes, and organizing forced labor drafts there, but villagers in Tubleché rejected Lara's demands, as well as rejecting his authority because he had been a soldier with the Kruso'ob. They apprehended Lara and his coconspirators, took him across the presumed border, and handed them over to Asunción Ek in San Pedro. A British Honduran arrest warrant had been issued for Lara and his associates related to the murder and conspiracy. Ek and a party of seventy San Pedro men in turn handed the suspects over to the BHC foreman at Yalbac, G. W. Hulse, who then turned them over to the police inspector for trial in Belize.[55]

The men from San Pedro transported Lara and his associates and guarded them at night. "You can depend on the San Pedro men to do their duty with honesty," Ek assured the police inspector. As the inspector's party was about to depart for Orange Walk, Ek approached him and the BHC foreman, asking them to "represent me to the Queen's Lieutenant Governor, that His Excellency may be graciously pleased to convey some authority on me over evildoers." Ek had a leadership problem, as he explained: "At San Pedro I try to keep them in subjection now but they sometimes laugh at me, because they say, I am not invested with any legal authority." Another headman with Ek (José Domingo) made a similar request. The inspector in turn recommended to the lieutenant governor that he appoint them as local constables.[56]

While Ek's role in subduing conspirators against the British Honduras Company and his suggestion that he be deputized within the British Honduran government might at first blush be interpreted as signs of Ek's submission to British authority, they represent rather clever political strategizing on his part. First, by turning over a Kruso'ob fighter to British Honduran authorities for trial, Ek essentially bent the colonial machinery to his will, by using the power of their court system to imprison a Social War enemy. Second, he could use the colonial bureaucracy to solidify his position as leader within the San Pedro Maya villages. While the personalistic, patron-client style of leadership of Maya military leaders at the time was somewhat fragile, backing from the British government might lend stability to his rule. Ek's third reason will soon be clear.

Hulse, the BHC foreman, saw an opportunity. Could the "friendly Indians" be employed as company guards? Since Ek and his men had already come to the aid of the BHC by capturing and subjugating a handful of anti-company conspirators, maybe they would do the same against others? Hulse had been warned that, under Luciano Tzuc's renewed leadership, a group from Chichanhá was expected to arrive in the San Pedro region to demand that the BHC pay the Chichanhá Pacíficos rent and fees for wood extracted. Hulse suggested that Seymour should give Ek some position of authority to "give [the company] every assistance." With the assistance of Ek and his men, he said, "I think we would manage matters here without further aid."[57]

The rumored imminent arrival of those from Chichanhá also alarmed the San Pedro–region Maya. At this time, Maya military leaders often made raids to capture deserters and press them once again into service. It was rumored that Tzuc's men would be coming to the San Pedro area in part to gather up those who had fled Chichanhá and force them back into the fight against the Kruso'ob. "Luciano Zuc, it is believed is not the man to submit to the secession of one half of the Indians of Chichenja without an effort to effect a reunion," wrote Seymour.[58] In addition, when Ek's group left Chichanhá, they had taken some muskets that Tzuc believed belonged to his group.[59] Ek's third reason for initiating an alliance with the British, therefore, would have been the hope that if Tzuc raided the San Pedro villages, the Maya might benefit from British assistance. A San Pedro–British Honduras alliance seemed a win-win arrangement.

Lieutenant Governor Seymour embraced Ek's suggestion, perceiving an alliance with the San Pedro Maya to be of mutual benefit. The British could use a third Maya group as an ally in the event of an attack by either the Kruso'ob or Chichanhá-region Pacíficos. After all, while ostensibly friendly, Kruso'ob aggressiveness against the mahogany companies, their sheer numbers, militancy, and the frequency of their raids across the Hondo regularly reminded Seymour of the possibility of an invasion.

Seymour was so impressed by the cooperation of the San Pedro villagers in apprehending the conspirators, even in the absence of payment, that he wrote to the governor: "All the Indians on the frontier behaved well; indeed it is the excess of their zeal which caused me to write."[60] There already was a fledgling system for appointing Indian officials within the British Honduran government. Having learned about *alcalde* traditions of local government in Mexico and Guatemala, in 1858, Seymour had proposed adapting them for British Honduras. In Yucatán, *alcaldes* were village commissioners, selected by the residents to represent them, to manage internal public affairs, and to keep the peace. Seymour proposed to the Legislative Council that *alcaldes* be designated in communities "where the inhabitants are Yucatecan or Indian race, and accustomed to Spanish polity." The resulting Alcaldes Jurisdiction Act of 1858, however, envisioned a scaled-down set of responsibilities for the *alcaldes*, imagining them solely as local sheriffs tasked with arresting and punishing criminal offenders.[61] In January 1859, an *alcalde* jurisdiction was to be created for a Labouring Creek District,[62] within which San Pedro was situated, although, as of 1862, no Indian *alcaldes* had been appointed.

Seymour's plan was two-fold. First, he sent a commissioner to the Yalbac district to deputize San Pedro Maya leaders within the *alcalde* system. Although in 1858 the *alcalde* role was essentially that of a sheriff, at this point, within the western region, Seymour added the roles of local administrator and frontier guardsman. The village *alcaldes* were to report to Belize about "any suspicious movements of the formidable tribes beyond."[63]

The commissioner dispatched to the San Pedro Maya villages was Edward Rhys, whom we have seen before. His background made him an appropriate intermediary: in 1848, he worked as an agent collecting mahogany duties on behalf of the Kruso'ob; he fought on the side of the Maya rebels prior to the Pacífico peace treaty; and he spoke the Maya language. Rhys estimated the population of the San Pedro Maya villages within the British limits at 900 people (see figure 3.2). San Pedro ("formerly called ceris") was the largest village, with an estimated population of 300. There, Asunción Ek was appointed Comandante over the other villages: "this title being given to him in consideration of his having been a General amongst them." Under Comandante Ek at San Pedro, and given the title of *alcalde*, was José María Vela. At other villages (Santo Domingo) or pairs of villages (Chorro/Tumbul, Chunkikhuntul/Holiuc, San Jose/Chumbalche, Naranjal/Isnocab), first and second *alcaldes* were appointed.[64]

Comandante Ek was to guard the frontier against foreign Indian invasions.[65] What "invasion" meant with respect to the Chichanhá Pacíficos and the Kruso'ob were somewhat different things, though. The Kruso'ob were primarily friendly to the British, so long as the munitions continued to flow northward. When they entered the supposed British territory in armed and menacing stances, their primary targets were Yucatecos (especially former Yucatecan comandantes and soldiers), deserters, and runaway debtors—all of whom ranked lower among British priorities (and would only continue to fall in British estimation). The Kruso'ob did threaten force against British timber company agents, but so long as rent payments were made, they desisted from inflicting violence. However, when the Pacíficos threatened violence within the supposed British territory, their primary targets were the British timber companies—which were the colony's ultimate reason for being. Moreover, the Pacíficos' rationale for doing so (that they rightfully controlled that land) posed an existential threat to the colony, which had never felt secure in its dominion. Consequently, even though the Kruso'ob were a military force ten times as powerful as the Pacíficos, the Pacíficos were the ones whom the British officials feared the most. The San Pedro Maya responsibility for protecting the western region against foreign Indian invasions, therefore, was critical for the colony's financial well-being. Perhaps more importantly, since these were Pacífico Maya who apparently were content not to assert collective Indian rights to the land and would even risk their own lives to protect the British companies' interests, these apparently submissive Indians lent legitimacy to the whole colonial project. Ek's additional duties included: "To catch all runaways accused of murder or escape from the Belize gaol gang. To respect the mahogany trees. To keep the peace, and to punish Indians who illtreated women or committed theft."[66] "We find the Indians very useful," affirmed Seymour to the governor.[67] While Ek and Seymour probably both considered Ek's responsibility of guarding the British Honduran frontier as of primary importance, Ek's task of arresting and punishing thieves would prove far more troublesome for him. He got far more than he had bargained for. It would be his Achilles' heel.

The regalia of office conferred upon the Maya officers were designed with care, reflecting the combination of imperial and local powers, as well as hierarchy within the colonial order.[68] Seymour did not issue a written commission to Ek, as: "A written document might commit me & would have no weight in the bush." He did, however, commission a staff of office which he thought would be "received with great import by the Indians." Comandante Ek's baton bore a gold head, adorned with symbols of the original Baymen who likewise "protected their properties against the attacks of Spaniards & Indians." The British lion and unicorn would not be appropriate, Seymour said, "nor will the Crown appear on the staff of the half savage Indians." Rather, the baton's head would be decorated with a mahogany tree and a woodcutter holding a shield.[69] The first *alcaldes* of the other villages also received staffs and the staff of the first *alcalde* under Ek at San Pedro bore a silver head, underscoring the prominence of that location.[70] With his new title and gold-headed staff embellished with symbols of imperial and local authority, Ek might have thought that people would no longer laugh at him. And he would have been wrong.

The second part of Seymour's plan was to ensure that Ek's authority over the Holmul cluster in Guatemala (Holmul, Axbalché, Toolines, Naclicab, and Tubleché) would remain strong. If that were the case, should the colony be attacked by Maya from the north, Ek's fighting force would remain undiminished.[71] Seymour initiated a series of communications with the Secretary of State for the Colonies and Guatemalan officials to press his case that Asunción Ek's authority over the seceding Chichanhás in Guatemala should be recognized.[72]

LUCIANO TZUC AND YOUNG, TOLEDO & CO., AGAIN

Ek's promise to defend the British logging companies in the case of an attack from Chichanhá became relevant probably sooner than he had anticipated. And it all began with a brawl in a drinking establishment. In January 1863, two of Ulúac's soldiers from Chichanhá had crossed the Blue Creek to go to Pablo Chan's where they got into an argument with woodcutters of Young, Toledo & Co. One woodcutter, Juan Chavín, threatened to slash the Chichanhá soldiers with his machete, and one of the soldiers fired a shot in the air. The bullet skimmed Chavín's hat, and a brawl broke out. Ulúac later apologized profusely to Stephen Panting, the YTC foreman—incidentally, the same Stephen Panting who had been kidnapped by Tzuc's crew at Blue Creek in 1856.[73] The following day, Juan Chavín and another woodcutter threatened that if the Chichanhá soldiers crossed the river again they would hack them into pieces and toss them into the river. Ulúac urged the foreman to make his workers cease the aggression, and if he did not do so, Luciano Tzuc and his soldiers would "take them on."[74] Seymour recognized the implications of this episode for the precarious balance of forces along Blue Creek. While Ulúac was "the nominal Chief of the residual Chichenjas," Luciano Tzuc was "the director of his Council and leader of his troops," and it seemed clear that Tzuc was gunning for the role of Comandante General. Rumors were circulating that Ulúac and Tzuc planned to enter the British settlement and forcibly demand rent from YTC. With Tzuc once again tussling with Young, Toledo & Co., it was a new refrain of an old tune.

Young, Toledo & Co. was used to paying rent to multiple parties when they harvested lumber from the northern side of Blue Creek. The company had prepaid the Mexican government £5,000 for a contract, but the Mexican government would not protect them against Indian attacks. Consequently, "they give an annual rent to Benancio Puc, the Chief of the Santa Cruz people & the real master of the territory. But then, when the Chichenjas occupy the country for a short time, it becomes theirs & they draw tribute also," Seymour explained to the governor. In February 1863, Toledo, however, did not want to make any additional payments to the Pacíficos at Chichanhá. Tzuc had apparently wrested control of Chichanhá leadership again. Toledo reasoned that since Tzuc "claims to represent Mexico and has a Mexican Alcalde in his camp," YTC payments to the Pacíficos were essentially dual payments to the Mexican government. Worried, of course, that the Pacífico threat to the mahogany companies would only worsen, Seymour felt somewhat reassured that Panting could head off any small-scale confrontation with a payoff to Tzuc. If a payoff failed, however, British Honduras could rely upon a divide-and-conquer strategy, reasoned Seymour. Venancio Puc had promised Panting that if he were threatened by the Chichanhá Pacíficos, he need only send up a signal and Kruso'ob fighters would arrive at Blue Creek within three days to provide defense.[75] How quickly these alliances could change.

THE INTERNATIONAL DIMENSIONS OF RENT DODGING

Also in 1863, another emerging dynamic with implications for Social War conflicts came into clearer view. Peasants of Maya and Spanish descent living on both sides of the Hondo River—seeking to maximize subsistence security and minimize physical risk—were becoming inveterate rent and debt dodgers, taking advantage of the multiple conflicts along the Hondo River. The dynamic becomes clearer if we consider what the various groups wanted.

First, Maya leaders—both Chichanhá and Kruso'ob—needed a supply of men who could be enticed or pressured into taking up arms. The Kruso'ob needed soldiers for confrontations with Yucatecan and Mexican armies and raids into villages for the purposes of plunder. In addition, both Chichanhá and Kruso'ob leaders needed fighters at the ready for armed conflicts with one another and also for shows of force designed to pry rent from British Honduran logging companies and other tenants on lands they claimed. To recruit soldiers, they could offer land for peasants to farm. Among the Kruso'ob, at least, male tenants were required to serve half of each month in the Kruso'ob army. They did not earn a wage, but they shared in the spoils of booty seized from villages they raided.[76]

Second, south of the Hondo, employers (whether in logging or in agriculture) needed a regular supply of workers. We have seen that they used a combination of control over lands plus the advance payment system to attract workers, and the truck and debt servitude systems to retain workers over time. They could not be too oppressive in their measures, however, because workers might abscond and try to find a new employer or pursue subsistence techniques in open lands.

For their part, Maya peasants obviously would have preferred the autonomy of milpa cultivation combined with hunting and foraging over indebted servitude. However, Yucatecan legislation in 1863 reaffirmed older laws (of 1843 and 1847) that authorized forced labor, ensuring that debt would continue to be used as a mechanism to retain workers.[77] Moreover, secure access to land was impeded by overwhelming land consolidation in Yucatán and within the British settlement and encroachment by logging companies in the latter. Following a centuries-old pattern, Maya peasants sought to escape debts (and the bondage thereby implied) when possible by fleeing from an employer, tenant, creditor, or tax collector.

As a consequence of these diverse goals and assets, by the 1860s, a unique pattern had developed in which large numbers of Mayas and mestizos were living south of the Hondo River, within putative British limits—a position that they valued because of the promise of security from Social War fighting. However, lacking access to land in the British settlement, they would cross the river to plant their fields on lands claimed by the Kruso'ob or Chichanhá Maya. The Maya leaders expected that these peasant farmers would both join them in armed conflicts and pay rent. Interestingly, at least in 1866, the Kruso'ob let some servants indebted to British employers make their milpa rent payments in gunpowder directly.[78] However, the peasant farmers often tried to avoid military conscription and paying rent by retreating to their homes on the British side. They seemed to have expected (or at least hoped) that Maya landlords would be wary of angering British officials by crossing the river to force them back into military service or to collect rent, and if they did so, that British officials would protect them. Many residents along the Hondo River did just this sort of opportunistic river hopping: farming to the north and living to the south, evading all sorts of debts and obligations along the way. The Maya leaders and British employers and officials, of course, were aggravated by such maneuvers. This was not just a clever strategy on the part of Maya peasants, but as it turns out, it had broad implications for the regional war.

This pattern (farming to the north and living to the south) became clear to British officials in the spring of 1863, through the following set of events. A group of Pacíficos (those under Pablo Encalada at Lochhá) had been collecting rent payments from people who lived "on the English side" but farmed on the opposite side of the river, on lands to which the Pacíficos laid claim.[79] The Kruso'ob felt entitled to those same lands, so in March 1863, they attacked Lochhá, killing many and imprisoning others. At the time, Encalada was then under Tzuc's command in the Pacífico hierarchy,[80] and consequently, when the six to eight hundred Kruso'ob were in retreat, Chichanhá soldiers followed in pursuit. Along the way, the Kruso'ob made a stop to collect rent. The soldiers crossed the Hondo to Albion Island, brandishing arms, and demanded that inhabitants who cultivated lands on the Yucatecan side should pay overdue rent. They captured one such debtor and promised to carry off others. The British were, of course, alarmed by this armed raid into their supposed colony.[81]

The conflict escalated. Those Chichanhá under Luciano Tzuc "rushed forward from their retreat with almost incredible rapidity and spread themselves in small bands along the river, levying money on every person they found in the Northern side, and destroying the timber and corn of all those who had a few days previously paid to Puc," according to Seymour. While the British characterized these armed rent-collection raids as "invasions" into their territory, they may be seen as predictable consequences of a regional system of labor exploitation complicated by a border dispute.[82]

Angered by "squatters" from Yucatán who farmed to the north and resided to the south, Seymour issued a proclamation that those residing in the British colony would not be sheltered by colonial forces if they failed to pay rent on the Yucatecan side.[83] Seymour recognized, however, that he was powerless to prevent raids by Maya leader-landlords. The Kruso'ob raid on Albion Island was "an unbearable act of aggression . . . [but] what were we to do?" he grumbled to the governor. No words of warning would work because Venancio Puc surely remembered that "his ill treatment of our last envoys [Plumridge and Twigge] was met by their actually kissing his feet." Pleading with the governor, once again, for a steamboat on the Hondo, he dismayed of Puc, saying: "The aggression he committed was after all not much more than people with savages on their frontier must occasionally endure."[84]

The proclamation was a paper tiger, as Seymour knew it would have little effect. Regardless, these armed rent-collection raids show once again that within the context of a regional war, even the small-scale, opportunistic, cross-border actions of individuals could stir up problems of international proportions, further entangling British officials in the sprawling melee. The raids are yet another reminder that in this massive, sprawling mess often given the simple, umbrella term "Caste War," there were a multiplicity of shifting groups and motivations. The outcomes of certain actions within the war laid the foundation for new sets of quarrels. Rent dodging was a foreseeable consequence of the monopolization of land and the depredations of war, but the fact that it might heighten the internecine struggle between groups of Maya and intensify the international border dispute was probably beyond what anyone might have predicted. In fact, Seymour did not anticipate how British inaction in response to Kruso'ob aggressions would be read by the Pacíficos.

ICAICHÉ GRIEVANCES

In addition to the Maya and mestizo farmers who were opportunistic river-crossers, trying to use residence within the British colony as a shield against Maya leaders to the north, logging subcontractors tried to pull a similar trick. In 1863, one of the worst offenders was Manuel Jesús Castillo, one of the wealthier Yucatecos who subcontracted with British logging companies, using Maya employees. Rather than harvesting timber solely within the British limits, he also sent his crews north of the river, into lands claimed by both Pacífico and Kruso'ob Maya. At the same time, he regularly sold munitions to the Kruso'ob.

Luciano Tzuc had recently relocated his headquarters from Chichanhá to Santa Clara Icaiché, which was closer to Blue Creek, but in a more easily defended location.[85] As Tzuc saw it, Seymour was allowing a British Honduran resident (Castillo) to inflict harm on Pacífico people, and he wrote to complain. First, the arms that Castillo sold to the Kruso'ob were used to attack and destroy Icaiché-region settlements. In addition, Castillo had been paying rent to the Kruso'ob for lands that should have been under Tzuc's control (as had many other tenants, he claimed). On those lands, Castillo had also set up a sugarcane mill. Invoking the 1853 Pacífico-Yucatán treaty, Tzuc scolded: "Your Excellence knows well that since the time of my father, D. Jose M. Zuc, the lands from Pucte to Blue Creek pertain to me and those from Pucte to the sea are in the jurisdiction of Bacalar." If Seymour did not take steps to prevent further such depredations, Tzuc would cross the river and "take care of it," he warned.[86]

Seymour expressed no regret for Icaiché losses, but instead worried that the weak British response to the invasion at Albion Island had led Tzuc to believe that he could act with impunity. In the meantime, Puc had written a letter of apology to the police magistrate at Corozal, which Seymour interpreted favorably. Seymour showed his partiality as he compared "a powerful and independent tribe making an honourable apology for a hasty act of violence; and those of a defeated upstart attempting to intimidate a friendly Government by threats of deliberate outrage." Exasperated, he wrote to the governor of Campeche, requesting that Tzuc be restrained.[87]

Vice Governor of Campeche, Tomás Aznar Barbachano, defended Tzuc, whom he recognized as the Comandante General of the Pacíficos. Given the long history of British Honduran munitions sales to the Kruso'ob—Barbachano chided Seymour—Campeche felt justified in arming the Pacíficos of the Icaiché region (as well as those of Mesapich) so that they could defend themselves against the Kruso'ob rebels.[88] Barbachano also wrote to Tzuc, with a copy to Seymour, in which he conferred on Tzuc the right to capture and punish Castillo according to Mexican law if he were found on Campeche soil, thereby communicating to Seymour that Campeche was not inclined to make concessions for British Honduras.[89]

Perhaps reassured by his backing from Campeche, Luciano Tzuc demanded payment of rent on lands deeper into the supposed British settlement than he had ever done before. In August 1863, Tzuc delivered a letter to the agent for the British Honduras Company, George Raboteau, demanding eight years' worth of back rent for woodcutting in the Booth's River region. These were Mexican lands, he said. The Booth's River region lay to the west of the British use-rights limits if going by the 1786 treaty with Spain. Tzuc would have understood these to have been assigned to the Pacíficos in the 1853 Pacífico-Yucatán treaty. In addition, since Spain had never permitted British use of this region, if Britain were to assert claim to these lands, that would have aggravated Mexico, and Tzuc knew that. Tzuc's secretary then visited John Hodge (the BHC manager) in Belize, whereupon Hodge showed him a map that designated Blue Creek as the boundary between British Honduras and Mexico. Since the Booth's River region was within British territory, said Hodge, the BHC would not pay any rent to the Icaiché. In Hodge's account, the secretary seemed to accept that explanation at the time and left.[90] Officials in Belize would not learn the details of this disagreement until three years later, but it was the seed from which would grow a major international dispute. Tzuc's insistence upon payment for the Booth's River region understood as Mexican territory would certainly have unnerved British officials once they learned of it. If they were to engage with Tzuc in armed conflict, that would force a response from Mexico and then force British Honduras into border negotiations with Mexico from a very weak bargaining position.

On a different note, these interactions point to the power of secretaries, scribes, and agents at this time. Tzuc delivered a letter to Raboteau by hand, perhaps indicating that he was unsure that he could communicate effectively without that written document. This would suggest that he was less than fluent in Spanish and/or English, and might also have been illiterate, and instead, his secretary translated and transcribed his communications. Tzuc also dispatched his secretary to communicate on his behalf. Almost all the Maya leaders at this time relied on secretaries for their written communications. We shall see that on more than one occasion, these intermediary figures took advantage of their bilingualism and literacy for personal gain.

REQUESTS FROM SAN PEDRO

Given Tzuc's goal of collecting rent on lands claimed by British Honduras and his willingness to use force in those efforts, all the more important, from the British Honduran perspective, were their new allies, the San Pedro–region Maya. The San Pedro Maya, as well, were alarmed by Tzuc's militancy and his desire to expand his sphere of control. In June 1863, Asunción Ek visited Seymour in Belize, whereupon the men met for the first time.

At this meeting, Ek delivered four letters to Seymour. (Here again, the fact that Ek delivered letters by hand indicates that he was not confident of his abilities to communicate effectively in conversation with Seymour, who, it would seem, spoke only English.) Despite Ek's efforts, people were still laughing at him, as the Guatemalan Consul who translated the first letter from Spanish to English added that it "might not be unworthy of a place in the next edition of 'Curiosities of Literature!'"[91] To the governor, Seymour characterized them as "four long letters in Spanish debased by Indian words."[92] In the first letter, Ek explained that he had heard rumors of an imminent attack on San Pedro by Luciano Tzuc, and he asked that they be sent gunpowder and shot to use in case of a surprise attack.[93] Seymour did not do so, but instructed that, if Indians were invading, Ek should send word, at which time Seymour would send powder, lead, and also military assistance.[94] Seymour surely knew that, given the difficulty of travel between San Pedro and Belize, if Ek dispatched a warning, British soldiers would never be able to arrive in time to aid in the defense. Seymour was being cagey, clearly not wanting to supply munitions to his new allies, and Ek surely sensed that.

Ek's second letter requested clarification of his duties. Seymour intentionally avoided writing them down, but he repeated them verbally. The third letter requested a school and school supplies for San Pedro. Seymour promised to send the supplies, but would not commit to creating a village school, simply referring the question to the Board of Education.[95] Seymour appeared rather unconcerned with his new allies.

Ek's fourth letter reported a serious problem with the British Honduras Company. All of the milpas at San Pedro (including all ninety-six men) had been destroyed by cattle belonging to the BHC crews. Recall that Chichanhá complaints to Young, Toledo & Co. in 1856 began with mahogany crew cattle destroying their milpas. How well, in fact, could milpa farming and commercial logging enterprises coexist in the same stretch of forest? Ek asked that the court compel the company to pay restitution, and indicated that the residents were so despondent that they wanted to resettle in the Petén district because they "[could] only sustain themselves with corn."[96] In response to this complaint, Seymour provided no restitution but merely instructed the timber crews to prevent the cattle from entering the milpas.[97] While Seymour was clearly glad for the San Pedro Maya alliance, this conflict with the mahogany crews may have left him wondering if more would follow. At the same time, from the perspective of the San Pedro–region Maya whose food supply was destroyed, the fact that the lieutenant governor cared so little for their survival must have made them question what kind of ally he in fact was.

At the end of 1863, shifting alliances, clashes over land and the rent payments represented therein, a proliferation of armed raids, and the ability of people to move back and forth across the Hondo with ease continued to hold British Honduran officials in a state of insecurity. The Chichanhá Pacíficos, now headquartered at Icaiché, were in a much stronger position, backed by the authority and military might of the new state of Campeche. Luciano Tzuc was intent on gaining control over more lands along the Hondo River and southward into the aspirational British territory, to collect rents thereupon and indirectly finance the Icaiché fight with the Kruso'ob. It was a chicken and egg question. Whether the groups were fighting with one another to control land or fighting to control land in order to maintain the fight—at this point, the question was moot, so entrenched was the self-sustaining cycle of war.

British Honduran officials knew that they would be in a delicate position in a potential Icaiché attack, because a military engagement would be interpreted by Mexico as a breach of international relations. British Honduras therefore needed Maya allies. The Kruso'ob were once again friendly with the British, although the regularity with which they used violence against British Honduran residents in pursuit of their military and financial goals ensured that as allies, they were less than reliable. Comandante Asunción Ek of San Pedro remained ready to defend the colony, but there were signs of trouble brewing with the British Honduras Company. As Lieutenant Governor Seymour was preparing to depart the colony toward the end of 1863, he repented of his earlier harsh criticism of Price's treatment of the Maya, writing: "I underestimated the difficulties with which he was involved and the manner in which he met them."[98] As for Asunción Ek, however, he may have wondered whether he could truly count upon his British allies in a time of crisis.

5

Maya Generals, Company Subcontractors, and the Battle of San Pedro (1864–1866)

Over the next three years, relations between the Icaiché and British Hondurans would deteriorate and reach a bloody end. What frequently began as hyper-local, interpersonal, financial disputes and grudges would snowball through retaliatory strikes and petitions made to more powerful agents and entities, and even blow up into international crises. While Comandantes Generales (including Luciano Tzuc, Marcos Canul, and Asunción Ek) were often center stage, directly engaging with British Honduran officials—behind the scenes, often stirring up discontent, were timber company subcontractors. Organizing labor and rent collection on their own terms, the subcontractors employed abusive techniques. Yet when discontent erupted into violence, they had the ear of British Honduran local magistrates and the lieutenant governor.

Emboldened by a Mexican imperial decree laying claim to territory that included British Honduras, a new Icaiché leader, Marcos Canul, would levy a series of rent demands upon British Honduran mahogany companies working throughout the western region. The San Pedro Maya were swept up into the disputes that ensued, culminating in a march by West India regimental troops on San Pedro in late 1866 and the effective dissolution of the San Pedro–British alliance. This chapter traces the interactions and events that contributed to this crisis, including grievances of San Pedro villagers against the British Honduras Company and its foremen. Amid the turmoil and skirmishes in the western villages, we see the fragility of personalistic leadership as Asunción Ek tried to maintain a peaceful alliance with the British,

https://doi.org/10.5876/9781646424634.c005

but ultimately was pushed out by representatives of the BHC, his own deputies, Marcos Canul, and West India regimental soldiers.

The year 1864 began in the shadow of mutiny. In January, word reached British officials that on the prior December 23, a group of Kruso'ob officers killed Venancio Puc and the ventriloquist youth who played the voice of the Talking Cross. The executions were reportedly motivated by horror at having witnessed the murder of many prisoners over the years, rejection of the Cross's demand for a new series of attacks on several Yucatecan towns as far as the capital, after which "every person they took should be killed, for it had been decreed by God that not a single white person should be left alive," and also a sense of betrayal felt upon learning that the voice of the Cross for the past sixteen years had been that of a ventriloquist.[1] The new Comandante General at Chan Santa Cruz, Dionisio Zapata, intended to surrender Bacalar to the Yucatecan government and negotiate for peace.[2] Some of his men, however, chased him out of Chan Santa Cruz, and while fleeing with his wife to safety in British Honduras, he and several traders from Corozal were also assassinated. His death left Bonifacio Novelo, Bernabel Cen, and Crescencio Poot in charge, all of whom, according to Magistrate Burke, were "distinguished by cruelty and thirst for human blood."[3]

And yet, when in May 1864, news reached the colony that Yucatecan forces, supported by Icaiché fighters, were planning an attack on the Kruso'ob at Bacalar, many mahogany workers along the Hondo were more sympathetic to the Kruso'ob, as they saw the Icaiché under Luciano Tzuc to be more of a threat to them. The new lieutenant governor, J. Gardiner Austin, agreed, reporting to Governor Eyre in Jamaica that Tzuc "is now so fallen in the estimation of the Indians as well as from his own bad character as his connection with the Merida Government, that his ill armed followers . . . subsist only on the plunder of those very mahogany works, which are rented from the Yucatan Government & pay to him as well as to the Santa Cruz Indians an annual tax or Black Mail."[4] In May 1864, Maximilian, the Archduke of Austria, had declared himself Emperor of Mexico (following upon Napoleon III's invasion of Mexico in 1861), although the implications of that for British Honduras were not yet clear.

WHEN IS A PERSONAL DEBT AN INTERNATIONAL AFFAIR?

In the spring and summer of 1864, a convoluted series of events that began with personal debts unfolded along the Hondo River, leveraging Social War hatred, and spiraling outward across several months, culminating in murders, mass kidnapping, and tense negotiations between British and Mexican officials. It resulted in heightened tensions between the Icaiché and British officials, and it revealed the immense power of Yucateco estate owners and subcontractors within the colony; it therefore merits wading through the details. The episode also demonstrates how, within the context of violence, crime, and fear of punishment or retaliation, misinformation multiplied in the form of strategic lies, threats, and rumors. If there were more than one version of a set of events, the version that was believed was not necessarily the one that was true, but rather the first version learned, hence there was an advantage in reaching out early and often to more powerful outsiders who might intervene to aid one's cause. Finally, the episode also reveals more about a man who will be very significant in the events in San Pedro in 1866: Florencio Vega.

The incident that is our focus began at the village of San Estevan (variously spelled San Esteban) on the New River, which was a large agricultural estate with primarily Yucatecan tenants (of Spanish and Maya descent). An 1857 census recorded a population of 1,300 at San Estevan, making it the third largest town in the British settlement, after Belize and Corozal.[5] The proprietor was Florencio Vega, whom we have now seen numerous times. A wealthier Yucatecan of Spanish descent, he had owned a sugarcane plantation in Tihosuco. When the war began, he and his family fled across the Hondo, and since the rebel secretary at Bacalar (José Teodoro Villanueva) was an "intimate friend," he pleaded for the rebels to be satisfied with the seizure of his property and spare his family's lives.[6] By 1849, he had become a merchant selling goods along the Hondo—munitions among them—and although he was suspected of smuggling munitions to rebel Maya, that does not seem likely, given his reasons for antipathy toward them.[7] Vega also became a subcontractor for timber companies harvesting logwood and mahogany, using Maya employees. In addition, his massive estate at San Estevan produced "a great quantity of corn, plantains, pigs, poultry, &c . . . for the supply of the district as well as Belize."[8]

One of Vega's tenants at San Estevan, Crisanto Carrillo (variously spelled Carillo), died indebted to Vega, who therefore took over Carrillo's estate with a business partner, Lucas Vasquez. In early May 1864, Carrillo's son (Inés), upset about the administration of his father's estate, took eight mules and crossed the Hondo into the region claimed by the Icaiché. Vega and Vasquez appealed to Luciano Tzuc, offering him $100 as a reward if he would capture and return Carrillo and the mules.[9]

At the same time, Basilio Grajales was the proprietor of an estate on British Honduras Company lands at the village of San Roman, on Albion Island in the Hondo River. Another wealthy Yucatecan of Spanish descent who had entered the British settlement during the war, Grajales was a BHC contractor, harvesting logwood and mahogany on the "Mexican side" of the river, using Maya laborers, many of whom were indebted "servants," as he called them. One of his servants, Susano Canul, was also Luciano Tzuc's brother-in-law. On May 10, Susano Canul killed Florencio Vega's son at San Estevan (motive unknown) and fled across the river into Icaiché territory. Vega elicited Basilio Grajales's help in tracking down Canul. Grajales had a second motive to track down Canul, which is that his servant—now a fugitive on the run—owed him $37. A third reason for Grajales's antipathy toward Susano Canul is that Canul had also requested that Grajales pay rent (presumably to the Icaiché Pacíficos) for timber extracted on the lands north of the river.[10]

When Canul precipitously fled across the river, he temporarily left behind three of his children, whom Grajales then placed in the care of Canul's compadre, who also lived at San Roman. Luciano Tzuc wrote to the compadre, asking him to hand over the children to Tzuc's comandante, the bearer of the letter, who was Marcos Canul, Susano Canul's brother (and the uncle of the children).[11] Apparently as compensation for his lost $37, Basilio Grajales had seized four cattle owned by Susano Canul, and Tzuc wrote that he should return those cattle, since Canul only owed Grajales "seven or eight dollars."[12]

On May 17, twenty-two armed Icaiché men arrived at San Roman with the two letters for Susano Canul's compadre and Grajales, intending to deliver the children and cattle to Susano Canul. Prior to the 1853 Pacífico-Yucatán treaty, family members frequently had been held as collateral to force repayment of a man's debt. The treaty ensured that Pacífico men could reclaim their family members without having to pay compensation. Grajales obviously felt this did not apply to him as a resident on British-claimed lands, and he refused to hand over his indebted employee's children without an order from the magistrate. In addition, he told the Northern District magistrate exactly where he could find and arrest Canul (at his residence at Achiote).[13]

On May 20, the two strands of this conflagration (the San Estevan and Canul strands) violently crashed into one another. Tzuc's men went to Negros on the northern side of the Hondo and seized the mules that Vega and Vasquez had asked them to recapture from Inés Carrillo.[14] Tzuc later explained that he had dispatched Comandante Marcos Canul and fifteen other men to capture the mules to return them to San Estevan, and also to arrest Carrillo and punish him because Carrillo was going to sell gunpowder to the Kruso'ob.[15] Magistrate Burke said that no one had ever alleged that Carrillo was a gunrunner prior to that, and he thought that rumor was just a "pretext."[16] Indeed, it seems possible that Vega just told Tzuc that rumor in order to incentivize Tzuc to capture Carrillo.

However, precisely at the time that Tzuc's men were seizing the mules and Carrillo, a larger, armed group from San Roman (obviously sent by Grajales) attacked Tzuc's men, and took off with Carrillo and the mules. One of Tzuc's men was killed, as was one from San Roman.[17]

How did Grajales's men know where to find Tzuc's group and that they should capture Carrillo and the mules? Who, in fact, knew that Tzuc's men would attempt to capture Carrillo and the mules and where they might be found? Presumably the men who dispatched them: Florencio Vega and Lucas Vasquez. Vega and Vasquez had lured Tzuc's men into a trap: sending them to Negros (incentivized by a reward and a rumor that Carrillo was going to sell gunpowder to their Kruso'ob enemies), all the while tipping off Grajales, who sent his men in pursuit of them.

Lieutenant Governor Austin was enraged with Grajales because the raid by Grajales's men across the river constituted a raid into Mexican territory, and Austin recognized the international sensitivity of that. He instructed the magistrate to warn Grajales that any residents within the British territory who wanted to maintain fields or otherwise work within Mexican territory "must take all the risks upon themselves." In addition, if their actions would "draw us into collision with the Indians," they would be deported. He directed Grajales to cease harvesting timber from the Mexican side of the river and to allow Susano Canul's children to be delivered to relatives.[18]

However, apparently not knowing that Susano Canul's children were to be delivered, and also angered about the attack at Negros, Tzuc sought revenge. The situation grew much graver. In early June, Tzuc's men descended upon San Roman, whereupon they looted, burned houses, killed three residents, and—not finding Grajales himself—they kidnapped twenty-four people in demand of ransom, including Grajales's son and servants.[19]

These events brought relations between British and Mexican officials to a new low. Austin learned that a certain degree of lawlessness of the Icaiché group could be blamed upon the Yucatecan government, since some of Tzuc's men were fugitive murderers and thieves from the British settlement and others were "lawless miscreants" from Corozal who had been enlisted by Yucatecan commissioners to join Tzuc's military force for pacification of the Kruso'ob.[20] Governor Eyre, in turn, sternly advised the Yucatecan governor to strip Tzuc of his title as Pacífico commander, and he promised that any future aggressive actions against the British colony would be taken up with the Emperor Maximilian.[21] The Supreme Political Prefect in Yucatán, however, denied any responsibility for Tzuc, reminding Eyre that the 1853 Pacífico-Yucatán treaty had not been ratified by the Mexican government. Moreover, "the pacific Indians of the South govern themselves in reality independent of the Yucatan Authorities"—that they neither paid taxes or fees nor submitted reports, no title was conferred upon their leader by the Yucatecan government, and neither was Tzuc issued any orders.[22] This was an astounding declaration, disavowing any responsibility for the Icaiché.

Following grim and protracted negotiations, ransom was paid and Luciano Tzuc returned all but two of the prisoners.[23] Grajales and his employees were arrested for their attack on Tzuc's party. Grajales, however, escaped and found refuge among the Kruso'ob (with whom he had good relations on account of his munitions sales to them). The Kruso'ob dispatched two (unsuccessful) parties to hunt down and punish Tzuc.[24]

In addition to undermining the relationship between British Honduras and Mexico, this incident at San Roman had several other significant consequences. First, British-Icaiché relations hit a nadir. The lieutenant governor was patently disgusted by Tzuc. Austin had only been lieutenant governor for half a year by this point, and he had not had much interaction with either of the northern Maya groups prior to this incident, but it clearly soured him on Tzuc. He compared the two: "Great indeed is the contrast between the Government party of 'Pacíficos,' as they are inappropriately called & the Santa Cruz Indians . . . [who] desire to avoid all interference with British territory or subjects, & seek seemingly but one object viz: the maintenance of that freedom which the tyranny of Yucatecan oppressors compelled them to conquer at the point of the sword."

The 1864 San Roman episode prompted Austin to immediately secure the northern border. He again implored the governor for a gunboat for the Hondo, and aimed to rebuild the garrison at Corozal.[25] Captain Peter Herbert Delamere and twenty-five men of his Third West India Regiment were dispatched to protect the British Honduran settlers at Albion Island and another fifty were to be permanently stationed at Corozal.[26] Efforts were made to organize a volunteer force for the defense of the northern border.[27]

At the same time, the 1864 San Roman incident and the prolonged negotiations allowed British officials to learn more about the Icaiché. The estimated Icaiché fighting force was a "half armed" force of 120, as half of the men carried only machetes.[28] The British also learned about struggles for power among the Pacíficos and the limited scope of Tzuc's influence. Pablo Encalada, Pacífico leader at Lochhá, called himself Commander in Chief (*comandante en jefe*) of the Pacíficos and considered Tzuc to be his subordinate and simply the comandante of the Icaiché district. To demonstrate his desire for good relations with the British, Encalada personally went to Icaiché to pressure Tzuc to hand the kidnapping victims over to the British authorities.[29] British officials would later exploit this division among the Pacíficos.

The British Hondurans also learned about the brittle relationship between Tzuc and his followers. Two of the kidnapping victims commented that Tzuc and his officers "quarreled for the proposed asking $1,500 ransom and his people said $2,500." John Hodge (of the BHC) added that "the want of control by Zuc over his men is a new view."[30] These reports align with what we have seen about personalistic leadership.

Finally, Marcos Canul, Tzuc's comandante, would have learned how lucrative the strategy of kidnapping prisoners for ransom was. (He would test these waters soon enough.) Toward the end of the year, Luciano Tzuc died and Marcos Canul (described as a "half caste or mestizo"[31]) ascended to his position as commander at Icaiché. Knowing of Canul's prominent role in the attack upon San Roman, Austin lamented that this change in leadership did not bode well for the British.[32] All in all, these events in 1864 demonstrated once again how people crossed the riverine boundary opportunistically, and they showed how personal feuds rooted in labor disputes, debts, and interpersonal crimes could spin out and escalate into international conflagrations. In this case, what started with the theft of mules, rumors, and a murder led to retaliatory attacks, a months-long armed standoff, and an international crisis.

THE MEXICAN IMPERIAL DECREE AND NEW RENT DEMANDS

In an extraordinary turn of events, relations between the British colony and Mexico were set aflame in late 1864. On September 19, the Imperial Commissioner of the Peninsula of Yucatán issued a decree claiming the entire peninsula for the empire.[33] The decree claimed for Yucatán the area that is currently within Mexico (the states of Yucatán, Campeche, and Quintana Roo) plus what is now the Petén district of Guatemala and all of what is now the country of Belize. The decree reaffirmed British logging rights in the same area "as has been conceded to them by treaties with Spain and Mexico," but of course recognized no British rights of dominion. This decree essentially rendered all of the extensive British settlements and logging work outside of the 1786 treaty limits as illegal trespasses on sovereign Mexican territory.[34] Residents in Belize panicked, wondering what this would mean for their security,[35] while some Yucatecans living in the British colony began crowing about which lands they would claim once the British were cast out by the Mexican imperial government.[36]

Austin worried what impact this imperial decree might have on Maya claims to the region. If Mexico's dominion encompassed the region of British Honduras, would the northern Maya groups feel empowered, as Mexican subjects, to claim lands south of the Hondo River, as well? The Icaiché were the first to strike. In February 1865, Marcos Canul, who referred to himself as Comandante General, and his second-in-command, Comandante Rafael Chan, wrote to British Honduras Company (BHC) foreman, George Raboteau, demanding that he pay for the wood cut on the "Mexican side" or else he would "suffer great harm."[37] Raboteau met with them and their agent (Santiago Cervera) at the mahogany works at Driving Camp on Río Bravo, whereupon he asked what Canul meant by Mexican land. Canul snapped that Raboteau had the map and knew which was which. When Raboteau told him that the British claimed as far north as the Blue Creek, Canul shrugged it off, saying in the Maya language: "When you have to cry, don't say that I did not give you notice."[38]

Canul and Chan then wrote to John Hodge, the BHC manager, demanding $2,000 for eight years' worth of back rent for extracting mahogany "on the Mexican side" ($250 per year), by which they meant lands between the Blue Creek and the Río Bravo.[39] Hodge sent Canul a map prepared by the Crown Surveyor, showing that the lands in question were grants to BHC from the British Crown issued three decades earlier (dating back to Superintendent MacDonald's tenure). Hodge refused to pay rent for prior years, but he offered to pay $250/year for future rent framed as protection money, stating that this rent was "subject to your protecting our Gang from any molestation from other parties" (in other words, from the Kruso'ob).[40] The political implications of framing rent as "protection money" are astonishing: Accepting the payment committed the Icaiché to fight against the Kruso'ob. Hodge thereby showed his willingness to exploit Social War hostilities to his own advantage.

ATTACKS AT QUALM HILL AND BETSON'S BANK

In the spring of 1866, all was quiet on the western front. Austin expressed no concern about the San Pedro Maya. Similarly, the British had reached an uneasy peace with the Kruso'ob. While Kruso'ob continued to occasionally cross the Hondo River and carry off or otherwise terrorize debtor tenants, Austin seemed content to let that slide.[41]

Austin instead remained fixated on the Icaiché threat, faulting the Mexican imperial decree for Canul's continued demands for rent in the region between the Blue Creek and the Río Bravo. At this time, the estimated Icaiché population was about one thousand, including two hundred men prepared to fight.[42] A Yucatecan Catholic missionary working in the Pacífico villages described the zone as a region of refuge from the war. Estimating the entire Pacífico region of southwestern Yucatán (fifteen square leagues) to have twenty-five thousand inhabitants, he described them as mainly "new settlers ... [who] live dispersed throughout the forests." "The area serves as a lair for the deserters, thieves, escaped servants, and every sort of criminal," he said, and there were "at least a thousand able-bodied white people living among them with their families, the majority of them deserters."[43] Others would soon echo this observation.

On April 27, 1866, Comandante General Canul made good on his threats, in events that British settlers interpreted as an armed invasion of the colony (at Qualm Hill). The episode revealed the growing tension between the Icaiché and the British Honduras Company and the overbearing power of the BHC in the colony, but also the extent to which BHC greed threatened the security of British Honduran settlers. Behind this particular episode was the fact that the BHC failed to pay the back rent that the Icaiché had requested the prior year, and moreover, the BHC also failed to pay even the $250 that John Hodge had promised in exchange for Icaiché "protection" of mahogany workers against the Kruso'ob.[44] General Canul and an estimated 125 Icaiché men, therefore, marched toward the Río Bravo "in martial array with fife playing and drum beating." They went, they said, to find company foreman George Raboteau and collect what they were owed. At the BHC settlements at Qualm Hill and nearby Betson's Bank, Canul's men killed two laborers, kidnapped fifty-nine people (men, women, and children), ransacked houses, and seized all the livestock (including 175 head of cattle) and other goods (including hatchets, machetes, liquor, pots, and other items). Among those kidnapped were Raboteau, his wife, and children. In the long march back to Icaiché, in which Canul rode upon Raboteau's stolen horse, the prisoners were tied in pairs and made to carry the stolen goods. The Icaiché then demanded $12,000 in ransom for the kidnapping victims.

Canul and Chan later explained that they had just been looking for Raboteau and they were fired upon first, which caused them to fire back and the incident escalated from there. However, the large size of their group and the fact that they went "in martial array with fife playing and drum beating," show that they were prepared to fight. This was the most serious Maya attack in the British settlement since the war had begun, measured both in human and financial costs.[45]

The $12,000 ransom demanded was an enormous sum, far more than the family members could pay. The family members pressured BHC to pay, while John Hodge felt that the colony should assist. Even the colonial government, however, did not have such an amount at its disposal.[46] The Mexican government should then pay, insisted Hodge, since they had supplied the muskets used by Tzuc's men.[47] Knowing that any attempt to hold the Mexican government responsible for the Icaiché would go nowhere, Austin sent commissioners (Gustav von Ohlafen and Edwin Adolphus) to Icaiché to negotiate for a reduced ransom payment, with the stipulation that it not be interpreted as recognition of rightful claim by the Icaiché to those lands worked by BHC below Blue Creek.[48] Following weeks of negotiations, Canul settled for a reduced ransom payment of $3,000, paid for by the colony, and the prisoners were released after two months in custody.[49]

Austin blamed the British Honduras Company and its agents for the whole lethal and costly incident. In addition to the ransom payments, BHC employees who had lost property in the attacks at Qualm Hill and Betson's Bank wanted the colony to reimburse them for those losses. An official investigation was launched. In the investigation, Santiago Cervera (the agent for the Icaiché who lived at Achiote) testified that all other representatives of mahogany companies (including Panting for YTC and Manuel Castillo, the subcontractor who worked at Cowpen) regularly paid both the Icaiché and the Kruso'ob rent for harvesting timber on lands those groups claimed. Only the BHC had been reluctant to pay, as Raboteau had told Cervera: "What can those damned cowardly Indians do. If the troops come from Belize they will reduce Ycaiche to ashes."[50] According to Cervera, when Canul learned that the BHC had no intention of making good on its promises, even after Canul had asked several times civilly, he and his men proceeded to Qualm Hill.[51]

When Austin saw that both George Raboteau and John Hodge had lied and each of them blamed the other, he grew infuriated. Upon the recommendation of the inspector, Austin accepted Raboteau's version of events, which was that Hodge told him not to pay Canul, except if harm were imminent, in which case Raboteau should forcibly defend the logging works. Austin faulted Hodge for creating an international incident that led to loss of life and property and that bore enormous diplomatic costs. John Hodge, he said, showed "very great impudence . . . in supposing that he alone could control events to which all others had bent."[52]

The attack at Qualm Hill and the hostage negotiations led to several developments of great significance. The first, of course, is that British Honduran officials, if they did not already, now viewed the Icaiché as incurable enemies of the colony. Austin asked the governor to send a warship to capture the "robber-chief" Canul and his men—the "vagabonds of the district binding together under the leadership of a Mexican half-caste."[53] Steps were taken to fortify the northern boundary against future invasion. The legislative assembly, seated in Belize, did not care to levy a tax to raise funds for the defense of the northern district. The lieutenant governor therefore pleaded with the governor to reach some sort of agreement with Mexico that each government would prevent its own "Indians" from invading the other.[54] In addition, twelve Yucatecans who were suspected of having abetted the Icaiché in the attack—including the agent Santiago Cervera, who was even suspected of masterminding the kidnapping and ransom negotiations—were ordered deported.[55] Finally, having learned that the Icaiché had been purchasing ammunition and gunpowder at Corozal, Austin issued a proclamation that, for a period of three months, no arms, gunpowder, or ammunition should be sold to foreigners without a license.[56] This ban on munitions sales would, predictably, create trouble for British Honduran relations with the Kruso'ob.

In addition, the Qualm Hill episode gave British officials new insights into Icaiché organization at the time. One of the hostages released from Icaiché described what he had witnessed. He estimated a total population of about four hundred people of diverse backgrounds: "Not pure Indians, but outcasts from all parts—part Spaniards—some African half-castes—Some Yucatecan Spaniards."[57] Reaffirming prior observations about the weakness of Icaiché leadership, one of the commissioners commented that he had to negotiate with Canul's agent because Canul had "no power or influence,—the Indians living under a state of anarchy, or rather pantarchy each man receiving his part of the booty, each man also has a voice in the matter."[58]

Moreover, the commissioner described the Icaiché as a group of bandits who had coalesced from different parts of the region. They were, he said, "but a body of half armed banditti (the fighting men being 150 in number) formed of the scum of all the surrounding communities, unrecognized by, and outlaws from the other border Indians,—savage and lazy, and ruled only by their wants and the desire of ardent spirits."[59] While we might write this off as exaggeratedly harsh criticism uttered under the extreme stress of hostage negotiations, it is worth considering whether the group being led by Canul at this point was, in fact, largely a gang devoted to living through extortion and armed robbery. After all, we have seen that, in 1864, Yucatecan commissioners recruited escaped prisoners from British Honduras and "miscreants" from Corozal to join the Icaiché army in their joint military campaign against the Kruso'ob. Also, the Catholic missionary described the Pacífico region in 1866 as "a lair for the deserters, thieves, escaped servants, and every sort of criminal." Finally, a few months hence, a Lochhá resident would explain that "Ycaiché is placed by order of the Imperial Government under the Command of Don Pablo Encalada, but lately they have revolted and are now simply wandering robbers. They captured my son lately and demanded $500 ransom for him."[60]

Suggesting that, in 1866, Canul was leading a band of robbers does not nullify legitimate claims by the Indigenous people to lands in the region, nor does it deny that the Maya had several legitimate grievances with British Hondurans, especially with the logging companies. However, the group that was under Canul's leadership in 1866 may have been quite different in composition from the Pacíficos under José María Tzuc's leadership who had signed the peace treaty in 1853. Certainly, it was smaller in size. In 1853, the estimated total Pacífico population was about twenty to twenty-five thousand.[61] In 1866, Canul was recognized as leader only at Icaiché, having revolted against the other Pacíficos under Pablo Encalada. Again, the former hostage estimated a total Icaiché population of four hundred people (men, women, and children). Given the mobility of people in the region at the time, the fragility of personalistic leadership (wherein people could push out or abandon a leader if he failed to meet his promises or if he put them in danger), and what we have already seen of Luciano Tzuc's and Marcos Canul's tactics, the notion that the people remaining with Canul at Icaiché at this time were largely interested in extortion and robbery does not seem out of the question. Such a conclusion certainly does not mean that all the Maya in the Pacífico region were bandits, but simply that by 1866, Canul—based at Icaiché, recognized as leader only there, and in conflict with the Pacífico Comandante

General—may have seen his role as one of making extortionist demands and organizing armed raids, and others were willing participants. We have already seen that the Chichanhá deposed Luciano Tzuc once and that another large group crossed the Hondo River because they rejected his leadership. Similarly, others who were disaffected with Marcos Canul might have gone elsewhere in the Pacífico region within Mexico or, like others before them, into Guatemala or the British-claimed zone.

One extraordinary piece of information that was revealed in the hostage negotiations relates to Icaiché understanding of geography. Since the old Anglo-Spanish treaties of 1783 and 1786 regarded the Hondo River as the northern limit of the British logging area, then, at issue, as we know, was the true source of the Hondo. While one of the hostage negotiators, Gustav von Ohlafen, insisted that the Blue Creek was its source, Canul told him that such was not the case, and furthermore, neither could the Río Bravo nor Booth's River be considered as such. This was, he reasoned, because when those treaties were drafted, the Río Bravo and Booth's River did not exist, but the region instead was swampland. They only became recognizable as rivers when Messrs. Hyde & Co. cut a canal through the swamp connecting them to the Hondo in the 1830s. Canul therefore concluded (in Austin's words) that: "that the Mexican claims extended from Achiote to the old Belize River to which he would march whenever it suited his convenience and levy rents on the occupants."[62] (Achiote was situated on the Hondo River just to the east of where Blue Creek and Booth's River pour into it.) This same understanding of geography, based upon a distinction between what was and what was not a river, would come into play later in the year, when Canul's men would place a demand for rent payment at Labouring Creek (near San Pedro), explaining that they knew it was their territory because "they had passed no river in coming."[63] In other words, the Icaiché did not consider the Bravo and Booth's as bodies of water upon which treaties could have been based because they were not true rivers. The Icaiché Pacíficos remained consistent in their claims to the lands to the west of the British usufruct timber zone as it had been delineated in the 1783 and 1786 Anglo-Spanish treaties, and thereby continued to remind the British that their own visions of territorial sovereignty for British Honduras were far from being realized.

Surprisingly, the Qualm Hill episode also pushed the lieutenant governor to flirt with the notion of creating a native homeland for the Icaiché in the region between the Río Bravo and Blue Creek. Since the British government would not provide proper defense for the colony, Austin wrote to the governor, the only way to guard against future Icaiché attacks lay in providing some concessions. He referred to Hodge's 1865 statement that: "the English Logwood cutters settled as high as the Bravo although the Indians were the possessors as they never would permit the Spaniards to take possession either before or since the Independence of

Mexico." Austin raised the idea of purchasing the lands between the Río Bravo and Blue Creek from Mexico, and subsequently paying the Icaichés annual subsidies to allow the logging companies to continue to work there based on the notion that the Indians were the "original possessors of the soil." Austin quickly scuttled this idea, however, because doing so would only generate squabbles over which Indian group were the original possessors and because such a concession would likely lead to other Indian demands down the line.[64] In essence, he recognized that the Icaiché had legitimate claims to the land but rejected acknowledging that publicly out of fear of opening a political Pandora's box.

The Qualm Hill episode also cracked open a fissure between the British Honduras Company and the British Honduran government. While officials in Belize had long considered their primary concern to be the prosperity and security of the logging companies, as the economy was beginning to diversify, not all political elites agreed. In defending to the governor his decision that the colony should pay the Qualm Hill ransom money (rather than forcing BHC to do so), Austin explained that the greatest progress made during his administration had been in stimulating agriculture, especially sugarcane production. The BHC was not looked on favorably by many of the settlers, and the Legislative Assembly only voted in favor of the resolution to pay the ransom money out of sympathy for the family members, he said.[65] Nevertheless, the BHC continued to wield enormous power. In response to the BHC employees who had lost property in the raid, the Attorney General explained that the colony could not reimburse them, but neither could the British government force the company to do so, despite Hodge's role in the fiasco, because the BHC was a favored client in London.[66]

One final outcome of the Qualm Hill episode was that Canul perceived, once again, that British defenses were pitifully weak and also that armed attacks on mahogany works could be immensely profitable. You see where this is heading...

WORK AT SAN PEDRO

Two weeks after the raid on Qualm Hill, Asunción Ek wrote to Austin that he had learned about the raid, which only heightened his concern because Canul had already threatened several times that he and his men from Icaiché were going to come to San Pedro and, in fact, would do so by the end of May. Ek wanted instructions from Austin about whether they at San Pedro should defend themselves in case of an Icaiché attack. The Legislative Assembly then resolved that Ek's group at San Pedro should be provided with arms and ammunition for such an eventuality.[67] Some time passed before the munitions were delivered, however, as Austin was undoubtedly focusing on the Qualm Hill hostage negotiations.

By this time, the lives of those at San Pedro were thoroughly intertwined with the British Honduras Company.[68] The subcontractor responsible for BHC work at San Pedro was Florencio Vega (also the proprietor at San Estevan), who had his own "plantation" at San Pedro. Maya tenants on BHC lands would have paid rent for the house and milpa plots with money they earned working for the company in some capacity, part-time or seasonally, or by providing a certain number of animals they raised or a portion of their crops.[69] Several Maya families at San Pedro owned cattle, and they may have raised them as part of their duties to the BHC landlord (or simply to sell them to the timber crews).[70]

Similarly, although sugarcane is not typically a milpa crop, it was grown in San Pedro milpas.[71] Just as many of Carmichael's tenants paid their rent in sugarcane, some of the San Pedro residents may have paid rent in sugarcane to BHC, which at that time was expanding beyond timber into sugar and rum production. At the time, Indian Church was the "crack Estate of the quarter."[72] Named after the Spanish colonial-period church, it had an advantageous position on the western bank of the New River Lagoon. On lands granted by Colonel MacDonald in 1837, and later owned by Hyde, Hodge & Co., the estate was subsequently absorbed by the British Honduras Company, and sugarcane was under production at the site at least by 1864. Sometime before 1868, a steam-powered mill was installed, one of the very few such mills in the colony at the time.[73] The plantation had a labor problem, however. Because it was difficult to retain Maya agricultural laborers for very long, under the colony's new immigration plan, the company arranged for the transfer from China of 150 indentured servants for this estate and another one in 1866. Within a few short months, however, the Chinese workers had escaped and had resettled among the Kruso'ob.[74] Consequently, BHC would have been eager to secure more workers or else have sugarcane provided by tenants.

THE COMPANY ENFORCER

When Asunción Ek asked the British Honduran lieutenant governor to "convey some authority on [him] over evildoers," he got much more than he had bargained for. Recall that, in his role as Comandante, Ek was responsible for administering justice in the San Pedro region. In the village, there was a court where criminal suspects were charged, a garrison where some of Ek's deputies were stationed, and barracks where prisoners were held. He had wanted authority over the migrants from the Chichanhá region, but he was unaware of the problems that role would create for him due to the fact that BHC claimed ownership of the land.

At San Pedro, Florencio Vega had stationed Yucateco foremen to oversee the work of the logging crews. However, there was a complicated organizational structure that predictably created disputes between Vega's foremen and the appointed leaders at San Pedro. Vega's men needed to rely upon Comandante Ek and his deputies for punishment of crimes against the company (such as theft—which would have included absconding while indebted to the employer). Vega's men also relied upon village leaders to keep the Maya workers "in order." Ek and his deputies, therefore, had dual roles as local police and company enforcers. What would happen in a case, however, in which one of Vega's managers happened to be the criminal offender? Would the comandante have to charge and punish the person who was, in effect, his immediate boss? Predictably, this dual role set up a struggle over authority.

One such tense confrontation unfolded in July 1866. Ek's deputies punished the manager of Vega's plantation at San Pedro—Claudio Manríquez—for striking a worker, José Remigio Pérez. (Pérez was the fugitive indebted servant of Carmichael, mentioned in chapter 2.) Pérez had come to Manríquez's house to have a word with the former *alcalde* (José Domingo Vela). According to the letter that Manríquez wrote to his employer (Florencio Vega), Pérez insulted the former *alcalde*, and when Manríquez told him not to use "bad language," Pérez then insulted Manríquez, who retaliated with "a slap and a blow." Two of Ek's deputies, Juan Balam and José María Dzul, hauled the manager (Manríquez) off to the barracks, where he was tied to a post overnight. Manríquez apparently sent word to Pérez's "master" for help, however, and the next day, John Carmichael Jr. arrived, had Manríquez released, and carried off Pérez.

Apparently incensed that the Maya leaders had the gall to punish him, Manríquez pushed Vega to have Ek stripped of his position as comandante. He charged, in essence, that Ek was costing Vega financially by allowing his deputies to use excessive force against employees. In one incident, three workers had stolen liquor; they were then tied up as punishment, but they escaped and ran away. Manríquez asked Vega to have Vela placed above the deputies as *alcalde* of San Pedro once again, or even to have him replace Ek. He needed, he said, to "put a stop to these illbred Indians."[75] This conflict between the manager/foreman and the appointed leaders at San Pedro would fester and have explosive consequences in just a few months' time.

RUMORS OF CANUL

Over the next few months, rumors about Canul's imminent invasion of the colony kept British officials and mahogany company agents on edge. Echoing Ek's earlier warning, John Hodge was advised in July that Canul's men were planning to march on San Pedro "within a week." Flush with ransom money from the Qualm Hill incident, the Icaiché had purchased a large quantity of goods in Achiote plus a large quantity of gunpowder in Belize.[76] Finally, then, as the Legislative Assembly had promised, ammunition and ten muskets were delivered to Ek at San Pedro in

August.[77] "What good would ten muskets do if the Icaiché raid us?" Ek likely wondered. "Is this all our lives are worth to the British?"

Canul's men did not set out "within a week"—but the rumors multiplied. At the beginning of September, Corozal Magistrate Edwin Adolphus was told that Canul and his men had already set out for San Pedro to retrieve some muskets that Ek's group had taken when they left Chichanhá years earlier,[78] but they in fact had not gone. In the middle of the month, word reached Adolphus that Canul was upset about not being able to purchase gunpowder in British Honduras (because of Austin's powder proclamation) and would go to Belize to find out why. Adolphus also was told that Canul and his men were upset that Santiago Cervera (the agent) had been arrested by British officials; they were threatening to go to Orange Walk and capture the magistrate as a hostage, pending Cervera's release.[79] Those were just rumors, as well. Later in September, Austin was told that Canul planned to attack the BHC works at Yalbac Creek and to force Ek and his group at San Pedro to join him. Another rumor held that Canul planned to attack the two sugar estates at Orange Walk; Austin took that seriously enough to dispatch a company of Third West India Regiment troops.[80] The detachment's commander, Captain Delamere, however, said there was no immediate threat from Canul, since Canul had just announced that he was organizing a big fiesta to be held in Icaiché, for which he was going to bring in the Catholic priest from Corozal and hire a band of musicians.[81]

Fearing an Icaiché attack, Austin even reached out to Pablo Encalada, Pacífico leader at Lochhá. Both Encalada at Lochhá and the Kruso'ob leaders blamed Canul for Austin's powder proclamation, which prevented them from buying the gunpowder they needed.[82] Some Lochhá residents told Austin they thought that Encalada would arrest all of the Qualm Hill conspirators, if Austin asked him to do so, whereupon Austin invited Encalada to meet with him to resume peaceful relations and trade.[83] To further gain favor with the British, Encalada told Austin that he had ordered Canul not to take any steps without his permission, as Encalada considered Canul his subordinate within the Pacífico hierarchy.[84] While the Secretary of State urged Austin to reinforce the powder proclamation across the board with a full trade embargo, Austin responded that he would only do so in the case of the Icaiché, but not the Santa Cruz or Lochhá groups because he needed their cooperation. They were really concerned only with the "150 to 200 marauding Indians, and half breeds assisted covertly by some traitorous Yucatecans residing on British territory," he explained.[85]

DISPUTES WITH FOREMEN

Many rumors hung in the air in late 1866, whipping up fear at every turn. Ignorance also played a supporting role. Vega's foremen and the appointed officers at San

Pedro had clashed several times over issues including the destruction of harvests, debt, theft, assault, and labor exploitation. The relationship between the Maya residents and BHC agents was strained to the point of breaking. Comandante Ek's dual role as local police and company enforcer had become untenable. Captain Delamere, however, knew none of this.

The first in a string of altercations occurred when—as had happened innumerable times before—the company cattle trampled through the farmers' milpa fields. That started a dispute with the foremen, but Claudio Manríquez, Vega's manager, reportedly liked to "torment the poor Indians" by threatening to have them arrested.[86] Captain Delamere, however, knew none of this.

In late September, Comandante Ek and his deputies once again wrangled with Manríquez. As it turns out, Manríquez himself was in arrears on a debt to his employer. Ek and eight of his deputies took Manríquez prisoner because of that overdue debt (now cast as "theft"). Manríquez escaped to Hill Bank, but Ek and five of his men returned to the house and seized his pigs, some poultry, furniture, and clothes.[87] Were these goods taken to be given over to Florencio Vega to settle the debt, or in part for revenge? We cannot know, but what is clear is that by this point, Manríquez had multiple reasons to wish ill on Ek and the other appointed officers at San Pedro. Captain Delamare, however, knew none of this.

Around the same time (in late September or early October), San Pedro residents clashed again with the "foreman" at San Pedro (probably still Manríquez). Austin was told in late October "that great dissatisfaction existed amongst the San Pedro Indians" because the BHC foreman had seized some of their cattle and they swore to retaliate.[88] One possibility is that, after having escaped from the San Pedro barracks, Manríquez—unable to return to his home, but needing some means of subsistence and also seeking revenge—stole the cattle and then sold them. Captain Delamere, however, knew none of this.

Austin wrote to Ek inquiring about the missing cattle. The ink on Ek's letter is faded and some parts are illegible, but he explained that an eyewitness saw cattlemen from the BHC works at Blue Water Bank with three bulls that had gone missing from San Pedro (one white and black, one red, and one spotted).[89] It seems possible that some at San Pedro accused the Blue Water Bank cattlemen of having stolen the bulls, which would have created a rift with that group. It is possible, as well, that others suspected Manríquez of having stolen the bulls, and the seizure of Manríquez's valuables was retribution for that. Whether either scenario or both scenarios were true, they are the sort of incident that might have brought down the ire of the proprietor, Florencio Vega. Someone sent word to the lieutenant governor about the disturbance, and Vega was the likely candidate, perhaps even asking for Ek to be punished or removed from his post (just as Manríquez had prompted him to do back in July). After all, how else would Manríquez's letter to Vega have ended up in the lieutenant governor's possession? Captain Delamere, however, knew none of this.

Meanwhile, the dispute of Ek and his deputies with Vega's men had grown far more serious and extended to include Vega himself. After Manríquez fled, his replacement as foreman at San Pedro also stole from his employer (Vega). (Who wasn't stealing from Vega?) The new foreman, Robert Manzanero, stole some of Vega's mules at San Pedro and fled to the Petén region (in Guatemala) on October 31. Vega dispatched Ek and his men (in their dual roles as local police and as company police) to capture Manzanero. They did so, but Vega paid them insufficiently for the risks they took to their lives in that mission. Ek complained publicly that Vega should pay all the soldiers for having captured him, or else Vega should come in person to "remove all his property from there, and they would settle the business with him."[90] Despite their official titles, Ek and the other appointed officials were ultimately just cogs in the company wheel, since the company subcontractor wielded control over their pay, their positions, and their physical safety. Ek may have wanted to be a lord of the land, but the company subcontractor had reduced him to the role of a hired brute. The fact that Florencio Vega was a sugarcane hacienda owner from Tihosuco—the type of man against whom the Social War rebels initially rose up—may have added insult to injury. Captain Delamere, of course, knew none of this.

Vega and two of his former foremen, in essence, had motives to bring down Ek. Vega also had a deep personal grudge against the Canuls, since Susano Canul had killed Vega's son, and Marcos Canul helped him escape. Captain Delamere, of course, knew none of this.

"I FEAR EK IS PLAYING FALSE."

OCTOBER 29: THE INFORMANT

On October 29, one of Vega's employees at San Pedro made a statement before Captain Delamere at Orange Walk, which propelled Delamare into action. José Carmen Hernández, a native of Tabasco, said that San Pedro residents were conspiring with Marcos Canul to rob the mahogany banks. He said that the second *alcalde* at San Pedro, Santiago Pech (fig. 5.1), had recently gone to Icaiché, and when he returned (about October 20), Pech reported that "the Icaiché and other Indians were coming to San Pedro and other mahogany banks in the neighborhood, and that they, the Indians of San Pedro, were not to be afraid, as they would not be molested, as the expedition was only directed against the English mahogany banks for the purpose of depredation & robbery." Hernández told Delamere that

Figure 5.1. Santiago Pech. Source: Enclosure with Henry Fowler dispatch no. 2, 15 Jan. 1884, CO 123/172. Credit: National Archives (UK).

people in San Pedro (including Ek) told him to keep that secret, that the group from Icaiché was expected to arrive on November 1, and that those in San Pedro had placed an order for food and rum to host the arrivals. In addition, a letter had been found attached to a post near San Pedro, from Canul to Ek, alerting him to his imminent arrival. Then, on Hernández's way to deliver pigs to San Estevan, he met a group who had just left their village of San Antonio in the Petén district, and they were leaving because Canul and his men were "levying forced contributions of men, having already collected the men belonging to the village of Tubusil and Celestun." Canul's group planned to attack the BHC mahogany works at Turnbull, Blue Water, and Swasey's Bank, it was said.[91]

"I fear Ek is playing false," Delamere wrote to Austin, sending along Hernández's statement. Without waiting for orders, and despite the heavy rains and muddy pathways, Delamare prepared to set out for San Pedro (by way of Hill Bank) with forty-three men (including two officers, forty privates, and one drummer) to catch Canul and head off any attacks on the mahogany banks.[92]

NOVEMBER 1: AUSTIN UNRUFFLED

Upon receiving Delamere's dispatch, Austin plainly did not believe that Ek was conspiring with Canul. The fiesta preparations were not suspicious because it was the time of year in which all the mahogany laborers ("whether Indians or Creoles") would be returning to their homes and celebrating. Moreover, as Austin learned about the alleged theft of Maya-owned cattle by a BHC foreman, he thought that public promises to seek revenge were just a matter of venting frustration. Austin was more concerned about the cattle theft, and "if wrong is done to [the Maya] by British subjects," he wrote to the governor, he wanted to "give redress."[93] To Captain Delamere's superior, Austin worried that the captain would antagonize Ek, in which case "we may have a perfectly harmless and well affected inhabitant turned into a designing and troublesome neighbor."[94] Austin had good cause for concern.

NOVEMBER 5: THE MESSENGER

Accompanying Captain Delamere was John Carmichael Jr., valued on the trek for his familiarity with the Maya language and the region. The soldiers took the overland route, arriving at Yalbac on November 5, whereupon they learned that Canul in fact had not arrived.[95] Carmichael dispatched a messenger with a letter to Ek, advising him that the soldiers were simply visiting the various banks and they were on their way to have a conversation with Ek about "the safety of these districts."[96] Their slow slog through the swampy and flooded terrain apparently gave the opportunity for someone else to travel by canoe and sound the alarm. Ek was told that police were coming to arrest him (which he might have assumed was related to their conflicts with the BHC agents) and he summoned eighty men from San Pedro and nearby villages to protect him.[97]

When Delamere's messenger finally arrived at San Pedro, he became suspicious, as he saw that a new road recently had been opened through the thick vegetation and an old one had been widened, the women and children had all vacated the village, and about one hundred armed Maya men were standing about the village, apparently on guard. Ek, who was himself armed with a gun and a machete, informed the messenger that he had the same number of men hidden as sentries in the forests. Ek's secretary, Calisto Medina, read Carmichael's letter aloud, whereupon the men at San Pedro "appeared much excited," presumably because those on the march were British troops, not just the police. They told the messenger that "if the troops came to arrest one of them, they would have to arrest all."[98]

Ek aimed to forestall any conflict. He sent a message to Carmichael thanking him for the notification, but also letting him know that when the troops arrived in San Pedro, they should not be alarmed to find the men armed. They were simply on guard because Canul was expected.[99] However, Ek remained distressed, asking the messenger again, privately, if the British could be trusted. He urged the messenger to tell Delamere and Carmichael not to arrive at night, because if they did, "there might arise a collision."[100]

NOVEMBER 6: CAPTAIN DELAMERE AT SAN PEDRO

When Delamere and his men arrived at San Pedro on November 6, they discovered the village in fully defensive mode. Everyone had been cleared out, except for some two hundred men on a hill above them, hiding behind fallen timber, armed with guns and machetes, and facing them directly. Ek was afraid to talk with Captain Delamere, and he and the other men on the hill talked excitedly for about an hour. Ek only stepped forward to talk with Delamere after his men promised that they would defend him, if need be. Ek explained that the villagers were afraid of the soldiers and that they were armed because they expected Canul and his men to arrive. Delamere expressed that he simply came to talk about "the future peace of the District."[101] The closest thing we have to Ek's version of the events is an account communicated two months later by his secretary, Calisto Medina, to a priest sent by the lieutenant governor. In that cross-cultural encounter in which the men might not have been able to understand one another's words, they would have been paying close attention to one another's behavior. Ek offered to let Delamere stay at his house. Ek then watched as Delamare and his soldiers drank from the creek that traversed the town and thereafter returned to the road. Apparently interpreting Delamere's behavior in terms of his own cultural expectations about hospitality, according to Medina, Ek took Delamere's hesitancy to enter his house as a sign that they did not trust him ("a manifestation of disconfidence") and "that he had fallen into disgrace with the English Governor."[102]

Ek then went to talk with the assembled *alcaldes* and other men on the hill, where they all spoke and argued excitedly, and it was another hour before Ek would return to talk with Delamere. Ek's response was: We need three hundred guns. That was what was needed if they were to defend themselves against Canul's men, he said. While there were three hundred armed with guns at San Pedro then, he said, he was expecting another three hundred to arrive in a matter of days, and they would need weapons.[103] (Did Delamere shake his head in disbelief?)

There might have been any number of reasons why some Maya people in the western Belize region at the time would have wanted to join up with Canul and collect rent from or rob the mahogany banks. To name a few: revenge against the logging companies for years of depredations, harassment, and exploitation; a belief that as original inhabitants of the region they had a right to live on the lands without owing anything to supposed private landowners; simple financial gain; intense pressure from Canul's armed soldiers or local allies; or any combination thereof. Once the British troops arrived on the scene, however, that added a new incentive. The troops' arrival and suspicious behavior convinced Ek (and probably others) that they were in danger and their best chances lay in joining up with Canul in a stand against the British. The excited talk amongst Ek, the *alcaldes*, and other men on the hill suggests strong disagreement among them about what to do. Ek's visible hesitancy and very slow response surely reflected internal confusion and feeling pressured from multiple sides. According to Medina, that is when Ek concluded that he could not salvage the situation with the lieutenant governor, and therefore, "not to be all alone in the affairs [Ek] put it into the hands of Canul who was his former enemy."[104] The request of three hundred guns would seem to have been a deceptive ploy. Ek knew they would be not delivered (after all, it had taken months for the Legislative Council to finally deliver ten rifles!), but Ek probably wagered that by making this request, he could signal to the Maya appointed leaders (including Medina) and the other gathered Maya men that he was on their side, while also buying some time with the British before engaging in armed conflict. Delamere's group departed, and in a later dispatch to the lieutenant governor, he concluded that: "Asumpcion Ek and his Indians are traitors and are only awaiting Kanul's at San Pedro to join him in a raid on English settlements, the limits of which cannot be foreseen." Carmichael agreed.[105]

NOVEMBER 7: INQUIRIES

After Captain Delamere's visit to San Pedro, but before he wrote to Austin, he made inquiries in the region to gather intelligence about Canul and to assess the honesty and intentions of Ek and the others at San Pedro. He took statements from a variety of people; however, all his informants had prior disputes with Ek, and therefore, not surprisingly, they cast Ek in a negative light. Was Delamere knowingly consulting only with people who would confirm his suspicions? As he was new in the region, how did he know with whom to talk? (Who pointed him toward those individuals?) How much influence did Carmichael have over Delamere? Recall that just a few months prior, Carmichael forcibly released Vega's manager whom Ek was holding prisoner (Manríquez). How much credit did Delamere give to rumors? As Austin suspected might have been the case, were some public threats against BHC agents mere expressions of anger that had been misinterpreted as actual intent to do harm?

Captain Delamere went first to the Blue Water Bank of the BHC, where the cattlemen had been accused of stealing San Pedro cattle and which was also one of the rumored Canul targets. The manager told Delamare that he had heard rumors that the Icaiché were on their way to San Pedro with the intention of raiding the mahogany banks (including his own), and also that the cattlemen at Yalbac had heard that the residents of San Pedro had hostile intentions toward the British. Ek was reported as having said: "that he would be glad if the Icaiché Indians would come as he had plenty of young bulls ready, and that had he only more guns he would show the English something."[106]

That same day, back in San Pedro, Ek took aside the new foreman for Florencio Vega, who had only been foreman for a few days. He told him that he wished him well, but that there was likely going to be trouble at San Pedro and that he should leave for his own protection.[107] Ek was certain that there would be trouble, although he did not know from which direction it would come from first.

NOVEMBER 9: EK'S PLEA

On November 9, Ek penned a panicked appeal to the lieutenant governor. He clearly had not yet given up on repairing the relationship with the British. He recounted details of the theft of San Pedro cattle and pleaded for the right of his townspeople to defend themselves against an Icaiché invasion: "I beseech you, because we are in grave danger here." Since there were so many paths leading to San Pedro, he explained, if the Icaiché approached at night, they could be caught in a surprise attack. Similarly, if the British were to come, they should send advance notice—implying that because the townspeople were on edge, if soldiers arrived unexpectedly, the San Pedro men would likely strike first out of fear and confusion.[108]

NOVEMBER 10: A COUP IN THE MAKING

Captain Delamere conducted more inquiries about Canul and Ek. Along the way, he learned exculpatory information about Ek, but that did not affect his assessment. Lorenzo Ortiz, a BHC worker at Guinea Grass, told Delamere that he had heard that Canul was recruiting men to plunder the mahogany banks at Blue Water Bank, Spanish Creek, Orange Walk, and San Estevan and kidnap victims for ransom. Ortiz revealed that there was a political division within San Pedro. Santiago Pech (the second *alcalde*), Juan Balam (one of Ek's deputies), "José Maria Xib" (probably the other one of Ek's deputies previously referred to as José María Dzul), and Calisto

Medina (Ek's secretary) were conspiring to join up with Canul, to kill Asunción Ek ("as he was too much a friend to the English"), and to name Juan Balam as comandante. According to Ortiz, one of the *alcaldes* (presumably Santiago Pech) had already made two visits to Icaiché to encourage Canul to come. San Pedro was to be the headquarters for their plundering forays. They planned to first kidnap someone from Blue Water (presumably the foreman) and hold him for twice the amount of Raboteau's ransom, then kidnap the foremen and workers from the various banks "from Duck Run down," and finally march on and burn the town of Belize. Ek knew of the conspiracy but felt powerless to stop it. Ortiz vouched for Ek: "I believe Don Asumpcion Ek is doing what he can to prevent the rising, but he told me himself that his men were too strong for him, and would not listen to him,—that he soon expected they would take his rod of office and burn it, and depose him."[109]

(Dear reader: You are probably as confused as I am. Since Medina was conspiring against Ek, can we fully trust his later statement about Ek's intentions? Since Medina was Ek's secretary, who therefore read and wrote all his correspondence, can we trust that all letters addressed from Ek at this time were authored by him? Did Medina ever misrepresent to Ek the content of communications addressed to him? We'll never know for certain. Let's press on.)

In his investigation, Captain Delamere then interviewed both Manríquez and his wife,[110] surely at the behest of Carmichael. Most troubling, Manríquez agreed with Ortiz's statement about Canul's plans for plunder, but he also named Ek as a coconspirator. Since Manríquez had escaped from San Pedro in late September or early October, he would have had no direct knowledge of their plans. Because of his prior disputes with Ek and his deputies, his statement should have been taken with a grain of salt. The fact that, knowing about those disputes, Delamere nevertheless used their statements to build a case against Ek suggests willful ignorance on his part (or the overweening influence of Carmichael). Delamere then returned to Orange Walk and wrote to the lieutenant governor that Ek was engaged in a treasonous plot to commit widespread plunder. Carmichael Jr. headed directly to Belize to raise a volunteer force for defense of the western region against Indian marauders.[111] Reflecting their own priorities, Robert Ferguson of the BHC, Carmichael Sr., and eight other estate and timber company owners and agents urged Austin to send a force to protect the northern districts, since their laborers (who were distressed about possible Indian attacks) were running off, and the signers of the letter might lose their harvests.[112]

NOVEMBER 13: A SECOND PLEA

A second plea was dispatched to Austin addressed from Asunción Ek and Calistro Medina. (Did Medina devise it and sign Ek's name?) Panicky, Ek asks "what fault [I] have committed" that caused the regimental soldiers and John Carmichael to come to arrest him. Their people were "in a state of alarm" that Icaiché men were on their way to San Pedro. The author(s) beg Austin to give them two days' advance warning if they should march on San Pedro. (The stated reason was that in a prior instance, the women and children had been sent into the forest overnight for protection, and when the men received notice that the British were coming, they were too afraid to go out into the dark to check on their family members.) For the good of their families, therefore, the author(s) asked for advance warning of a British march. Similarly, if they heard that the Icaiché were headed to San Pedro, they would alert the British in Belize.[113] Was this Ek acting in good faith—and being afraid simultaneously of the British, the Icaiché, his deputies, and the dark? Or was Medina using Ek's name to forestall and compromise a British advance?

November 20: "I Should be Tempted to Visit You"

On November 20, having received Ek's two letters and Captain Delamere's report, Austin tried to de-escalate the situation. He simply did not believe Delamere's accusations. Austin wrote to reassure Ek that the captain truly had not been sent to arrest anyone at San Pedro. Austin had advised Delamare that he fully trusted Ek, believing him and his people to be loyal, and he promised Ek that the British only wanted "to give to the Indians the little protection we are able to afford at such a great distance." Poignantly, his letter ended with a gesture of friendship: "Captain Delamere has brought me a very glowing account of the beauty of the plain of Yalbac, and if I could manage to ride in one day from Hill Bank to San Pedro when the weather is fine say in March or April next I think I should be tempted to visit you. I suppose that you could have the road cleared before hand."[114]

Behind Austin's affection for Ek and against Canul was more than a touch of racism, as revealed in his dispatch to the governor. Austin was not afraid that the "Indians" would cause trouble, he explained, but he had "no great confidence in many half-caste Indians and Yucatecans living with Canul or on the banks of the Hondo." After all, he reasoned, "the poor Maya Indians, who if guilty of many acts of barbarism when seeking freedom at the point of the sword are naturally docile and were not anything as bad as the educated revolutionaries of France."[115] Despite Austin's sentimental musings, a military confrontation seemed imminent, as a company of Fourth West India regimental soldiers, under the command of Major McKay, had been dispatched for defense against an Icaiché invasion, and one detachment of regimental soldiers was sent to Orange Walk (New River).[116]

EK'S PREDICAMENT

Meanwhile, back in San Pedro, Ek was being shoved out of his position as regional comandante. Details were reported to the magistrate by one of Vega's employees who had been sent to capture the foreman (Roberto Manzanero) who had stolen Vega's mules. When Vega's employee arrived in San Pedro on November 19, he found roughly three hundred armed men, including boys armed with machetes. Ek was cautious, kept to himself, and would not talk openly with him. When the group went in hot pursuit of Manzanero, Calisto Medina (Ek's secretary and one of the reported conspirators against him), shot one of the other members of the posse—a sign that the internal political struggle had burst wide open. Medina was seized, and he was being guarded by four men with his arms bound behind his back. With Ek marginalized, other men at San Pedro told Vega's employee that they were preparing to fight the British.[117] By the end of the month, Ek had been decisively pushed out as comandante and Juan Balam claimed the title. Balam sent a message to Icaiché via Santiago Pech, and according to someone who was then imprisoned at San Pedro, the message invited those at Icaiché "to come and fight against the English and that he and Ek would give a help."[118] Was the prisoner lying about Balam's letter, was Balam lying about Ek's intentions, or had Ek—afraid of the British, pressured by the other San Pedro leaders, and perceiving the inevitability of Canul's arrival—decided by this point that his safest bet was to join in the conspiracy?

CANUL'S MEN AT SAN PEDRO

On December 1, Canul dispatched his right-hand man, Comandante Rafael Chan, his secretary, Virginio Cámara,[119] and about one hundred men from Icaiché (including "several savage Indians") to San Pedro, appointing Chan to serve as the regional Comandante (rather than Balam or Ek). Chan and his officers summoned another two hundred men from other San Pedro–region villages, including San Jose, Santa Teresa, Chorro, Xmul, Holiuc, and Naclicab. Some of these men undoubtedly joined willingly, while others might have enjoyed the same fate as San Pedro, which was, according to one account, surrounded and "Ek and all the people were taken and tied and pressed into the service of the Invading Indians." Ek was demoted to the position of sentry.[120] One of those recruited from Guatemala was Lino Lara,[121] the alleged murderer whom Asunción Ek had remanded for punishment in Belize back in 1862.

Although it seems that Marcos Canul was never present in San Pedro in December 1866 (but that he just sent Chan in his stead), a letter drafted by his secretary (Virginio Cámara) addressed from Canul and Chan to Austin said that he had arrived at San Pedro not with the intention of harming anyone, but because he had heard that British troops were there, trespassing on Yucatecan lands and harassing the Indians, and they had come to investigate.[122] Once settled in at San Pedro, Comandante Chan and others set about their rent collection activities. A group of fifty of Canul's men, armed with guns, machetes, and knives, captured James Phillips, the foreman of the crew working at Labouring Creek, demanding back payment for the mahogany that Phillips had taken out over a period of years. Not having the sum on hand, Phillips sent a letter asking his brother to deliver it. In an oddly gentle scene, Canul's men hung their hammocks and slept at Phillips's house overnight, and they asked him for six pairs of moccasins, for which they promised to repay him. The men took his shot and his gun and he was held at San Pedro between December 5–10 while awaiting his ransom payment, but he was grateful that he was allowed to take with him one of his servants, a "Carib" (Garifuna) man named Simon.[123]

The question, "What did the San Pedro Maya people want?" would be the wrong question. Within the miasma of anger, frustration, alarm, and suspicion, there would have been hundreds of different views and reactions, evolving by the minute and by circumstance. Clearly, some at San Pedro and neighboring villages wanted to collect rent and timber fees from the companies, and some (notably Santiago Pech, Juan Balam, and Calisto Medina) were willing to use force to that end, even joining up with Canul. Others probably became convinced to seek Icaiché help once Captain Delamere arrived and they feared arrest or military attack by the British. Ek held out the longest, trying to maintain the peace with the British, probably in part because of his own prior conflicts with Chichanhá leadership, and perhaps in part because he enjoyed his elevated status as comandante as an auxiliary to the British Honduran government. His friendliness with the British, however, led to his usurpation by Juan Balam and other appointed leaders. He was pressed on three sides—from Icaiché, British officials, and his own deputies. In late November, having been deposed and perhaps fearing for his life, he apparently gave in to pressure from Balam and Pech and consented to the letter that invited Canul and his men to come to San Pedro.

However reticent Ek might have been to invite Canul's help, once he opened that Pandora's box, he could not shut it. The consequences of that decision were beyond his control. Rafael Chan did not stop with the kidnapping of James Phillips, but schemes were set in motion to kidnap the foremen of other timber gangs (including Swasey, Wagner, and August). Demands for rent payments were sent to Mr. Toledo (of YTC), James Swasey (YTC foreman at Young Girl), and Francisco Pat (subcontractor at Spanish Creek).[124] Canul's men kidnapped John Samuel August, foreman at the mahogany works at Orange Walk (Belize River), demanding $600 for past rent.[125] They took him to Duck Run, where they also set upon the Corregidor of Petén, and stole his horse and those of his traveling companions. They also took August's horse, for which—curiously—they handed him a receipt.[126] Finally, men headquartering at San Pedro raided the BHC Blue Water Bank, demanding rent and stealing equipment, including axes and machetes—clearly gearing up for a fight.[127]

The British struck back. Having learned that James Phillips had been kidnapped, Austin ordered Major McKay of the Fourth West India Regiment to dispatch 50 men to Swasey's Bank (near Orange Walk on the Belize River) on December 8—although the major lacked the men necessary for the march.[128] Frustrated, Austin complained bitterly to the governor that Delamere was the one to blame for the new alliance between the Icaiché and San Pedro. As he saw it, when Delamere left San Pedro without having arrested Ek, that would have led the Indians to believe that reinforcing troops would arrive, which "cause[d] them to make those proposals to Canul which had ended in an invasion of the Colony."[129] As he saw it, only a major show of military force would put an end to the marauding, and he ordered Major McKay to march toward San Pedro with 446 troops.[130] At Swasey's Bank, British troops seized two of Chan's messengers who were suspected as spies and sent them to Belize.[131] Belize prepared for an escalation, as town residents battened down the hatches, arming themselves and keeping guard by night.[132]

Now that Austin had lost his strongest ally, he scrambled to fortify other alliances. Carmichael Jr. was in Orange Walk (New River) discussing the possible cooperation of Pacífico Comandante General Pablo Encalada against those from Icaiché.[133] Pushing back against pressure from the Secretary of State for the Colonies to enforce the powder proclamation, Austin explained to the governor that, given the Icaiché threat, he could not do so with respect to the Lochhá or the Kruso'ob, because he needed their friendship. The circumstances now were quite different, he added, since Pablo Encalada was "a shrewd and temperate man" who was willing to "control the robber gang," and since Bonifacio Novelo, the leader of the Kruso'ob, was a "Spiritual Chief" and "in every way dissimilar to Puc, seeking to rule in the cloister thro' superstitious influence." Austin pressed for latitude to make an official alliance with the Kruso'ob against the Icaiché.[134]

BATTLE AT SAN PEDRO

On December 20, Major McKay and a detachment of 120 troops set out on an overnight march over the thirteen miles from Orange Walk (Belize River) toward San Pedro. With the officers on horseback, the other soldiers went on foot, as did the hired porters carrying rocket tubes, rockets, and medical supplies.[135] With them went Edward Rhys as a commissioner to broker the peace, although Rhys worried that going to San Pedro might end up "creating difficulties rather than dissipating them."[136]

The next morning, exhausted after having walked and slogged all night through the thick mud, the troops approached San Pedro on the road from Orange Walk. According to Canul and Chan, James Swasey had never responded to either of their letters demanding back rent (on the land "which belongs to Mexico") and their two messengers had never returned, presumably being held against their will. That same morning, Ek, Chan, and some thirty of Chan's men departed San Pedro and were heading toward Orange Walk to collect rent from Swasey and rescue the messengers. A meeting on the road was quite unexpected.[137]

When the regimental soldiers and Chan's group encountered one another on the road about a mile outside of San Pedro, a battle commenced. Unsurprisingly, both groups later reported the other side had fired first. Rafael Chan said he placed his gun on his head and said, in Maya, "I come for peace, for peace," and others in his group pointed their guns downward, in a show of good will. Most of the "Indians" ran to fire from the woods and only twelve stood to face the British in battle.[138] It was a short skirmish, and Major McKay sounded the retreat only fifteen to twenty minutes later.[139]

The men at San Pedro withdrew first as their small supply of gunpowder was quickly depleted. Chan had been wounded in the knee. Chan's contingent had been woefully armed. Only the front line had guns, and they were merely "old muskets and some with fowling pieces," and the others simply had machetes and sticks. A British inspection of shots in the trees revealed the Indians had slugs rather than bullets.[140]

Nevertheless, the British retreat was chaotic. McKay sounded the bugle, but his soldiers continued fighting. When he sounded it again, the officers fled, leaving behind the soldiers and Commissioner Rhys. Three or four WIR soldiers had been killed on the spot, and the surviving troops fled back to Orange Walk in groups of two and three. The military and medical supplies and water kegs were all abandoned in the retreat, strewn across the road, since the soldiers had been so fatigued by the overnight march through the soggy terrain. By the next morning, though, the major ordered a full-scale retreat back to Belize, since the soldiers had been too weakened by the ordeal to withstand any subsequent attack.[141] A total of six colonial soldiers died, either in the field or from wounds suffered therein. Rhys had been shot,[142] although his body was never recovered.

Following the bungled retreat from San Pedro, Austin called a Council meeting and martial law was proclaimed on December 28. John Carmichael Jr. was to command a volunteer colonial militia to "defend the western frontier." Fuming about the British loss, Austin blamed McKay for the sloppy defeat. Neither did the Indians consider this a win, however. Infuriated at Ek for having called upon the Icaiché to fight when they lacked sufficient gunpowder, Rafael Chan left San Pedro and returned to Icaiché.[143]

At the end of 1866, the British were in a sorry state: beaten and vulnerable to attack from all sides. They had suffered a humiliating defeat by poorly armed Maya on the western frontier, including by a regional comandante and *alcaldes* who had been trusted and deputized within the British Honduran government. Moreover, the northern frontier appeared impossible to defend from the Icaiché under Marcos Canul, who had, over the course of the year, taken ever-bolder actions of raiding, armed robbery, and kidnapping to collect rent from British Honduran timber companies working on lands he believed the Pacíficos rightfully controlled, assured by the 1853 Pacífico-Yucatán treaty, and reinforced by the Mexican imperial decree. Meanwhile, friendly Maya groups to the north, including the Pacíficos under Pablo Encalada and the Kruso'ob, were frustrated that Icaiché raids had led to a ban on the sale of munitions to them from British Honduran merchants. A Santa Cruz comandante threatened a Corozal merchant that if British Honduras officials did "persist in closing the sale of powder we will go . . . not only to Corosal, but also to Belize."[144]

As for the people in San Pedro, Asunción Ek surely knew that that skirmish on December 21 was a harbinger of things to come. Officials in Belize had twice dispatched West India regimental troops to the western region. They would surely send more, freshly equipped, and more knowledgeable of the terrain. San Pedro residents were unprepared to receive them, as Canul's deputy had abandoned them and they had no gunpowder, nor ready access to more.

6

Flight, Deserters, and Canul's Last Stand (1867–1872)

The battle at San Pedro marked a turning point in Maya-British relations in the region. The San Pedro–British alliance was irrevocably broken. Over the next few months, British troops would burn the villages in the western region in retaliation, and survivors would flee across the line into Guatemala. Harsh terms of surrender were issued, and in the British view, the San Pedro Maya were thereafter associated with the Icaiché threat.

Shortly thereafter, fighting escalated between the Icaiché and the Kruso'ob, as both groups engaged in creative diplomacy—with the British and officials in Campeche—to secure a steady flow of arms and gunpowder. Perhaps thousands more Maya people resettled south of the Hondo River over the next several years, to evade rent (and the indebted servitude thereby implied) and forced military service in one of the Maya armed forces. The Maya leaders, however, needing a steady supply of funding and foot soldiers, conducted raids into the presumed British territory to recapture those whom they considered runaway debtors and deserters. These new settlers in the British settlement were, in terms of their experiences and goals, much like the San Pedro Maya. This time, however, they were deemed less useful to the British, who treated them with an indifference that was lethal.

GUNPOWDER PLOTS

Over the next several months following the battle at San Pedro—panicky about the possibility of another attack from Icaiché or the western region—Lieutenant

https://doi.org/10.5876/9781646424634.c006

Governor Austin would go around the Executive Council to use the promise of munitions as a bargaining chip. Both the Kruso'ob and Lochhá groups depended almost exclusively on munitions from British Honduran merchants, and Austin could use that to British advantage. On January 3, 1867, the Executive Council extended the powder proclamation—which prohibited the sale of guns and powder to all foreigners and Indians—for another three months.[1] However, immediately thereafter, Austin wrote to leaders of both the Kruso'ob and Lochhá telling them that the intention was not to stop the flow of munitions to them, and there still might be a way for them to acquire those goods. He devised a plan to bypass the ban by issuing select commercial licenses. To John Carmichael, who traded and had very friendly relations with the Kruso'ob, Austin confided that he would use the promise of renewed munitions sales as an incentive to encourage the Kruso'ob and Lochhá to suppress the Icaiché and San Pedro Maya. He directed Carmichael to facilitate such an arrangement with Kruso'ob leaders.[2] When, later that month, the governor asked the lieutenant governor whether there might be a way to maintain the powder proclamation publicly while secretly providing munitions to their Indian allies, Austin told him of his licensing scheme, already underway.[3] In February, with the greatest of secrecy, Austin granted Carmichael an export certificate to ship gunpowder to Bacalar, as Kruso'ob leaders had requested.[4]

Meanwhile, Austin continued to enlist the help of Pablo Encalada and the Lochhá Pacíficos to rein in Marcos Canul. As a show of support to Austin, Encalada ordered Canul to Lochhá to explain his actions. Expecting a quid pro quo, commissioners from Lochhá simultaneously delivered Encalada's request for gunpowder.[5]

MEDINA'S EXPLANATION

The western border continued to vex Austin. Wray's survey work had to be halted because of the troubles in the west and also to benefit those two mahogany companies (BHC and YTC) whose claims extended beyond British Honduras's presumed western border—and whose claims to those lands would surely be disrupted by a survey that would reveal those encroachments into Guatemalan territory. At the same time, however, Austin worried that a border not clearly marked gave the Maya confidence in their land claims, and he therefore wanted a sixty-foot-wide bank cleared along the length of it.[6]

Even while British troops were mobilizing, Austin attempted to reestablish peaceful relations with San Pedro by dispatching two Catholic priests as intermediaries there in late January.[7] Juan Balam had recently boasted to Austin that the Icaiché leaders had appointed him as comandante of the western region,[8] but Austin ignored Balam and continued to try to reach Ek. When the priests arrived, however,

Ek was away, so they talked with Balam and Calisto Medina, among others. It was at this meeting when Medina offered his explanation of Ek's actions—how BHC cattle had been trampling their milpas, which triggered a dispute with the foremen, and how Manríquez took pleasure in threatening to have them arrested. Those at San Pedro became alarmed when they learned that soldiers were on the way, and Ek read Delamere's refusal to enter his house and the troops' physical distancing as signs of antagonism. Ek became convinced that Austin had turned against him, and therefore reached out to Canul for protection. Medina then shifted the blame, stating that since then, "all that has happened is by Canul's commands."[9]

Canul had sent instructions that his men stationed at San Pedro should insist on payment of rent by the timber companies since the 1853 Pacífico-Yucatán treaty clarified that "all the right bank of the river Belize belongs to the Indians." Father Avvaro, however, told those assembled at San Pedro that the British Honduran maps reflected a different understanding. At that point, two Indian men stood up, announcing that they had accompanied José María Tzuc to the treaty negotiations in Belize in 1853. On that trip, they had "seen the marks of the boundaries placed, one at Punta Gorda on the New River, where Pancho [Francisco] Pat lived, and which still exists; and the other in Black Creek, which old Mr. Oscia caused to be taken up and thrown into the river." Given their proper claim to the land, therefore, the men told the priests that if the appropriate rents were paid, all would be resolved. To Austin, Father Avvaro suggested a peace conference, requesting that no more troops be sent until after that meeting.[10] By the time Austin received the priests' reports and learned that peace negotiations might have been possible, however, it was too late. Troops were already on the march.

Austin fretted over what the Pacífico-Yucatán treaty would mean for British Honduras. He knew of the old boundary markers. Conveying the priests' accounts, he told the governor: "The Indians were now determined under the advice of the Yucatecos who were with them to hold all the territory up to the Old Spanish Crosses."[11] Austin worried enough about the treaty that he asked Magistrate Adolphus about it, and Adolphus responded that he knew of it, but none of its details.[12] In the end, Austin blamed Claudio Manríquez ("one of these traitorous employees") for creating the conflicts at San Pedro, conspiring to depose Ek, and ultimately setting in motion the march by Delamere's troops that led to the alliance with Canul.[13]

ATTACKS AT MOUNT HOPE AND INDIAN CHURCH

Austin's realization came too late. Sides had been established, anger ignited, and British troops had already been ordered into position by Governor Grant. Initially, most of the Chichanhá-region Pacíficos who seceded and moved into the aspirational British settlement had farmed peaceably, worked for landlord-employers, and did not make moves to collect rent. It was perhaps only after Canul's financial success at Qualm Hill that more decided that rent collection was a worthwhile (if risky) pursuit. After officials in Belize sent in the military, however, the calculus changed. A clash with the British was inevitable—they might have reasoned—so why not get as much as they could in the meantime? Having already lost the favor of British Honduran officials and left exposed to company depredations and indignities, they pressed ahead with demands.

The British military plan was two-fold. To prevent an Icaiché invasion, Captain Delamere's troops were to be stationed at Panting's bank at Blue Creek. Then, on January 30, Lt. Col. Harley of the Third West India Regiment led a march toward San Pedro. With a group of pitpans that had been seized under martial law, the troops proceeded up the Belize River to Orange Walk, from which they would trek overland to San Pedro.[14]

However, before Harley's troops could reach San Pedro, on February 4, a group of about fifty men raided the YTC mahogany works at Mount Hope and also the BHC sugar estate at Indian Church.[15] While initial reports pointed the blame at men from San Jose and San Pedro, the diversity of participants—"pure Indians," "Spanish Indians," "Yucateco Spaniards," and "Creoles," including some former employees at Indian Church—suggests that the motives went beyond payment of rent and that others in the region joined in the raiding party for motivations ranging from profit to revenge on former employers. They were led by Domingo Tzuc and Antonio Hernández (the latter of whom lived in Belize and "appeared to be more of a Spaniard than an Indian").[16]

Curiously, the party was expected at Indian Church, and John Carmichael had laid a trap: aniseed liquor in a demijohn laced with poison. Spies had forewarned the party, though, so when they arrived, they took one man prisoner and made him drink the aniseed liquor, which made him very sick. He then ate salt and lemon juice, forcing himself to vomit out the poison. The raiding party engaged in a fight with special constables, two of whom were killed. The party burned three buildings and ran off with quinine and other medicines, sixty guns, forty pounds of gunpowder, twenty to forty mules, and all the cattle. They presented a letter addressed from Ek and Balam, threatening that if payment of $400 for rent of land at Indian Church were not received within fifteen days, they would return to destroy the estate. Rent demands were issued for several other locations along the New River, Old (Belize) River, and the Hondo River, to the sum of $400 for sugar estates, $1,000 for mahogany and logwood works, $10,000 for the town of Belize, $4,000 for Orange Walk, and $5,000 for Corozal, and the sums were to be annual.

A judge would later conclude that the party at Indian Church had come peacefully to collect rent and had not intended to kill anyone, but that they were fired upon first by the constables, provoking the incident.[17] Austin did not know that at the time, however, and he saw these raids as evidence of an alarming uprising that was regional in scope. He ordered Captain Carmichael's militia to head from Corozal to Orange Walk (New River) to help extinguish the uprising.[18]

DESTRUCTION OF SAN PEDRO

At Orange Walk (Belize River), a fruitless search for guides to take Lt. Col. Harley to San Pedro and then on to Blue Creek revealed how few non-Maya were familiar with the area, one officer calling it: "a portion of the Colony that is known to very few people excepting Indians themselves." The soldier's meager supplies were supplemented by the timber companies, which contributed horses, mules, and men to the colonial military effort.[19] After nearly a week of traveling and slogging through the mud ("after a march so trying, as well from the depth of the mud as the entangling of bushes and roots above and below ground, a description would scarce be possible"), the porters who had been pressed into service deserted.

When the troops finally reached San Pedro on February 9, the village was empty, everyone having fled.[20] Lt. Col. Harley described it as having around fifty houses—accommodating an estimated three to four hundred people—with some larger buildings including a fiesta hall and chapel. After the troops set the village on fire, "nothing of San Pedro remains except the Chapel," reported Harley with satisfaction.[21]

In the fiesta hall, the soldiers had discovered letters they seized as evidence of a conspiracy. One addressed from Ek to Austin claimed that the Indians had a treaty-backed right to "the whole territory from the capital of Yucatan to the Belize River." In another, Canul told Ek that he knew the substance of the treaty, but he did not have a copy of it.[22] Lt. Col. Harley left a letter for Ek in the church, commanding total surrender. Allowing his men to fire upon British soldiers and to kill a peace commissioner amounted to treason, Harley wrote. Ek would never be allowed to live in San Pedro again unless he surrendered himself at Belize.[23] On the road out of town, Harley and his troops then destroyed the "rich and ample provision grounds" and granaries of San Pedro.[24]

Curiously—perhaps because of his prior good relations with British Honduran officials, and perhaps because of the statements offered by the priests—officials in Belize blamed Asunción Ek less so than others. The Legislative Assembly passed twelve wartime resolutions related to restrictions on munitions sales, military and volunteer forces, martial law, expanded powers of detection and deportation, and a request for additional support from Jamaica. The eleventh resolution offered bounties for the capture of the "more prominent among the marauders," including "Marcos Canul, Juan Balam, Virginio Camara, Rafael Chan, Caliste Medina, Reon [Santiago?] Pech," but excluding Asunción Ek.[25]

SCORCHED EARTH

Harley and his troops then set out "to demand the surrender of any of the followers of Ascension Ek" in the region. They first marched on San Jose on February 12. The villagers were caught completely by surprise, as stew pots were perched over cooking fires. The soldiers were fired upon first, and several rockets were lobbed at the houses in return. The villagers fled and when the soldiers inspected, they discovered evidence that some had participated in the raid on Indian Church, including bits of Fourth WIR uniforms, firearms, bags of ammunition, mules, and many other of the stolen items. Captain Rogers then "deservedly punished them by the destruction of their town."[26]

The following day, Captain Edmunds and his troops marched on Santa Teresa, to which Asunción Ek was said to have escaped. Once again, the residents fled, and the troops burned the entire village, sparing only its church. They burned, as well, the granary, with its stores of corn and rock salt, to prevent the villagers from returning.[27]

However, the British faced threats from multiple directions. On February 16, John Carmichael's boat (the "Secret"), carrying the promised shipment of forty arrobas of gunpowder to Bacalar (intended for the Kruso'ob), was alighted upon by five "Yucatecans" who stole their goods and were presumed to be heading to San Pedro.[28] Although it later became clear that the gunpowder was not destined for San Pedro, this robbery in fact reignited the Kruso'ob competition with the Icaiché. On the northern bank of the Hondo, men from Chan Santa Cruz posted notices in the various villages, telling residents that they should no longer pay rent to Marcos Canul, but rather to Chan Santa Cruz. Eager to secure the continued flow of munitions northward, the Kruso'ob promised that anyone who took up arms against the British would be killed.[29]

To guard the western frontier in case the Maya should return, Lt. Col. Harley established a temporary military outpost at San Pedro, equipped with three officers and eighty men.[30] In the meantime, Juan Balam and a group of Icaiché were said to have kidnapped some families who had escaped to Guinea Grass and they were camping out at nearby Isla Limones. Rumors also reached Magistrate Downer that the Icaiché were conspiring to burn Orange Walk (New River) and commit other atrocities with that stolen gunpowder.[31]

THE TERMS OF PEACE

In late February, Austin issued terms of peace to be delivered to Asunción Ek. The requirements amounted to total surrender and the dissolution of the San Pedro regional alliance. The Maya, if they were to live in the western region, had to recognize British sovereignty and essentially to relinquish all autonomous rights as original inhabitants. The Maya would lose rights to land, self-governance, and defense.

In addition, Austin's statement misrepresented Anglo-Spanish treaties and was therefore a document of deceit and trickery. Pretending as though a treaty offering usufruct rights translated to outright sovereignty, Austin stated as fact that the Spanish king "gave by Treaties to the English all lands from the Sarstoon to the Hondo, the latter river from its source to the head of Blue Creek being the dividing line between the Yucatan and British Honduras." After Mexico became an independent country, he asserted, there was no need to renegotiate the boundary between Mexico and British Honduras, and the western boundary had since been settled by treaty with Guatemala. "This is the territory we are entitled to, and intend to hold, and it is an absurdity in the Indians to suppose that the authorities at Yucatan did or could give them or any body else a right to hold the lands on this side of the Hondo and Blue Creek," he wrote. If the Indians persisted in charging rent or otherwise bothering British subjects on British land, they would be deemed enemies subject to expulsion. However, if Asunción Ek "and his Indians" were to accept British authority and promise to abide by British law, they would be allowed to live in the British territory. Ek was also commanded to hand over his staff of office as well as the ten muskets that the government had provided the year before.[32]

The terms of peace gutted the regional alliance. Recalling Ek's gold-headed staff of office symbolized the dissolution of the position of Comandante over the San Pedro region. Never again would the British Honduran government appoint a regional Comandante or bestow the gold-headed staff of office upon an Indian leader. Without common lands, a copy of the treaty document, or a recognized regional political structure, the ability of the western-region Maya to wield power or influence was anemic. The list of regulations that those who surrendered would have to abide by was extensive. All residents in the British territory would be required to pay rent to the landlord—whether the Crown or private landowner—for house plots and milpa lots. (No mention was made of the possibility of Indian ownership of land.) Indian villagers could still select their *alcaldes* who would be responsible for arresting criminals, but the *alcaldes* would then remand them over to government-appointed magistrates and policemen for punishment. Indians were required to apply for licenses for any firearms and to maintain local roads. Perhaps the only benefit for the western Maya would have been the promise of religious instruction through a resident priest.[33] If the San Pedro Maya were to have accepted these terms of surrender, they stood to gain little more than freedom from British military attack.

At Austin's request, Father Eugenio Biffi wrote an earnest, affectionate letter to Ek and his wife, Irenies, urging them to surrender. Leveraging sentiments of faith and futility, Biffi encouraged them to accept the terms, since Canul did not have a copy of the Pacífico-Yucatán treaty. "Moreover, if what the English say is true," the priest wrote, and Spain had granted all of that land to the British, then "it would be wrong in you to wish to deprive them of it; and God will not protect you because God does not defend Injustice." The priest promised that the government would provide a magistrate and school in every village and also a priest in San Pedro.[34]

One of Father Biffi's promises would have been immensely significant. The priest conveyed that the British Honduran government had expropriated some land from the British Honduras Company so that the lands upon which the village of San Pedro was situated would no longer be private property. The villagers would no longer have to deal with the company foremen, he said, "and nobody will dare to trouble you."[35] Not being forced to pay rent or other form of compensation to the company as landlord would have been an enormous step toward Maya security and autonomy. It remains doubtful, however, that the promise to expropriate company lands for the San Pedro Maya villages—presented here as a *fait accompli*—was in fact ever fulfilled.[36]

The olive branch of Biffi's letter was unconvincing, however, since the British did not wait for a response but instead forged ahead with the military campaign. On March 9, Captain Delamere's troops marched on Cerro—between Naranjal and San Jose—where escapees from those villages were said to have fled. The inhabitants fled to Chorro, and Delamere's troops burned Naranjal and Cerro, along with Cerro's milpas and a large granary.[37] Captain Carmichael's volunteer militia then destroyed Santa Cruz and Chumbalche.[38] Nearly all the villages within British Honduras that had been identified in 1862 as under Ek's leadership were now obliterated. How many villagers died and how many ran away? The British documents are silent about those facts. With their villages now destroyed, trust broken, and the terms of peace so stringent and absolute, those western-region Maya who survived this scorched earth campaign stayed away for quite some time.

SHORING UP DEFENSES—AND WHEN IS A RIVER NOT A RIVER?

Austin took further measures to fortify the western and northern boundaries of his aspirational colony. Pacífico General Pablo Encalada—upset that Icaiché involvement in the uprising in the Yalbac Hills region might have damaged his reputation and good relations with the British—was determined to prove himself of use. He effected another quid pro quo: in March, Encalada's men captured and took Canul and Chan into custody, and Austin rewarded Encalada by allowing him to purchase thirty arrobas of gunpowder.[39] By April, small detachments of British troops were stationed at Orange Walk (New River), Indian Church, Corozal, and Blue Creek, in addition to San Pedro. Raiding had ceased, and Austin prepared to lift martial law.[40] Determined to protect the British Honduran settlement from "Indian" threats, the magistrates adopted a system of passports for all who wished to cross their aspirational borders.[41]

At the same time, as part of a more ambitious plan to promote the cultivation of food crops for domestic consumption and to fortify the colony's defenses, British officials invited American Confederates to settle there. Not only was the colonial population small, wrote Austin, "but it is also apathetic to a degree which can scarce be credited."[42] Young, Toledo & Co. offered to give one hundred acres of land free of charge to "every male adult from the Southern States of America or of Anglo Saxon Origin who will settle on those lands on the Western Frontier."[43] One B. R. Duval applied for a large land grant in the western frontier, where he intended to place a settlement of Confederates.[44]

To the west, naval officer Lt. E. C. Abbs was cutting the western boundary line from Blue Creek to Garbutt's Falls.[45] To facilitate surveillance along the river, Lt. Abbs also set about to clean the bank of the Blue Creek with the help of Chinese laborers. The work to clear and define the northern boundary came to an abrupt halt, though, when the surveying revealed unwanted information. More water in fact flowed through the Río Bravo than the Blue Creek. That would have made the Bravo the true source of the Hondo, thereby potentially placing the northern limit of the British colony much farther south. Austin engaged in torturous, circuitous logic, however, to figure out a way to continue to argue that the Blue Creek was the true source of the Hondo. He in fact used Canul's understanding of historical geography against him. First, Austin argued, in 1837, Col. MacDonald observed that the Bravo was not a river ("it then small meandering exit to the Hondo at Fish Creek having been dried up") and more water flowed through Blue Creek. That would have been the case, as well, noted Austin, when the treaties with Spain were drafted. Accordingly, during the negotiations following the raid on Qualm Hill the prior year, Canul had stated that the Bravo was "not a natural river on which treaty rights could be founded." The Río Bravo and Booth's River had only become recognizable as rivers when Messrs. Hyde & Co. cut a canal ("at an expense of about £10,000") so that all the water stretching across a large swampland would pour into the Hondo River. The Crown Surveyor and John Hodge confirmed Canul's recollection about the canal and the transformation of the Bravo. Since "we must in defining our rights under the treaty with Spain be guided by the then existing state of Facts," reasoned Austin, the Blue Creek therefore should be considered as the true source of the Hondo River. In essence, although it was true in 1867 that more water flowed through the Bravo than the Blue Creek, when the Anglo-Spanish treaty had been signed, the opposite was true, and therefore the Blue Creek, as the true source, should represent the northern limit of the British colony.[46] Lt. Abbs thereafter resumed the survey of the northern boundary line and finished it in April (see figure 2.1).[47]

EXODUS

Lt. Col. Harley expressed the "honour" he felt that the military operations he led in the spring of 1867 had resulted in "the almost complete Exodus of Indians from the Territory."[48] In April, Maya villagers from San Pedro, Santa Teresa, and Chorro were discovered to be living at Santa Rita in Guatemala.[49] Pacífico General Pablo Encalada continued to seek the favor—and munitions—of the British, and he dispatched three commissioners to the mountains of the Petén region to capture Asunción Ek, Juan Balam, and other accused leaders of the uprising.[50] The western-region Maya may have wearied of being on the run, however, and Austin soon received word that they wanted to resume "full enjoyment of peace and trade."[51] In Santa Rita, Ek was selling horses, mules, and cattle, and a group of bounty hunters planned to capture him by offering to buy his livestock.[52] However, Austin sent the surveyor (J. H. Faber) and the Belize magistrate (Samuel Cockburn) as commissioners to let the San Pedro–region people know that they could safely return to the British colony should they accept the terms of peace. Faber was under orders, as well, to begin surveying the western boundary.[53]

In the meantime, John Carmichael's militia had set a trap and captured two men from San Jose who were charged with murders committed during the raid on Indian Church. Again, the judge concluded that the party had not set out to commit murder, but instead had acted in defense after the police shot at them. Interestingly, the land claims question figured into the trial. "There was not sufficient evidence of any territorial right in the Crown over the Locus in quo," argued the defense lawyer, "and thus the demand of the Indians for rent was not merely colourable but to a considerable extent a justifiable demand." Since the Indians were subjects of the British Crown, continued the lawyer, they should have been read the Riot Act rather than having been fired upon straightaway. The lawyer's strategy succeeded in part. One suspect was convicted and sentenced to death by hanging while the other was acquitted.[54] Asunción Ek and the western-region Maya largely disappeared from British official communications for a few years after that. Staying out of the fray obviously seemed to them the best solution.

The clash of the San Pedro–region Maya and British troops stirred up fears of "Indian" attacks among other British Honduran residents, however. Throughout the western region, timber and agricultural workers fled en masse, mahogany extraction efforts had to be suspended, and exports declined.[55] By August 1867, timber extraction in the western region had been renewed only at Indian Church.[56] Nearly all villages on the southern side of the Hondo River had been abandoned.[57] Florencio Vega's San Estevan estate was also decimated. By 1869, San Estevan had lost 92 percent of its population. While it had an estimated thirteen hundred tenants in 1857, in 1869 it had an estimated two hundred houses, but only about one hundred inhabitants ("chiefly Logwood cutters and builders of bungays and other small craft") and it was said "not [to be] in a very flourishing condition just now."[58] When Florencio Vega died in July 1869, all of his assets were seized by his employer (the BHC), except for a small house and furniture left for his widow and young children.[59] While Vega's actions in part precipitated the 1866 standoff at San Pedro, the military conflict that ensued led to his financial ruination.

GAINING FAVOR

While from the perspective of the western-region Maya, the destruction of their villages by British forces was cataclysmic, Marcos Canul seems to have shrugged it off. He had other, more pressing concerns. The Kruso'ob, who had ready access to munitions through the British Hondurans, were continuing to raid into Icaiché territory; timber company agents who paid rent to the Kruso'ob were therefore indirectly financing those assaults. The worst, from Canul's perspective, were those timber company subcontractors who also sold munitions to the Kruso'ob, including Manuel Castillo. At the beginning of May 1867, Canul somehow escaped or was freed from Encalada's captivity, and he went directly to Yo Creek to confront Castillo.[60]

Still wary of Canul, Austin sought to strengthen relations with his Kruso'ob allies. He proposed reducing tariffs on imports of pigs, poultry, and corn into Corozal, hoping that in addition the Kruso'ob might send back the absconded Chinese laborers. Austin even went so far as to consider lifting all duties on trade with both the Kruso'ob and Lochhá.[61] The Kruso'ob were all too eager to strengthen this alliance against the Icaiché. Kruso'ob commanders charged that one San Roman resident (Sisto Campos) had ferried Canul to Yo Creek for the "purpose of committing robbery and murder" at Orange Walk, San Antonio, and Chunaba. Unable to find the ferryman, they captured his son to deliver him to the British, instead.[62] In another instance, a group of Icaiché had crossed the Hondo to go to Dos Cocos supposedly to trade, although it was feared that they also meant to attack Manuel

Castillo's bank. Kruso'ob fighters set upon those from Icaiché, killing most of them and seizing their property.[63] The British, however, would not look favorably on these "invasions" of British territory.

For his part, John Carmichael took an outsize role in cementing good relations with the Kruso'ob and advocating for them with British Honduran officials. Having promised to sell them 220 arrobas of powder, he asked Austin to issue a purchasing license to them (in violation of the powder proclamation), and he even loaned them his boat to transport the powder.[64] Carmichael also urged Austin to waive import tariffs at Corozal on horses, cattle, rice, beans, straw hats, grinding stones, henequen rope, and dried peppers, all for the benefit of Kruso'ob traders.[65]

In the meantime—in what might have appeared to be a gain for the British—the Pacíficos of the Lochhá region were thrown into political turmoil. Pablo Encalada had been deposed, and those at Lochhá were now allied with the Kruso'ob.[66] In 1867, the mighty Kruso'ob fighting force therefore consisted of eleven thousand men plus another four thousand from Lochhá and Macanche (formerly of the Pacíficos).[67] The Icaiché could not stand a chance against those combined forces who moreover had privileged access to British Honduran munitions.

Kruso'ob leaders continued to seek favor with the British. In October, the Kruso'ob warned that the Icaiché were headed to Corozal and requested permission—should the Icaiché cross the Hondo River—to cross the river as well and engage them in battle. Should they find Canul, they promised to arrest him and turn him over to the British.[68] When the powder proclamations expired on October 17, they were not renewed, and British Honduran merchants could resume selling gunpowder and arms to any paying customers.[69] The Kruso'ob plan had worked.

Whether John Carmichael Jr., the Corozal-based merchant and militia captain, was motivated primarily by pecuniary gain or whether he fashioned himself a military adventurer, we will never truly know. What is known, however, is that his and his father's strong alliance with and advocacy for the Kruso'ob put the British in a compromising situation. In November 1867, Carmichael Jr. reported to the new lieutenant governor, J. R. Longden, about a recent lengthy stay at the rebel headquarters in Chan Santa Cruz. He reassured Longden that the Kruso'ob wanted friendly relations with the British and their only goal was to recapture lands that had belonged to their ancestors. Carmichael described General Bonifacio Novelo as respectful, intelligent, and a kind and fair leader. Under prior leadership, he conceded, a ventriloquist speaking for the Cross had been used to trick "the ever credulous Indians to commit deeds of unparalleled barbarity and ferocity." Now, however, the Indians were simply "taught to worship the Divine Being through the cross alone." Novelo had even expressed a willingness for Kruso'ob territory to be annexed by British Honduras.[70] Longden, however, disapproved of being too conciliatory with the Kruso'ob or the Lochhá, and he was annoyed that Carmichael took the liberty of discussing annexation when he had no official government role and seemed to be acting "entirely on his own or his father's business."[71]

DESERTERS—AND A PRECARIOUS BALANCE

In the month of December, the Icaiché and Kruso'ob collided once again, the Icaiché first attacking and burning the village of Esteves. A force of 240 Kruso'ob soldiers, in turn, marched on and burned Icaiché itself.[72] Raids and counterraids by the Icaiché and the Kruso'ob thereafter set the tone for social and political life throughout southern Yucatán and Campeche in the 1860s and 1870s.

A glimpse into what these raids might have felt like is revealed through stories that residents in the Pacífico region passed on to their descendants. María Torres's mother, who lived in Icaiché, said that people moved southward into the British settlement because of the Kruso'ob raids: "Every six months . . . the Santa Krusilo'ob would go there and take people's animals—their cows, pigs, whatever. If you didn't give it to them, they would shoot and kill you."[73] Pedro Ortega described how "the Kruso'ob used to come down and make war with the poor people, the Icaiche'o'ob. They could come and rob and then go away. They would kill one another."[74] Another man explained that his parents and other relatives left Yucatán to get away from the war altogether (some fleeing to Belize and others to the Petén region of Guatemala). They were being "run over by the rebels . . . who did not accept Mexican rule and thought themselves independent," but they were also worn out by the Icaiché. The Kruso'ob and Icaiché "would attack and rob one another." Marcos Canul, he explained, liked to lead attacks "here and in Quintana Roo [and they] would come here to rob." In effect: "The people came here to get away from all of that."[75]

However, as the conflict between the Kruso'ob and Icaiché escalated, both sides needed foot soldiers. The leaders would call up their tenants for military service, including those who had deserted to the opposite side of the river. In their efforts to bring deserters back into the military fold, the Maya leaders used tactics not unlike those used by employers to recapture absconded servants.

For example, feeling empowered, perhaps, by their cozy relationship with the Carmichaels, a large group of Kruso'ob led by Isidoro Aké (Comandante of Ramonal) crossed the Hondo to chase down nearly thirty people considered deserters and their family members in Corozal and other nearby settlements. While the voices of Maya civilians so rarely come through in the archival documents, the testimonies later offered by witnesses to the raid offer vivid details about wartime capture. María Juan testified that when they were on their way home to Patchakan, her husband was carrying their child. Isidoro Aké and three of his men accosted her husband and made him hand the child over to her. They ordered her to gather provisions for their trip but she stood firm, saying, "I will follow my husband." Aké went to Carmichael's house to get permission to take her, erroneously calling him the "magistrate"—all signaling Carmichael's immense power in Corozal at the time. Nevertheless, her husband was taken away by Aké. José María Chan then described the looting that characterized such raids, testifying that Aké's men "entered [Manuel] Chuc's House, plundered it, and chopped his trunk to pieces also the Hammocks, they carried away with them 3 large turkeys and everything that the house contained." The deserters were tied up and made to carry the stolen goods back to the Kruso'ob region. British officials were none too happy with what they considered to be a Kruso'ob raid into their territory, and Aké and eight other Kruso'ob soldiers were arrested and jailed in Corozal. The fact that the Kruso'ob soldiers told the captives that they had permission from John Carmichael to take them away certainly complicated the matter.[76]

The substantial backing provided to the Kruso'ob and the Icaiché by diverse outsiders (including British Honduran officials, merchants, and landlords; Yucatecos in British Honduras; and Yucatecan and Campechano officials) had turned the Social War into a sprawling, intractable regional conflagration. Perhaps seeking revenge against his long-time foe (Canul), Manuel Castillo warned the magistrate at Orange Walk that the Icaiché had given up on fighting the powerful Santa Cruz and intended "to direct their attacks in future against the English." According to Castillo, following the Aké raid, Canul heard that the British had given the Kruso'ob permission to cross into the settlement to take captives, and he took this news to the governor of Campeche. Reportedly possessing "certain letters of Mr Carmichael of Corosal and other English subjects . . . sympathizing with and professing attachment to the Santa Cruz Indians," Canul requested arms from Campechano officials for the purposes of defense against British-backed Kruso'ob raiders.[77]

By this time, the battle lines were clear. In the war between the Icaiché and the Kruso'ob, they were backed, respectively, by officials in Campeche and British Honduras. The Icaiché and Kruso'ob were, to a certain degree, pawns. The British did not have to directly engage in fighting the Icaiché if they could empower the Kruso'ob to do so; similarly, arming Icaiché fighters to put up a defense relieved the burden of the Campechano regular forces.

With their supplies having been replenished in Campeche, a group of Icaiché crossed south of the Hondo River to capture some deserters, but the Kruso'ob set upon them, killing seventy-six Icaiché men. Kruso'ob General Crescencio Poot also warned Carmichael that the Icaichés intended to attack Corozal on Christmas Day, and he provided a list of residents in the British settlement who were suspected of spying for the Icaiché.[78]

The governor and lieutenant governor were alarmed by the impunity with which Kruso'ob soldiers crossed the Hondo River in pursuit of enemies and deserters (in what they considered to be invasions of British territory). While British officials had often sought not to display too much friendliness toward the Kruso'ob or the Icaiché, so as not to rile the others, the Carmichaels had tipped the balance. Their favoritism of the Kruso'ob had pushed Canul to seek reinforcement from a larger, more powerful ally. Moreover, Carmichael's alleged letter expressing such favoritism would be read by the Campechano governor (and probably Mexican federal officials, as well) as direct British support for those in rebellion against them. Now the British did not have to worry just about the Icaiché, but also the Campechano governor and the Mexican government, as well.

Carmichael Sr. was called to answer for his actions. Longden blamed Carmichael and his son for having created the crisis with the Kruso'ob by having encouraged them in the first place. Under the gun, Carmichael tried to downplay the seriousness of the Aké raid. Four of the men who were seized by the Kruso'ob had returned "to complete their military service voluntarily," he protested, implausibly. Defending his allies, Carmichael reminded the lieutenant governor that the Kruso'ob had taken eight hundred men to fight at Icaiché, for which the British might be grateful. Because the British had imprisoned Aké and his men, "the most excitable feeling prevails among the Indians in Bacalar at present," Carmichael explained, since they saw the imprisonment as "an act of treachery on our part." Carmichael urged Longden to make amends with the Kruso'ob. He pleaded innocence, but resigned as Commissioner, nevertheless.[79]

In short order, yet another group of Kruso'ob, under the comandante of Sabidos, had been leading similar raids across the Hondo to capture deserters. Ultimately, however, Lt. Gov. Longden blamed the victims of the raids for their own misfortune. He was convinced that opportunistic border-crossing destabilized the northern region, leading to raids and skirmishes along the river as Kruso'ob and Icaiché soldiers went to capture those whom they considered deserters and rent dodgers. He was particularly irked that many of those deserters had not been born within the limits of British Honduras, but had, as he saw it, brought trouble with them. During the 1866 panic, he explained to the governor, they had gone north of the Hondo to avoid being called for military duty, and there they farmed on lands controlled by Maya leaders, but they later returned to the southern side went their rent was due. They were "squatting wherever they find unoccupied land and moving off when required to pay rent or service," he grumbled.[80]

VILLAGE RESERVES?

In the spring of 1868, Longden cast about for ideas on how to reduce the threat posed by Maya land claims. He returned to an idea that had been tossed about by Lt. Gov. Austin when he set the terms of surrender for the San Pedro Maya—that of setting aside a bit of land for Indian villages, in effect, a type of community land grant. Writing to the governor, he noted that prior to the regimental forces having chased the San Pedro Maya out of the western region, the villages had been on lands claimed by BHC and YTC. He proposed no changes to that arrangement—at any rate, the point was moot since the villages lay empty. He proposed, however, that in cases in which Indian villages were situated on Crown Lands: "I think the villages and a sufficient surrounding space should be reserved in the hands of the Crown for the use of the Indians,—no marketable title being issued to them to enable them to dispose of such lands,—but the land being divided amongst them, from time to time, by the alcalde or chief man amongst them, as may be most convenient."[81]

What did such an idea signify? On the one hand, it would have granted villagers freedom from paying rent to a private landlord. In addition, it would have provided a degree of economic security if the lands were extensive enough to support the farming, hunting, and natural resource collection needs of the residents.

On the other hand, Longden's idea for village reserves would have represented significant setbacks for Indigenous rights. Such village reserves would have rendered the Indigenous people an official minoritized and dependent subpopulation, insofar as the lands would have remained Crown Lands. The residents would not have controlled the land outright, nor would they have been granted titles to use the land any way they saw fit—such as by collecting rent or fees from companies intending to extract resources. In addition, by apportioning the lands to individual villages, such village reserves would have sabotaged the power of the regional San Pedro Maya alliance. Each individual village would have had its own lands, administered by the village *alcalde*. Longden was not proposing a large-scale regional reservation (of the type more often seen in the United States). His village reserves, instead, would have been akin to the *ejido* community land grants apportioned in Yucatán first during the sixteenth century—which similarly broke up broader alliances of *bataboʼob* under a common *jalach winik*. Longden's village reserve plan would have been, in effect, a colonial strategy that gave one concession (community land grants) while forcing two others (powerful regional alliances and claims to regional territories). Furthermore, while at first glance this type of village reserve might be seen as recognition of the idea that Indigenous people possessed rights to land by virtue of aboriginal occupation, in context, it is clear that such was not Longden's understanding. In the following sentence, he includes the "Caribs" among the "Indians," while emphasizing that they were not aboriginal to the region, but were "a very mixed race who were transported from St. Vincent to Honduras." In the next paragraph, he moves on to Crown Lands grants for former West India regimental soldiers. In other words, his concern was for managing different sub-populations within a colony rather than acknowledging group rights.

Longden may have thought that offering village reserves would have at least put an end to the Indian land claims (which were often wrapped within extortionist threats). Regardless, this plan would not have had much effect in the northwestern quadrant—in the region that the San Pedro Maya had inhabited—since those villages had been situated on lands with private titles. In the end, Longden simply floated this idea for Indian village lands—and nothing came of it for several years.

BORDERING PRACTICES

Also in the spring of 1868, Longden felt certain that security in the western region depended upon clearly demarcating and protecting the colony's borders. On the west, the Crown Surveyor was clearing a line from Garbutt's Falls northward. He had reached the point of forty-two miles south of Lt. Abbs's marker (cairn) at the 18th latitude parallel (near the Belize River). At that point, he stopped the work, however, recommending that the remaining portion be taken up by soldiers since it passed through Maya settlements and "lands disputed by the Indians."[82] To make matters worse, the border dispute with Mexico could not be resolved since Mexico had cut off all communication with Britain. After Emperor Maximilian was executed in June 1867 and President Benito Juárez resumed power of the resurrected Republic of Mexico, Juárez's administration severed diplomatic relations with any nation that had dealt with the emperor.[83]

For Longden, frequent movement across the Hondo River represented a threat to colonial security. With the Icaiché and Kruso'ob fighting once more, settlers on the British side feared incursions into the supposed British territory. Irrepressible John Carmichael, ever eager to be involved, petitioned to have a permanent garrison placed in Corozal.[84] Lt. Col. Harley, however, assured the lieutenant governor that the western region was safe and British Honduran settlers had little need to fear an Indian raid. Harley faulted the rumor mongers who stirred up anxiety because they profited from military supply contracts and the rent of buildings.[85] He did not need to name names, because Longden well recognized Carmichael's financial motivation, as Carmichael owned the town and had profited "many hundreds of pounds" each year that the troops maintained a garrison at Corozal.[86] Meanwhile, Carmichael continued to ship hundreds of arrobas of gunpowder at a time from Belize to the Kruso'ob at Bacalar.[87]

Longden then aimed to put a stop to the movement back and forth across the Hondo by establishing a frontier police force. Headquarters would be maintained at

Achiote, where the Icaiché would stop before crossing the Hondo River. The police force would consist of an inspector, sergeant, two corporals, and twenty privates, all of whom would be armed and many of whom would be mounted on horseback.[88] Longden intended to imprison for six months any British Honduran residents who owned or cultivated land on "Indian territory" (i.e., north of the river) without a license; similarly, any British Honduran residents who emigrated to that territory would be forcibly returned.[89] Tenants behind on their rent on the northern side were subjected to threats, confiscation of property, or capture by the Icaiché or Kruso'ob, depending upon the location. If tenants paid rent to the Kruso'ob on lands claimed by the Icaiché, they would be pressured to make a second payment to them, as well.[90]

Meanwhile, residents along the Hondo, seeking protection from one group or another, continued to set the Icaiché and Kruso'ob against one another. Many of those passing along rumors were aligned with one side or another or had a direct financial interest in certain outcomes, and consequently the truth of a matter is often murky. For example, the BHC hired Liberato Robelo to work as a River Clerk, during which he was to spy on the Icaiché.[91] Robelo told the Orange Walk magistrate that Manuel Castillo and three other residents on the southern side of the Hondo, fearing an Icaiché attack, had written to the Kruso'ob, asking them to attack the Icaiché first. In retaliation, Campeche officials put out a $3,000 bounty on Castillo's head.[92] As the owner of mahogany works and estates on the northern side of the river, Castillo would have been one of those people whom the Icaiché accused of utilizing lands in their territories, all the while living on the "British side" where they could avoid paying rent.

INDIOS PACÍFICOS DE CAMPECHE—AND FRESH RENT DEMANDS

At some point prior to February 1868, the Icaiché and Lochhá Maya retained an agreement in which they were officially recognized by the Campeche government as "Indios Pacíficos." Pacífico leaders could collect rent within their territories for their own purposes, and the Pacíficos did not have to pay taxes, but they were obliged to assist the state government in containing the Kruso'ob rebels. "Canul is a commissioned officer of the Campeche Government," wrote a BHC representative—and he bore the title of Comandante General and the chief of the Canton of Icaiché. Similarly, Encalada was recognized as the chief of the Lochhá district. The state government apportioned to them some munitions as part of the war effort.[93] Canul and his men had even recently joined a Mexican military campaign against the Kruso'ob.[94]

However, in the spring of 1868, British military acts of boundary maintenance directly threatened the Icaiché. Lt. Abbs was clearing a boundary line in the north at the 18th parallel, and a portion of the line in fact extended north of Blue Creek. It reached within nine miles of Icaiché, in an area "never before claimed by the English," according to Canul (see figure 2.1). Longden fretted that he had not intended to "give fresh cause of umbrage," and defending that land "may cause infinitely more expense than any profit which could possibly ever be derived from it."⁹⁵ Indeed.

In April 1868, Icaiché leaders then turned their attention from the Hondo River to the rent collection in the western region of the supposed British territory once again, alarming logging crews that were beginning to return to the region. Were Icaiché leaders emboldened by their official support from the Campechano governor? Possibly yes. Were they upset about British military officers clearing a boundary line so close to their capital? Probably that, as well.

First, Maya men were pressing residents at Chorro (near the Guatemalan line) into military service, with the goal of making a show of force to collect rent from the timber companies. They stopped first at Turnbull Bank on the Belize River, claimed as the private property of YTC. Lt. Col. Harley advised Longden that British troops should not intervene, saying, "We are not at War with these people, nor have they as far that I am aware of committed any fresh depradations [sic] since peace has been restored." Not wanting to stir up fresh trouble, he recommended that the newly formed frontier police investigate.⁹⁶

Frontier Police Inspector Plumridge then met with Manuel Rosado, Marcos Canul's new secretary, who handed over a list of places within the supposed British limits for which rent was owed to the Icaiché Pacíficos, and he asked that the lieutenant governor notify company agents in those locations of their debts. Canul claimed to have permission from the Campechano governor to collect rent in those places all along the Belize River and New River, and YTC and BHC were the major debtors. Rosado indicated that Canul hoped to have the matter settled amicably, but if not, they would "march with a hundred men to insist upon payment."⁹⁷ Panicky about Rosado's list, BHC's manager and attorney, John Hodge, contacted the lieutenant governor. Canul was only making those claims—said Hodge—because the Emperor Maximilian had claimed the British Honduran region for Mexico and granted the Icaiché permission to collect rent on Mexican lands. Hodge asked Longden's permission for the company to send a representative to deal directly with Campechano governor Pablo García. Letters were dispatched ahead of the visit.⁹⁸

Having learned of British displeasure over Icaiché rent demands, Governor García wrote to Longden that his powers were limited, as he, merely a governor, had no influence over boundary disputes between the nation of Mexico and the British colony. Nonetheless, he would give orders to the Indian "chiefs" who recognized his government (including Canul) not to disturb the British. He expected that, similarly, the British should order the Kruso'ob to stop conducting war against

Yucatán and Campeche and the British should cease selling munitions to the "barbarians" and "savages" of Chan Santa Cruz. British Honduras was their sole source of such powder—said García—which prolonged the war and all of its destructiveness.[99] García thereafter instructed Canul that in order to ensure that the British put a halt to the sale of munitions to the Kruso'ob, he should "respect . . . the possessions and British Settlements."[100] Limply, Longden replied to García that he was unable to control the trade in gunpowder because Ascension Bay and other eastern ports were controlled by the Kruso'ob.[101]

Subsequently, in his visit with J. I. Blockley (BHC's representative), García assured him of his efforts to rein in Canul. He reminded him, though, that the Mexican government held the British responsible for the deaths of over one hundred thousand Mexican citizens because of their munitions sales to rebels—and worse, they sold these munitions in exchange for monies the rebels had accrued through stealing from other Mexican citizens in armed raids. When Blockley dared to raise the specific issue of the western boundary—to suss out whether BHC crews would be working on lands claimed by Mexico—the Campechano governor repeated that he could not know exactly how far south Campeche extended, but that it did encompass the Petén region (implying that it extended into the British-claimed zone, as well). Flustered by this most unwelcome news, Blockley urged that the British and Mexican governments should resolve the boundary problem as quickly as possible.[102]

NORMALIZING RELATIONS

In an abrupt change of tone, in the summer of 1868, British and Icaiché officials both made overt gestures of peace. Icaiché leaders would be allowed to issue temporary permits for their subjects to visit the British colony for private business.[103] Of enormous significance, Inspector Plumridge again permitted the sale of gunpowder and shot to buyers from Icaiché.[104]

In turn, Canul and Chan also signaled a desire for peace with the British. Domingo Tzuc had been one of the leaders of the party that raided Indian Church the prior year. In July 1868, he was living in Yaloch (across the presumed western border in Guatemala) and bore the title of comandante of the western-region Maya within the Icaiché leadership. Tzuc led a group of about twenty-five men over the Guatemalan line, bearing letters (addressed from Canul, Chan, and Tzuc) demanding the payment of rent by the timber companies (including BHC).[105] Canul and Chan, however, quickly denied that they had dispatched Tzuc and they promised the lieutenant governor that he would be stripped of his commission.[106] Tzuc was arrested in Yaloch by an Icaiché-appointed captain (José Justo Chan) and was sent to Icaiché, where the captain assumed that he would be executed for his treachery.[107]

Longden concluded that Tzuc's men merely had set out before Canul received the cease-and-desist letter from the Campechano governor, but since Canul aborted the mission, Longden considered the problem resolved.[108] "The Ycayche Indians wish to be at peace with the English Colonists," affirmed Chan, and they would "leave the boundary line to be settled by the Mexican & English Commissioners altho' they do not consider the present line is correct."[109]

Curiously, Chan also said that the Icaiché secretary, Manuel Rosado, did not have permission to circulate the list of rent demands that he did.[110] Longden believed him. He compared the three lists and found they were all penned in Rosado's hand, rather than Canul's. "It is not the least of the difficulties which impede any understanding with the Indian Chiefs," Longden explained to the governor, "that the Chiefs themselves, speaking no language but the Maya, are unable to read or write even in that language, are entirely dependent on their secretaries." They were susceptible, therefore, to being deceived and having their communications forged. Longden assured the governor that peace with Canul had been established and the British had nothing to fear from the Icaiché at that time.[111]

RETURN TO THE "ENGLISH SIDE"

Thereafter, more Icaiché-aligned Maya living in Guatemala sought entry into the British region. Captain José Justo Chan at Yaloch wrote to John August (YTC foreman) and demonstrated his goodwill toward the British by reporting that he and his men were the ones who had apprehended Domingo Tzuc and delivered him to Icaiché for punishment. Captain Chan wanted to move his village of twenty-five people to the "English side," and he hoped that August would intervene on his behalf. He expressed that Tzuc's leadership was oppressive and he would not let them go. "I do not want to continue in this [Icaiché] military career," wrote Chan, "and the people are tired of all of the work that befalls the poor."[112] Given the prevailing governmental institution of forced labor in the Petén district, life in the British region might have seemed preferable.

Longden asked both the BHC and YTC if they would consider allowing the Indians from Yaloch to settle on their lands as tenants. John Hodge replied that, some months before, he had invited hundreds of Maya from Yaloch and neighboring villages to settle and work on the BHC sugar estates at Indian Church in exchange for a wage, plus rent-free use of provision grounds. Some did come, while others were prevented from doing so by Tzuc. After Tzuc was deposed, however, one of the Maya from Yaloch then working at Indian Church had returned to invite others to relocate. "Those Indians, in general, are good Agricultural Labourers," Hodge commented happily.[113]

At the end of 1868, Longden was feeling optimistic enough about peace in the western region to withdraw the military detachment at Young Girl.[114] In January of the following year, Longden happily reported that Maya of the western frontier who had fled in 1867 were gradually resettling the region "in a quiet and peaceful manner." He planned an expedition to visit them without a military escort as "it would tend greatly to restore confidence and a feeling of security."[115]

INDEBTED LABOR AND CROSS-BORDER RAIDS

In early 1869, Samuel Cockburn (magistrate at Belize) set out on an important expedition along the New River to assess the prospects for expanding sugarcane cultivation in the colony. His report—at first circulated only privately—partially blamed the systematic exploitation of Maya workers within British Honduras for the prior Icaiché attacks. Recall that Cockburn was one of the two commissioners dispatched in May 1867 to offer amnesty to those western-region Maya who had fled to Guatemala and wanted to return. In that visit, he likely became aware of their complaints and concerns.

In his report (dated March 1), Cockburn concluded that one of the greatest obstacles to commercial farming in the colony was an integrated system of labor exploitation. He described the widespread and standardized mechanisms of labor exploitation discussed in chapter 2: the wage advances provided with contracts; the payment of wages in cash and kind, with the goods assigned inflated values; similarly, if away at a timber camp, the worker would have to buy items from the company "truck," once again, at marked-up prices. Cockburn identified, as well, the predictable and inevitable consequences: the accumulation of debt on the part of workers; the incentive that created for a laborer to abscond from one employer and enter a contract with another one; and the hunting down and corporal punishment of indebted servants. While the advance and truck systems were first developed within the timber industry, they were also utilized, according to Cockburn, on the landed estates. This included the many smaller "ranchos" in the sugarcane production sites in Corozal, Caledonia, Orange Walk, and Indian Church, which also cultivated corn, rice, other food crops, and distilled rum. These ranchos were under the proprietorship of Yucatecans of Spanish descent and operated at low cost "as their labourers are chiefly their own countrymen (native Indians) who are content with but little pay and no rations." The proprietors, he wrote, would sometimes supply rations of corn and coconut oil to their Indian laborers. However, if the laborers needed other things, "in the shape of printed calicoes, estrevillas, mantuas, &c., for clothing of himself, his wife and family," for example, the employer would sell them such goods at a 200 percent markup, and the laborer would fall further into debt.

The longer he remained in a position, the further he would fall into debt. Neither did the death of the "master" make any difference, because "the debt is sold and bought with the land as assets of the Estate, and the 'mozos' transferred to the purchaser as goods and chattels,—serfs, attached to the soil and irrevocably doomed to perpetual slavery!"[116]

Significantly, Cockburn linked the system of labor exploitation to regional violence. Not only was it an "evil" set of practices, but it was also a threat to British Honduran security, he concluded: "Thus imposed upon by his own countrymen, over-reached by the mahogany cutters, and despised and contemned by all, is it surprising that he sometimes escapes over the border to his tribe and instigates them to raids and forays in retaliation and revenge?"[117] Which were those occasions in which Maya "mozos" instigated members of their "tribe" to raid and foray in retaliation and revenge? Was Cockburn referring to the 1864 conflict at San Ramon, in which Icaiché leaders directed violence against Yucateco estate proprietors and timber subcontractors (Vega and Grajales) and perhaps also to the 1866 conflict at San Pedro, triggered by depredations by Vega's agents? Quite possibly so—or he may have been referring to any other such occasions about which we have no knowledge. Were labor exploitation and cross-border violence part of a self-reinforcing system along the Hondo River? Exploitation led to flight, which led to raids and counter-raids, and so on. (Is every border both the locus of and generative of violence?) Cockburn shared his report with the lieutenant governor, who passed it along to the governor, and then ... nothing happened.

DEPORTING VASSALS

Thereafter, British Honduran officials arguably made the situation worse. Rather than trying to improve labor relations, British frontier police became directly involved in deporting deserters and rent dodgers, sending them back to face forced military service and, likely, indebted labor. They did so at the request of Maya military leaders.

A new law passed in November 1868 in the state of Campeche affirmed and formalized the system of debt peonage, which would have made escape across the Hondo River even more enticing for Campechano peasants.[118] At this time, many people who had newly crossed the Hondo River were welcomed by the British as contributors to the colonial economy. Many were absorbed into the mahogany and logwood cutting crews at banks that had been abandoned in 1867. BHC once again had three hundred or so men employed in mahogany at Cacao Creek, Betson's Bank, and Qualm Hill, and Manuel Castillo employed about one hundred logwood workers at Corozalito. The new tenants added to the rent rolls, and BHC had doubled the amount of rent it collected on houses and farmlands between 1867 and 1868. In addition, Maya from Yucatán were bringing hogs, cattle, horses, and agricultural produce to sell in the northern markets.[119]

However, those settling (or resettling) within the supposed British limits to avoid forced military service or rent payments to the Pacíficos or Kruso'ob continued to create headaches for British officials.[120] Canul and Chan complained that their "vassals" (*vasallos*) were deserting them for the British territory, and, curiously, they asked Plumridge for help from the frontier police in returning them. If the frontier police could not return the deserters, Canul and Chan hoped that they would at least confiscate and return their guns to Icaiché headquarters.[121] Plumridge tried to figure out how to respond to this request. An influx of deserters and indebted tenants from the Kruso'ob region would not pose a security problem for the British colony—Plumridge reasoned—because the Kruso'ob depended upon trade with the British and would do nothing to jeopardize that relationship. On the other hand, the Icaiché could trade freely with Campeche and Yucatán and acquire munitions there, and consequently, the Icaiché leaders would be less concerned about antagonizing the British. Plumridge worried that if people living in the British settlement failed to pay rent for fields they cultivated on Icaiché lands, Canul would raid for plunder and kidnapping victims.[122] Plumridge decided that it would be better to help Canul control his "vassals" rather than incur his ire. He therefore drew up lists of all residents on the British side who farmed land on the "Spanish side" between Douglas and Achiote, and Longden suggested that Canul should appoint a river agent to collect rent payments.[123]

Kruso'ob leaders also pressured the British officials for help, and by June, Plumridge was trying to help both the Icaiché and Kruso'ob collect rents owed to them by British Honduran residents for cultivation on lands the Maya leaders claimed north of the river. Plumridge even proposed that a bill be introduced into the British Honduran legislature to put an end to cross-border rent evasion.[124] While the rent evaders included Yucatecans of both Maya and Spanish descent, the case of Spanish-descended Yucatecans was particularly problematic, Plumridge reasoned, as the British colony should not be seen to be allowing Yucatecos to continue practicing "rascality . . . on the Indians."[125]

By November, most of the small villages on the southern side of the Hondo were composed of settlers who had fled the Kruso'ob and Icaiché areas to escape obligatory military service and debts of one kind or another. During the Christmas season, the Kruso'ob often came to Corozal to trade and purchase gunpowder, and on their rent-collection excursions, they frequently stopped in Consejo to drink as they had cash in hand. On one such trip, a band of armed Kruso'ob fighters kidnapped a husband and wife at Consejo, carrying them off to Bacalar.[126] Magistrate

Adolphus blamed the kidnapped couple for their own misfortune, stating "the miserable Yucatecos who have for many years past made Br. Honduras their asylum," by cultivating lands to the north of the river and living south of it, were wholly responsible for creating the situation in which the Indians felt they could raid into the British territory "to enforce their rights."[127] Typically eager to assist his Kruso'ob friends, John Carmichael—always in the thick of things—was then selected by the Kruso'ob leaders to serve as their debt collections agent in Corozal.[128]

In late 1869, access to munitions and foot soldiers was of critical importance, for both Icaiché and Kruso'ob leaders. Icaiché leaders loaded up on gunpowder and supplies in Orange Walk to thereafter join General Eugenio Arana of Xkanhá (whom the Campeche government recognized as the General of the Pacíficos) and two thousand of his men in an attack on Bacalar. A large force of Kruso'ob retaliated by marching on Icaiché.[129] In the midst of this fighting to the north, British Honduran officials conceded to the Maya leaders' requests for assistance in recapturing deserters and debtors, even when it meant they were complicit in sending Maya peasants to the front lines. British obsession about territorial control led them to disregard the fact that allowing rent evaders and deserters to be hauled off by Maya leaders threatened their lives. Obsession with a border is its own form of violence. "Every border implies the violence of its maintenance," wrote Ayesha A. Siddiqi.[130]

"THE PURE NECESSITIES OF THE CASE"

Having read Samuel Cockburn's private report of March 1, 1869, in November of that year, Earl Granville concluded that the dissatisfaction of laborers in the British colony was a matter for concern. Tasked with investigating, Longden solicited responses from the magistrates of the Corozal and Orange Walk districts (Edwin Adolphus and Robert Downer, respectively). Their reactions were to downplay the seriousness of the issues, deflect blame, and shrug in resignation.

The magistrates affirmed that the Maya in the colony were nearly always indebted to their employers. Adolphus quibbled that Cockburn had exaggerated the amount by which goods provided by employers were marked up.[131] Magistrate Downer conceded that they were marked up, but that it was the Indians' fault. They were lazy by nature, he insisted. (His statement about how they would "remain at home and squat in their houses, or lounge in their hammocks, the whole live long day" is quoted in chapter 2.) They could not be persuaded to work for wages unless they were given "enormous advances," he averred. For him, the matter was personal: "I speak from a personal knowledge of the habits of these people, as I frequently have to employ them, which I am forced to do at their own exorbitant price." "The Indian is not so easily imposed upon," he insisted, "[and] in nine cases out of ten the employer is the sufferer." The employers, he said, had to charge high prices to make up for the advances paid out.[132] (That does not follow logically, of course.)

Adolphus and Longden blamed tradition and precedent, but they concluded that the colonial government need not take any action. Adolphus blamed the "Spanish system of hiring, or as I may truly call it semi-slavery," for having been introduced by the Yucatecan refugees, although he admitted it was universally utilized.[133] Longden thought that no government intervention was necessary, since indebted servitude would phase out on its own. The "truck system had its origin in the pure necessities of the case," he explained to the governor, since workers taken on crews into the forest could not access food for themselves but needed to be given rations and advances on the cash part of their pay. Since rations need not be provided to agricultural laborers (who could purchase their own food from another source)—he reasoned—the practice of giving them rations would die out eventually. It was unnecessary to abolish the truck and advance systems by law—he added—since they were purely a matter of custom and could be dispensed with by employers on their own accord at any time. Finally, indebted servitude on agricultural estates would disappear on its own because British law prohibited slavery, he asserted.[134]

Reflecting willful ignorance of the dangers faced by Maya peasants, Adolphus and Longden suggested that if the Maya laborers were discontented, they could simply cross the river into Icaiché or Kruso'ob territory. The system of advances really worked to the disadvantage of the employers, said Adolphus, since the employers could not risk having the workers arrested, because "the recently punished Indians will take the earliest opportunity of crossing the border into Yucatan, but a few miles distant, where the Indian Commandants gladly receive them, and where they have rich ground for cultivation freely granted them on rendering, when called upon, their services for raids against the unprotected towns and villages of Yucatan or for fights with their Ycaiches."[135] Longden agreed that a natural check was placed upon debt peonage because a discontented Indian worker "simply joins his wild countrymen on the other side of the Hondo." Moreover, since the Indians' labor was in high demand and since they had the opportunity of "evading all oppression by crossing the river . . . there is no ground for believing them to be ill-treated in any way," concluded Longden.[136] In essence, the existence of the border (and the possibility of flight) provided the justification for continued exploitation of labor. Downplaying the dangers Maya peasants faced north of the river (indebted servitude and obligatory military service, not to mention being subjected to raids by the other warring faction) reflected a willful disregard for their lives. It was this disregard that would have helped ease British officials' minds about deporting peasant refugees.

MARCH ON COROZAL

In the spring of 1870, Icaiché-British relations took a turn for the worse. In March, the lieutenant governor thought the issues with the Icaiché had been resolved, since all the mahogany crews working in the area of the Upper Hondo, Río Bravo, Booth's River, and Blue Creek had been withdrawn.[137] As it turned out, that was not exactly true, and Longden should have known that the mahogany crews would not have been Canul's only complaint.

Icaiché villages continued to be raided and pillaged by Kruso'ob fighters. Beaten down by the powerful Kruso'ob, Canul and Chan were desperate to put a stop to the British Honduran arms sales to their attackers. They drew up a long list of 122 British Honduran residents whose actions in support of the Kruso'ob were deeply injurious to their people. The list included 6 "allies," 3 former Yucatecan comandantes, 34 merchants, and 79 other people who were not identified by name because their surnames were unknown. Number one on the list, of course, was John Carmichael, the primary arms supplier for the Kruso'ob and the Kruso'ob's main advocate before the lieutenant governor. Canul and Chan were additionally frustrated that the British Honduran import taxes on Icaiché goods were too high, and they wanted a more favorable trade agreement.[138]

On April 16, Canul and Chan led a group of about 120 armed Icaiché men in a march on Corozal, for the expressed purpose of negotiating reduced import taxes and the unrestricted right to enter the colony for trade. They crossed the river at Achiote and marched to Orange Walk, from whence they intended to travel up the New River to Corozal. In Orange Walk, they had a tense standoff with Magistrate Robert Downer, who must also have been the most prosperous resident, living in a home with multiple rooms, decorated with several pieces of mahogany furniture, cut decanters, and pieces fashioned from silver, gold, and bronze. Canul and Chan entered his house, placed sentries at the door, and demanded that Downer provision them with boats, indicating that that was the usual procedure when an army was on the march. Downer argued with them for "entering the Colony with an armed force," and the situation was resolved when others went in search of boats for their trip, but Canul "left in a very surly manner." Then, as they neared Corozal, the police inspector and others on horseback told them to put down their weapons. Canul sent a message ahead to the Corozal magistrate asking for permission to enter peacefully to negotiate, but no one would meet with him: "All was a farce—all were speaking—and I could get no one to direct me," he later bitterly complained.[139]

Once in Corozal, the Icaiché leaders demanded $3,000 of John Carmichael as compensation for the damages that his arms sales had done to the Icaiché people.[140] According to Canul and Chan, however, the magistrate and police inspector offered them $3,000 to leave without harming anyone, as did officers at the garrison.

Frustrated that no one seemed to understand him, Canul took his men and left, but subsequently asked for the $3,000 to be delivered.[141]

After the march on Corozal, laborers throughout the northern region fled to safety, fearing an Icaiché attack. John Carmichael and nine other British Honduran planters or merchants who had lost their workers (or suffered other business losses) characterized the march as an invasion "by an armed and organized body of Indians under . . . a person holding a commission as a military officer under the Mexican Government, who crossed the frontier and entered the colony in regular military array . . . creating terror and consternation on every side." These citizens demanded compensation from the colonial administration for financial losses incurred—a total of $177,031, representing lost harvests and the depreciation of the value of their properties. (Carmichael's own demand was for $62,500, or one-third of the total.) Downer's own wife and servants had run away to a nearby village that had become "crowded to excess with refugees from Orange Walk." British troops were dispatched to the northern district, but in June, the agricultural laborers still had not returned.[142]

By this time, the added costs of policing the Hondo River and protecting the northern districts had overwhelmed the fledging colony. Although a permanent garrison had been proposed for the Hondo River region near Achiote, where the Icaiché would cross on their way to Orange Walk, Longden had advised against it because the Hondo waters were prone to spreading dysentery. Meanwhile, the act that had established the Frontier Police expired after the designated two-year period in August 1870, and it was discontinued for lack of funds.[143] The public debt had reached $150,000. While the logging companies and landed estates in the north bore the brunt of any Maya raids, the merchants in Belize were relatively unaffected and consequently were uninterested in levying a tax on commerce to increase public revenues. Consequently, the Legislative Assembly voted to dissolve itself so that British Honduras could be transformed into a Crown Colony (which it was in 1871). The settlers in effect sacrificed a degree of self-governance in exchange for imperial protection.[144]

Commerce and security often work at cross-purposes, however. Scarcity of labor continued to be a problem for planters and timber subcontractors, to such an extent that they would hire whoever volunteered to work, even if British officials might look on them askance. Orange Walk, with its advantageous position on the New River, had become a major center for logwood harvesting and transport. Three of the wealthiest residents ("principal inhabitants") were Yucateco logwood subcontractors and, collectively, they owned more than half of the town's lands, which they would rent out.[145] Some of the Maya who showed up for work were not residents of British Honduras, but rather Icaiché-region men who would enter the colony, particularly around Orange Walk, to work for weeks at a time, in logwood harvesting and many other types of jobs.[146] Through these temporary stays in the Orange Walk area, they came to know Magistrate Downer, and they would, he said, "from habits of intemperance, when excited by liquor, become insolent and violent." Harley commended Downer for performing his duty related to these Indians "with intelligence and energy," as it required "both discretion and tact."[147] Downer's role as magistrate—meting out punishment to those who disrupted the peace, such as rowdy woodcutters—would not have engendered good feelings over time.

ATTACK ON ORANGE WALK

Throughout 1871, relations between the Icaiché leaders and the British continued to deteriorate. Canul continued to resent how British policies put his people in danger from the Kruso'ob. In one new such wrinkle, British policy required that when the Icaiché entered the colony to trade, they had to leave their weapons behind. Doing so, however, made them vulnerable to Kruso'ob attacks. In one instance at Achiote in April 1871, Icaiché men entered the colony unarmed, whereupon Kruso'ob troops killed one of Canul's men and stole four arrobas of gunpowder from the group.[148] Later that year, Canul and forty soldiers crossed the Hondo River on their way to Santa Cruz to collect rent from residents who cultivated lands on their side of the river. A dorey operator refused to give them free passage and he insulted them, and for that he should be punished, Canul urged Magistrate Downer. Downer did not take well to this directive about how he should dispense justice.[149] In the context of these tense relations, a First West India Regiment detachment was dispatched from Jamaica to Orange Walk in December.[150]

In 1872, Icaiché-British relations fundamentally imploded. It turned out that the mahogany companies had not in fact halted timber extraction in the western region claimed by the Maya. By this time, the villages of Santa Teresa, San Pedro, and San Jose—which had been destroyed by British troops in 1867—had been resettled. On January 2, Icaiché leaders complained that George Raboteau (of the British Honduras Company) had been harvesting timber for four years near those three villages without applying to Canul for a license nor paying rent, and that Raboteau should have done so because they were "Mexican" lands. Raboteau objected that BHC would not pay rent because they were "English" lands and, further, he intended to post policemen there.[151] (Recall that it was Raboteau's reluctance to pay rent that triggered the Icaiché raids at Qualm Hill and Betson's Bank in 1866.) Lt. Col. R. W. Harley (who had ordered the destruction of San Pedro and San Jose in 1867) was now the Administrator of the Government, and his reply was most officious and stern. Harley warned the Icaiché leaders that the places in which Raboteau was harvesting timber (around Victoria Creek, Río Bravo, and Blue Water) were within the boundaries of the British colony, and the boundaries had been "settled in 1867." Therefore, the BHC owed the Icaiché nothing and they should desist from making further demands.[152]

Harley was concerned enough to make a trip to take stock of the colony's northern defenses, accompanied by the WIR commanding major. Of particular concern was Orange Walk. The WIR detachment in Orange Walk consisted of the commanding lieutenant, two sergeants, and thirty-eight rank-and-file soldiers, and the small barracks had recently been repaired. A major problem, he noted, were the lack of roads, which meant that transport of military wagons, horses, and soldiers was exceedingly slow. Troops traveling from Corozal to Orange Walk (thirty-one miles; fifty kilometers) would typically take three days. An eighteen-mile road had just been built from Corozal to Caledonia (halfway to Orange Walk), rendering it passable during the dry season, but during the rainy season, it remained "impassible for horse or man."[153] In the summer of 1872, the "principal inhabitants" of the town had heard no rumblings of a potential Icaiché invasion. One exception was logwood subcontractor and shopkeeper Francisco Escalante, who often overheard his Icaiché employees "when they [were] in liquor threatening that they are coming to attack the town," but he did not pay this any heed.[154] He might have later regretted his nonchalance.

Subsequently, in August, Orange Walk Magistrate Downer violated the Icaiché sense of political autonomy. On the twelfth of the month, a prosperous Yucatecan who lived at Water Bank (José Eugenio Gonzáles) issued a complaint with Downer at the courthouse that a man from Icaiché, looking for an Icaiché woman who was living at Gonzáles's house, stormed through the house, assaulting his employee and wife in the process. At the courthouse, while fifteen Icaiché men looked on threateningly, Downer said that he would listen to testimony the following morning. The men issued the "most violent threats . . . toward Gonzáles," said Downer, and: "I at once in a loud tone ordered silence & then through the Interpreter told the Indians that I would have every one of them arrested & would punish them if they misbehaved." Downer later sentenced the assailant to hard labor, but he soon escaped.[155] An Icaiché leader later explained that by convention, a person who had committed a crime within the British settlement should have been extradited to Icaiché territory for prosecution.[156]

In late August 1872, Icaiché leaders apparently could no longer abide the many ways in which British Honduran action threatened their lives and liberties. Loggers were extracting wood from the disputed lands without paying for the privilege. British Honduran merchants continued to provide their Kruso'ob enemies with munitions that they used in raids throughout the Pacífico region. And now

Magistrate Downer had unfairly treated a suspected criminal and disrespected them in the process.

On August 31, Marcos Canul and a force of about 150 men crossed the Hondo River and proceeded to Gonzáles's house in Water Bank. Not finding him right away, they robbed the house, searched in other homes, and once they found him, they carried him away and killed him with machetes, his body subsequently being discovered by his servant. The following day, around eight in the morning, the group from Icaiché went straight to Magistrate Downer's house in Orange Walk. With the apparent motives of kidnapping and plunder, a group of men set upon him in his bedroom, slashed at him a few times with machetes, tied him up with ropes, and pulled him into the sitting room, threatening to kill him and demanding the key to his desk. One of the men reminded Downer that he had previously thrown him in jail. Downer believed his wife saved his life, as she put her body between his and theirs, and speaking the Maya language, she promised to pay them $3,000 if they would let him live. Others grabbed his valuables, whereupon two armed policemen and the military rations supplier entered the house and chased them away; one Icaiché man was still trying to drag Downer with him, but he was shot dead. The WIR detachment of forty-one soldiers hardly stood a chance. Several large stacks of logwood readied for riverine transport provided excellent cover for the Icaiché fighters, who then began firing on the military barracks from three sides. Another large group of Icaiché men ran through the town, ransacking and looting shops and houses, and they set fire to several buildings, including Downer's house (valued at $1555.75), the officers' quarters, the police station, the barracks' kitchen, and the military ration supplies. The shooting continued all day, until around 2:30 p.m., at which time the attackers retreated. Lives were lost on both sides.[157]

Marcos Canul was mortally wounded in the fight and his body was carried back to Icaiché. Soon thereafter, Canul's successor, Rafael Chan, begged for the Queen's pardon and promised that no additional attacks would be made on the colony. Even though he had been Canul's second-in-command for at least seven years, he dodged all culpability, saying that Canul "at that time governed and we had to obey him. . . . It was not the wish of all of us against your Colony, but it was alone the folly of our Chief who died."[158]

The attack on Orange Walk would prove to be the last Maya attack on the British settlement. At the time, however, it was not at all clear that that would be the case. Since Canul had had about 150 men with him, had Icaiché been aided by residents of villages within the supposed British limits? A military officer advised the lieutenant governor to "send some trustworthy person to watch the Ycaiché Indians of 'San Pedro' in the Old River District. These Indians cannot be trusted after what has taken place."[159] In 1887, the Assistant Surveyor-General stated that the western region Maya had conducted the raid on Orange Walk,[160] but since no contemporaneous sources reached that conclusion, it remains doubtful—or perhaps only a small number participated as opposed to a wholesale, coordinated effort.

The most significant outcome of the raid on Orange Walk was that British racial animosity hardened—toward Yucatecans of both Maya and Spanish descent. Rather than helping to put up a defense, all the Yucateco logwood contractors and Maya town residents had fled. Two who rushed to defend the British soldiers were American Confederates, including John Wallace Price, the proprietor of the Tower Hill estates, and his visitor from Louisiana.[161] In taking stock of the prospects for future defense, Colonial Secretary Mitchell betrayed a dismal view:

> The excitement and terror consequent on the very determined raid of the Ycaichés on this town having... subsided, the Yucatecos and other inhabitants are rapidly subsiding into their customary state of insouciance.... The Spanish speaking population of the District (three fourths of the whole)... view any reverse to our arms or peril to our Government with opinions varying from indifference to absolute satisfaction.... As to the Indian inhabitants of our territory, the question of allegiance to... any Government appears to convey no meaning. They have probably crossed our border because employment was more easily obtained on British territory, to avoid the forced military service of the trans-Hondo tribes or to escape the consequences of some blood-feud.[162]

The colonial secretary properly understood the motivations of Maya peasants who crossed the Hondo River, and his indifference to the lives of people seeking safety and employment is remarkable. This indifference was by now a studied indifference, cemented into official policy. It was, however, a predictable consequence of the British fetishization of territory.

Any process of nation-building in British Honduras was far off in the distance. In 1872, the residents within the aspirational colonial borders were not united by any shared identity or sense of loyalty. Within the span of twenty-five years, the population had been completely transformed. In 1845, just prior to the outbreak of the Social War, the enumerated population of the British settlement was 9,809 people, including a miniscule number of "whites" (399 people, or 4%) in government, commerce, and timber; a tiny and slow-growing Creole middle class; their poor Creole, Carib (Garífuna), and Indigenous laborers; and an unknown number of "Indians" who largely remained at a distance from Belize, in the forests of the interior. By 1871, the total enumerated population had nearly tripled to 24,710, and the number of whites had been overwhelmed by Yucatecans of Maya and Spanish descent,[163] who were variously seeking safety from war, military drafts, and exploitative conditions of land alienation, heavy taxation, and debt peonage. Although Maya peasants had crossed the Hondo River, those same problems hounded them. South of the river, overlapping patterns of labor exploitation awaited them, as the monopolization of land abetted by laws drafted in London in favor of British settlers gave Maya migrants few places where they might live and work free from the overreaching demands of landlords, generals, and employers.

Epilogue

Placing Boundary Markers

The Crown Lands Ordinance announced in November 1872 was, for the San Pedro Maya, a matter of too little, too late. A passage within the ordinance included a formalization of the idea for "Indian and Charib" village reserves that Lt. Gov. Longden had proposed in 1868. On the one hand, it might have been interpreted as lending credence to the notion that Indigenous people bear rights to land based on aboriginal occupation. On the other hand, the way that the reservations were designed seriously undermined those rights. The lands around a village were to be "reserved to them under the protectorate of the Crown"—in other words, they would not own or control them outright, neither as a collectivity nor as individuals. The *alcaldes* of the villages were to assign permits ("location tickets") to villagers that would allow them to occupy and utilize certain plots within the reservation; the permits had to be renewed every year and could be canceled by the lieutenant governor. In addition, according to the ordinance, Crown Lands utilized through such permits "shall not be transferable by sale, lease, or otherwise, without the written consent of the Colonial Secretary."[1] In other words, these lands could not be used by the community or the individual to charge rent or fees for the extraction of natural resources by others. Furthermore, by apportioning land grants to individual villages, administered by village *alcaldes*, the system would have eroded larger regional and cultural alliances.

Furthermore, the British Honduran reservation system was not in fact grounded in a notion of land rights derived from aboriginal possession. The *terra nullius*

https://doi.org/10.5876/9781646424634.c007

mythology (discussed in chapter 1) that the lands of Belize were essentially vacant at the time of the original British settlement had been repeated so often throughout British colonial communications that it became accepted as fact. The various Indigenous groups in the colony were all cast as latter-day immigrants from elsewhere. In 1912, Acting Governor Wilfred Collet reported that there were no Indigenous groups who could make legitimate land claims: "The only aboriginal natives of America in the Colony are either immigrants or the descendants of persons who came to the Colony after it became a British possession. No natives seem to have been dispossessed."[2] Later, in 1941, the Report of the Interdepartmental Committee on Maya Welfare echoed that: "The present-day Indian inhabitants are, without exception, the descendants of immigrants from the neighboring republics since the early days of British settlement."[3] Given that erroneous preconception, colonial officials might have felt little moral pressure to set aside reserves.

Finally, in terms of implementation, the ordinance can be seen to have failed miserably. Since the San Pedro Maya villages were on privately owned lands, no reserves were ever established in the northwestern quadrant of the colony.[4] By 1895, the only reserves created for Maya people were the towns of Benque Viejo and Succotz on the Belize River, near the Guatemalan border. These were populated primarily by Maya people from Yucatán who had first settled in the Petén during the Social War. In the far northeast, around Chetumal Bay, some community lands were targeted to be set aside for the villages of other refugees from the Social War. Otherwise, the colonial government had largely given up on the idea of establishing Indian reserves in the northern half of the colony. In the southern half, where more Crown Lands were located, more reservations were later established for people of Mopan and Kekchi Maya and Garifuna descent. Joel Wainwright observed that the three tiny areas originally identified for reserves (the far north, the far west, and southwestern corner) represented a general strategy of containment of the Indians at the far edges of the colony.[5]

Nigel Bolland and Assad Shoman rightly concluded that the creation first of Crown Lands and secondly of reserves on Crown Lands was a two-step method of "dispossession of the [Maya and Garifuna people] from their lands."[6] The Indigenous people were not outright forbidden from owning land—they just were not allowed to fully own or control territory as a group. Maya people could in theory purchase individual plots of land, and some did,[7] but again, the vast monopolization of land in the north, in combination with the high purchase price of Crown Lands, prevented that from becoming a widespread practice. Throughout the northern half of British Honduras through the mid-twentieth century, the Maya overwhelmingly remained tenants on privately owned lands, which facilitated their incorporation into the economy as paid laborers.[8]

Maya people did not so easily give up their claims to the western region, however. In 1874, General Eugenio Arana, the head of the Pacíficos in Xkanhá, established friendly relations with the British, while at the same time complaining that
people were farming lands without paying rent at San Pedro, which he considered
to belong to Mexico.[9] By 1875, Asunción Ek and others had repopulated the villages of the western region, and San Pedro, San Jose, Santa Teresa, Chorro, Santa
Cruz, Hololtunich, Yalbac, and Little Yalbac (as well as some villages in Guatemala)
were aligned politically with Icaiché. Icaiché leaders appointed their own *alcaldes*,
and while the British never again appointed or recognized a regional comandante,
Asunción Ek was recognized within the Icaiché hierarchy as comandante in the
western region.[10] In 1875, the Icaiché secretary was again demanding the payment
of fees for mahogany and cedar harvested in the western region (specifically at
Hololtunich), and had kidnapped a subcontractor to force payment from Messrs.
Phillips & Co. Other timber agents made regular rent payments to keep the peace,
including even the formerly recalcitrant George Raboteau of the BHC.[11]

The Icaiché and western-region Maya felt so assured in their land claims that
they fixed them in stone. They placed boundary markers at three points along the
Belize River—at Saturday Creek, Bermudian Landing, and at Black Creek—and
reminded a company surveyor of their claim to the lands north of those points.
These boundary markers were consistent with the land claims that the Pacíficos
had been voicing since 1853, if not long before. Pacífico general Arana reminded
the lieutenant governor that Hololtunich was on Mexican lands (in the state of
Campeche), "in accordance with the treaties, as can be seen on the maps."[12]

The boundary dispute between Mexico and British Honduras would not be
resolved until the end of the nineteenth century. In the meantime, the Icaiché and
western-region Maya would continue on occasion to demand payment of rent for
use of their lands by British Honduran loggers for years to come: in 1876, 1879, 1882,
1884, and 1885, at least. Santiago Pech (figure 5.1), who in 1866 had invited Marcos
Canul to use San Pedro as a headquarters for rent-collection activities, was rewarded
among the Pacíficos; in 1878, General Arana replaced Rafael Chan with Pech as
Comandante General at Icaiché.[13] Negotiators in Mexico and Britain recognized
that the boundary dispute could not be resolved without a simultaneous commit-
ment on the part of British Honduras to halt munitions sales to the Kruso'ob rebels.
So long as the British continued to support the Kruso'ob, the rebels threatened the
Pacíficos and other residents of Yucatán and Campeche. Consequently, Mexico had
no incentive to try to stop the Maya from collecting rent within the aspirational
British limits; indeed, some Mexican officials might have seen those rent collection
activities as just payback for British support of the rebels. The Spencer-Mariscal
treaty, signed in 1893 and ratified in 1898, indicated that Mexico would concede to

the British demand and stipulate the Hondo River (and its Blue Creek tributary) as the boundary between Mexico and British Honduras. In return, the British promised to stop the flow of munitions to the Kruso'ob. This was the beginning of the end for the Kruso'ob rebellion, which is considered to have come to a close in 1901, when General Ignacio Bravo's troops seized Chan Santa Cruz.[14]

The Icaiché threat to the British was greatly diminished after epidemics of smallpox and whooping cough in 1892 halved the town's population (to about five hundred people).[15] The border treaty did not put an end to the Pacíficos' southern claims, however. In 1900, Pacíficos at Xkanhá still claimed Kaxiluinic (British Honduras) and Yaloch (Guatemala) as theirs.[16] Moreover, neither the border treaty nor the end of the war stopped the southern migration of Yucatecan peasants seeking freedom from debt bondage. That continued well into the twentieth century.

As industrial uses for henequen fiber soared in the late nineteenth century, haciendas in northwestern Yucatán were transformed into large-scale henequen plantations. The westernmost third of the state of Yucatán became a vast henequen zone, and the most common type of worker on these plantations were indebted peons, tied to the estate (*peones acasillados*). Henequen was king, and "sooner or later, most of the villagers based in the zone went to work on the henequen estates as tenants, part-time workers, or, most commonly, *peones acasillados*," according to Allen Wells and Gilbert Joseph.[17] Indebted peons regularly ran off, even though escapees were pursued by bounty hunters. Ironically, for decades, the ongoing Kruso'ob rebellion discouraged some from fleeing, because being an indebted tenant was one of the only ways that a Yucatecan peasant could escape the rotating military draft and being sent to fight the Kruso'ob.[18] Debt peonage remained the linchpin of the Yucatecan rural economy until it was finally abolished in 1914.[19]

Some of the parents and grandparents of people who lived in San Jose as children fled to British Honduras during this period often called the "Epoch of Slavery." They told their descendants about the "*esclavitud*" they experienced. Tomasa Ortega's grandfather, from the Mérida region, recounted to her that *esclavitud* was the reason why many "poor people" came down to San Jose and other villages in the area, including Chorro.[20] María Torres's father-in-law, also from the Mérida region, ran away from *esclavitud* as a youth, along with his parents. "You would be hit. You couldn't leave," he recalled. "I will never forget them telling me," she half-whispered.[21] Jorge Tun's grandfather ran away from *esclavitud* in Yucatán, which Mr. Tun described as: "the rich people would steal from the poor and force them to work and hit them." Mr. Tun's grandfather, his wife, and children fled to a small place in the forest called Xmabax, where there were stands of *mabax* (hog plum) trees with fruit to eat. Five soldiers caught up with him, tied him up, and carried him back to the estate. He escaped again, was reunited with his family, and they went to Icaiché, then later to Ch'och'kitam (in Guatemala), and later Kaxiluinic (British Honduras).[22]

Felix Ortega (the father of Pedro Ortega) also left Yucatán "because of the *esclavitud*." Many people did so at the time, traveling in groups: "They said to their *padrinos* [godparents], let's go." They went to the British region, Mr. Ortega said, because "there was forest" (to plant milpa): "There was fruit, there was stuff to eat. Up there, there was nothing, there were no breadnut trees, there was nothing." Breadnut (Spanish: *ramón*) is a famine food, and its absence underscores how desperate the situation in Yucatán was, and that their lives were more comfortable in the western Belize region.[23]

However, in the late nineteenth century, the northwestern quadrant of British Honduras was nearly entirely owned by the Belize Estate and Produce Company (the successor to the British Honduras Company).[24] For those who settled and lived in San Jose, as mahogany stands became depleted elsewhere and the company intensified their timber harvesting in the area in the 1920s, the company began to dominate their lives. Needing to pay rent for house and milpa lots, many worked for the company (either in timber or chicle extraction), until they were finally evicted and removed to a reservation in San Jose Palmar in 1936. That, however, is an account for another day.

Chronology

1544. Spanish villa of (Salamanca de) Bacalar founded; *encomiendas* assigned.

1697. Spanish conquest of the last independent Maya (Itzá) kingdom, at Nojpeten.

1707. Remaining Tipuans ordered to be resettled in the Spanish settlements of the Petén.

1763. Treaty of Paris reasserts Spanish dominion over the Bay of Honduras, while granting British usufruct rights to extract logwood for export.

1783. Treaty of Versailles reaffirms Spanish dominion over the Bay of Honduras, plus British usufruct rights to extract logwood for export, but within more precisely defined limits.
Town of Belize is founded at the mouth of the Belize (Old) River.

1786. Convention of London expands the allowable area of British logging and permits extraction of any type of wood.

1821. Mexico gains and Guatemala declares independence from Spain.

1826. Treaty of Amity, Commerce, and Navigation between Great Britain and Mexico reaffirms British logging use rights within the same region.

https://doi.org/10.5876/9781646424634.c008

1837. Superintendent Alexander MacDonald explores the western Hondo River and declares the Blue Creek to be its source; on that basis, distributes grants in the western region, beyond treaty limits.

1847. The Social War begins in eastern Yucatán.

1848. Great Britain adopts position of neutrality.

Bacalar seized by Maya rebels; Yucatecans of Spanish and Maya descent flee to British settlement in the Bay of Honduras.

1849. Chichanhá becomes an important rebel base and thoroughfare for munitions.

Under pressure from Mexico, British officials attempt to halt the flow of munitions to the Indians.

Bacalar recaptured by Yucatecan forces.

1850. Chan Santa Cruz becomes headquarters for Maya rebels and worship of the Talking Cross.

1851. Chichanhá offers declaration of peace to the Yucatecan government; Kruso'ob burn Chichanhá in retaliation.

1853. Chichanhá and other towns and villages sign peace treaty with Yucatecan government.

1854. British Honduras adopts a constitution and a Legislative Assembly.

1856. Chichanhá leader Luciano Tzuc demands rent payments from Young, Toledo & Co. at Blue Creek Bank, under threat of force.

1857. Thousands of Chichanhá-region Maya have resettled in the Booth's River region, as far south as Labouring Creek.

Kruso'ob demand payment of rent from Young, Toledo & Co.

1858. Kruso'ob seize Bacalar again and take prisoners for ransom; West India regimental soldiers on hostage rescue mission witness massacre.

1859. Anglo-Guatemalan Treaty establishes borders between Guatemala and the British settlement in the Bay of Honduras.

British Honduras Company is registered.

1860. Kruso'ob and Chichanhá Pacíficos clash over land; Chichanhá is burned.

1861. José Ulúac and Luciano Tzuc of Chichanhá secure approval and arms from Pablo García (of Campeche) to recapture Bacalar from the Santa Cruz.

Contingent from the Chichanhá region, led by Asunción Ek, resettles in Yalbac district and Petén.

Honduras Land Titles Act is finalized, enabling large-scale land monopolization.

1862. British Honduras becomes a colony.

Asunción Ek offers to defend British Honduras and the British Honduras Company against attacks by Chichanhá and Kruso'ob Maya.

Appointments of *alcaldes* in San Pedro Maya villages.

1863. Luciano Tzuc of Chichanhá demands rent payments from Young, Toledo & Co. and the British Honduras Company, as far south as Booth's River.

Tzuc establishes new headquarters at Icaiché.

1864. Raids by and on San Roman, Albion Island; Icaiché Pacíficos take hostages.

Imperial Commissioner of the Peninsula of Yucatán issues decree claiming British Honduras for the Mexican Empire.

Marcos Canul becomes Comandante General at Icaiché following the death of Luciano Tzuc.

1865. Icaiché demand back rent from British Honduras Company for mahogany harvested between Blue Creek and the Río Bravo.

1866.

APRIL 27–28. Icaiché raid and take hostages at BHC mahogany works at Qualm Hill and Betson's Bank.
MAY 10. Asunción Ek warns of Canul's plan to descend upon San Pedro.
NOVEMBER 6. Captain Delamere visits San Pedro.
DECEMBER 1. Canul's men arrive at San Pedro.
DECEMBER 21. Skirmish at San Pedro.

1867.

FEBRUARY 4. Raids at Indian Church and Mount Hope.
FEBRUARY 9. Destruction of San Pedro, San Jose, and Santa Teresa.
MARCH. Destruction of Cerro, Naranjal, Santa Cruz, and Chumbalche.

MAY. Terms of surrender delivered to western-region Maya.

DECEMBER. Town of Icaiché burned by Kruso'ob soldiers.

1868.

FEBRUARY. British Honduran frontier police formed.

APRIL. Lt. Abbs's boundary line reaches within nine miles of Icaiché.
Renewed Icaiché rent demands in the western region.

1869. Frontier police begin deporting vassals and deserters.

1870. Icaiché march on Corozal.

1871. British Honduras becomes a Crown Colony.

1872. San Pedro, San Jose, and Santa Teresa now resettled.
Icaiché attack on Orange Walk. Death of Marcos Canul.

Notes

PREFACE: A NOTE ON LANGUAGE

1. Matthew Restall and Wolfgang Gabbert, "Maya Ethnogenesis and Group Identity in Yucatán, 1500–1900," in *"The Only True People": Linking Maya Identities Past and Present*, ed. Bethany J. Beyyette and Lisa J. LeCount (Boulder: University Press of Colorado, 2017), 91–131.

2. Fidencio Briceño Chel and Gerónimo Ricardo Can Tec, eds., *U nu'ukbesajil u ts'íibta'al maayat'aan: Normas de escritura para la lengua maya* (México: Secretaría de Cultura, Instituto Nacional de Lenguas Indígenas, 2014).

INTRODUCTION

1. Cocom to Fancourt, 11 May 1848, Belize Archives and Records Service (hereafter cited as BARS) 28.

2. Cocom to Fancourt, 11 May 1848, BARS 28.

3. Don E. Dumond, *The Machete and the Cross: Campesino Rebellion in Yucatán* (Lincoln: University of Nebraska Press, 1997), 237–38.

4. The phrase *guerra de castas* was used at least as early as January 1847. A group of Campechano-led federalists resisting the reincorporation of Yucatán into Mexico launched an attack on Valladolid, and large numbers of "Indian" fighters joined in. A Yucatecan official saw this as evidence of an impending *guerra de castas* (Serapio Baqueiro, *Ensayo histórico sobre las revoluciones de Yucatán desde el año de 1840 hasta 1864, tomo I* [Mérida, Yucatán:

Imprenta de Manuel Heredia Argüelles, 1878], 527). Nineteenth-century historian Eligio Ancona attributed the rebellion to "a three-centuries-old hatred between the two principal races of the peninsula" (*Historia de Yucatán desde la época mas remota hasta nuestros días*, Vol. 4, *La guerra social* [Mérida, Yucatán: Imprenta de M. Heredía Argüelles, 1880], 10).

5. Gabbert, "Of Friends and Foes: The Caste War and Ethnicity in Yucatan," *Journal of Latin American Anthropology* 9, no. 1 (2004): 90–118, https://doi.org/10.1525/jlca.2004.9.1.90. Three works that use the term "Social War" include Ramón Berzunza Pinto, *Guerra social en Yucatán (Guerra de Castas)* (Mérida, Yucatán: Maldonado Editores/Gobierno del Estado de Yucatán, Secretaría de Educación, 1997); Jorge Alberto Canto Alcocer, "Las otras castas de la guerra: Bonifacio Novelo y los mestizos de Valladolid en la guerra social de 1847," in *La ventana de Zací: Otras miradas de la Guerra de Castas*, ed. Jorge Canto Alcocer and Terry Rugeley (Valladolid, Yucatán: Universidad de Oriente, 2013); Alejandra Badillo Sánchez, "Memorial de la Guerra Social Maya," accessed June 15, 2022, https://memorialguerrasocialmaya.org. On the multiethnic origins of some rebel leaders, see also Nelson A. Reed, "White and Mestizo Leadership of the Cruzoob," *Saastun: Revista de Cultura Maya*, 9 (1997): 63–88.

6. Book-length treatments of the war include: Victoria Reifler Bricker, *The Indian Christ, the Indian King: The Historical Substrate of Maya Myth and Ritual* (Austin: University of Texas Press, 1981); Dumond, *Machete*; Wolfgang Gabbert, *Violence and the Caste War of Yucatán* (Cambridge: Cambridge University Press, 2019); Moisés González Navarro, *Raza y tierra: La guerra de castas y el henequén* (México, D. F.: Colegio de México, 1970); Marie Lapointe, *Los mayas rebeldes de Yucatán* (Mérida, Yucatán: Maldonado Editores, 1997); Nelson A. Reed, *The Caste War of Yucatán*, rev. ed. (Stanford, CA: Stanford University Press, 2001); Douglas W. Richmond, *Conflict and Carnage in Yucatán: Liberals, the Second Empire, and Maya Revolutionaries, 1855–1876* (Tuscaloosa: University of Alabama Press, 2015); Terry Rugeley, *Rebellion Now and Forever: Mayas, Hispanics, and Caste War Violence in Yucatán, 1800–1880* (Stanford, CA: Stanford University Press, 2009); Terry Rugeley, *Yucatán's Maya Peasantry and the Origins of the Caste War* (Austin: University of Texas Press, 1996); Terry Rugeley, ed., *Maya Wars: Ethnographic Accounts from Nineteenth-Century Yucatán* (Norman: University of Oklahoma Press, 2001).

7. Nancy M. Farriss, "Nucleation versus Dispersal: The Dynamics of Population Movement in Colonial Yucatan," *Hispanic American Historical Review* 58, no. 2 (1978): 202, http://www.jstor.org/stable/2513085.

8. Mark W. Lentz, "Black Belizeans and Fugitive Mayas: Interracial Encounters on the Edge of Empire, 1750–1803," *Americas* 70, no. 4 (2014): 645–75, https://www.jstor.org/stable/43189294; Matthew Restall, "Crossing to Safety? Frontier Flight in Eighteenth-Century Belize and Yucatan," *Hispanic American Historical Review* 94, no. 3 (2014): 385, https://doi.org/10.1215/00182168-2694300.

9. About the western Belize region during the period of the Social War, historians and historical anthropologists have produced a significant body of scholarship upon which to

build. O. Nigel Bolland's ("Maya Settlements in the Upper Belize River Valley and Yalbac Hills: An Ethnohistorical View," *Journal of Belizean Affairs* 3 [1974]: 3–23) and Grant D. Jones's ("Levels of Settlement Alliance among the San Pedro Maya of Western Belize and Eastern Petén, 1857–1936," in *Anthropology and History in Yucatán*, ed. Grant D. Jones [Austin: University of Texas Press, 1977], 139–89) pioneering work in the Belizean archives revealed the migration southward of the San Pedro Maya and critical features of San Pedro Maya-British relations. Bolland fleshed out key details of British policy with respect to the Pacíficos in "Alcaldes and Reservations: British Policy towards the Maya in Late Nineteenth Century Belize," *América Indígena* 57, no. 1 (1987): 33–75; *The Formation of a Colonial Society: Belize, from Conquest to Crown Colony* (Baltimore: Johns Hopkins University Press, 1977); "The Maya and the Colonization of Belize in the Nineteenth Century," in *Anthropology and History in Yucatán*, ed. Grant D. Jones (Austin: University of Texas Press, 1977), 69–99. As part of her work on Pacífico politics throughout the length of the war, Lean Sweeney outlined the position of the San Pedro Maya with respect to the Chichanhá/Icaiché groups in Sweeney, *La supervivencia de los bandidos: Los mayas icaichés y la política fronteriza del sureste de la peninsula de Yucatán, 1847–1904* (Mérida, Yucatán: Universidad Nacional Autónoma de México, 2006). Angel Eduardo Cal's dissertation added a critical political economic perspective, charting the development of an enclave economy in nineteenth-century British Honduras that was both colonial and capitalist, and he analyzed timber extraction, commercial agriculture, and subsistence farming as an interrelated system of capital, land, and labor ("Rural Society and Economic Development: British Mercantile Capital in Nineteenth-Century Belize" [PhD diss., University of Arizona, 1991]). A basic outline of the 1866–1867 San Pedro Maya-British clash emerges within: Jones, "Levels of Settlement Alliance," 149–51; Bolland, "Alcaldes and Reservations," 40–41; Angel Eduardo Cal, "Anglo Maya Contact in Northern Belize: A Study of British Policy toward the Maya during the Caste War of Yucatán, 1847–1872" (MA thesis, University of Calgary, 1983), 172–84; Dumond, *Machete*, 275–79; Rajeshwari Dutt, *Empire on Edge: The British Struggle for Order in Belize during Yucatán's Caste War, 1847–1901* (Cambridge: Cambridge University Press, 2020), 81–89. In his final dissertation chapter, Cal ("Rural Society," 327–68) began to characterize the conflict between the Pacíficos/San Pedro Maya and the British in relationship to the wider political economy. Rajeshwari Dutt's *Empire on Edge* charts how British political strategies changed with respect to the various Maya groups as the war evolved.

10. Shepard Krech III, *The Ecological Indian: Myth and History* (New York: W. W. Norton, 1999).

11. Matthew Restall, *The Maya World: Yucatec Culture and Society, 1550–1850* (Stanford, CA: Stanford University Press, 1997), 207.

12. Rugeley, *Yucatán's Maya Peasantry*, 68–72, 78–84.

13. Farriss, "Nucleation versus Dispersal," 203. "As much as thirty percent of a community's population at one time might be what were termed *nachilcahob* (outsiders)," she noted.

14. Rugeley, *Yucatán's Maya Peasantry*, 78–84.

15. Restall, "Crossing to Safety?," 385.

16. Dutt, *Empire on Edge*.

17. Hayden White, *The Content of the Form: Narrative Discourse and Historical Representation* (Baltimore: Johns Hopkins University Press, 1987).

18. Lila Abu-Lughod, "Writing against Culture," in *Recapturing Anthropology: Working in the Present*, ed. Richard G. Fox (Santa Fe, NM: School of American Research Press, 1991).

19. John Van Maanen, *Tales of the Field: On Writing Ethnography*, 2nd ed. (Chicago: University of Chicago Press, 2011).

20. Tim Ingold, *Being Alive: Essays on Movement, Knowledge and Description* (London: Routledge, 2011), 160, 162.

21. Abu-Lughod, "Writing against Culture."

22. Van Maanen, *Tales of the Field*, 101–24, quote on 119.

23. Carolyn Nordstrom, *A Different Kind of War Story* (Philadelphia: University of Pennsylvania Press, 1997).

24. While the first edition of Nelson Reed's *The Caste War of Yucatán* (Stanford, CA: Stanford University Press, 1964) was praised for an animated writing style that brought historical characters north of the Hondo River to life, recreating the drama and emotion of the conflict, it could not stand as authoritative because, writing for a general audience, Reed did not regularly cite his sources. Dumond's *The Machete and the Cross* is carefully detailed, painstaking in its scholarship, and sweeping in scope, and yet it takes on an encyclopedic style, such that the personalities, motivations, and bravado of individuals, and the terror and anguish of decisions made are lost along the way. Angel Cal's dissertation ("Rural Society") added an essential political economic perspective to the analysis of events in nineteenth-century British Honduras. His tight systemic analysis, however, hides some of the uniqueness and agency of individuals.

25. In the documents consulted, women rarely are named. When they are mentioned (also rarely), they almost always appear in aggregate form ("women and children") and as passive recipients and victims of the actions of (named) men. Alejandra Badillo Sánchez is doing important work to recapture the experiences of women and children in the Social War in her collaborative web project ("Memorial de la Guerra Social Maya").

26. Archives Officer Mary Alpuche, email communication, 5 Feb. 2020. Cal similarly reported that "R. 5, 55, 57, and R. 68, p. 1–510 . . . are missing" (Cal, "Rural Society," 410).

27. Major Sir John Alder Burdon, ed., *Archives of British Honduras* (London: Sifton Praed, 1931–1935). For this work, I did not consult archival records in Yucatán or Guatemala, and future researchers might find these fruitful avenues of inquiry.

28. This might seem an unfair conclusion, but as we shall see, several important documents that would have put the British in a bad light were selectively edited or appear to have gone missing. This might have occurred at any point in time before, during, or after

Operation Legacy. As discussed by Ian Cobain, in the 1950s–70s, as the UK government prepared for the eventual independence of its many colonies in Africa, Asia, and the Caribbean, it rolled out Operation Legacy, in which documents that were deemed to be damaging to Britain's legacy—should they fall into the hands of former colonials—were systematically culled from the records and removed to a top-secret location in Britain or else destroyed. In 1962 in Belize, according to Cobain: "There was a shortage of trustworthy officials 'of European descent' who were considered qualified to perform the task of weeding and destroying documents. The task was left to a visiting MI5 officer, who decided that every sensitive file should be destroyed: 'In this he was assisted by the Royal Navy and several gallons of petrol'" (Cobain, *The History Thieves: Secrets, Lies and the Shaping of a Modern Nation* [London: Portobello Books, 2016], 101–35, quote on 127). The Public Records Acts of 1958 stipulates conditions under which documents might be removed from the Public Records Office and destroyed. One example of a sensitive document that was destroyed is "Reports the removal of the Maya village of San Jose to a new site," which would have been the official account of the eviction of the people of San Jose by order of the Belize Estate and Produce Company and with the assistance of the colonial government in 1936. The index CO 348/22 [1936–1937] at the National Archives (UK) refers to the document (number 66682, from Gov. 78, dated 30 March 1936), but a stamp at the top marks it "DESTROYED UNDER STATUTE."

29. Lt. Gov. J. Gardiner Austin to Gov. Edward John Eyre, 13 July 1864, no. 83, BARS 81.

30. These interviews were conducted as part of the larger San Pedro Maya Project, mentioned in the acknowledgments. The eviction is briefly discussed in Christine A. Kray, Minette C. Church, and Jason Yaeger, "Designs on/of the Land: Competing Visions, Displacement, and Landscape Memory in Colonial British Honduras," in *Legacies of Space and Intangible Heritage: Archaeology, Ethnohistory, and the Politics of Cultural Continuity in the Americas*, ed. Fernando Armstrong-Fumero and Julio Hoil Gutiérrez (Boulder: University Press of Colorado, 2017), 53–77.

CHAPTER 1: IMPERIAL RIVALRY AND MAYA
RESISTANCE IN THE PENINSULA'S SOUTHEAST

1. Robert Redfield and Alfonso Villa Rojas, *Chan Kom: A Maya Village* (Reprint, Chicago: Chicago University Press, 1962; first published 1934); Farriss, *Maya Society*; Matthew Restall, *The Maya World: Yucatec Culture and Society, 1550–1850* (Stanford, CA: Stanford University Press, 1997).

2. Thomas W. F. Gann, *The Maya Indians of Southern Yucatan and Northern British Honduras*. Smithsonian Institution, US Bureau of American Ethnology, Bulletin 64 (Washington, DC: Government Printing Office, 1918), 28.

3. Redfield and Villa Rojas, *Chan Kom*, 24; Farriss, "Nucleation versus Dispersal," 207–9. The idea for discussing the mobility facilitated by milpa cultivation was Minette

Church's, and we elaborated on this in Minette C. Church, Christine A. Kray, and Jason Yaeger, "Landscapes of Strategic Mobility in Central America: San Pedro Siris during the Caste War," in *Routledge Handbook of the Archaeology of Indigenous-Colonial Interaction in the Americas*, ed. Lee M. Panich and Sara L. Gonzalez (New York: Routledge, 2021), 308–23. In the twenty-first century, milpa agriculture continues as a subsistence practice, although by a smaller percentage of families.

4. Grant D. Jones, *The Conquest of the Last Maya Kingdom* (Stanford, CA: Stanford University Press, 1998), 9–13.

5. Grant D. Jones, *Maya Resistance to Spanish Rule: Time and History on a Colonial Frontier* (Albuquerque: University of New Mexico Press, 1989), 10–11.

6. Ralph L. Roys, *The Political Geography of the Yucatan Maya* (Washington, DC: Carnegie Institution of Washington, 1957, Publication 613), 3, 159–65.

7. Sergio Quezada, *Maya Lords and Lordship: The Formation of Colonial Society in Yucatán, 1350–1600*, trans. Terry Rugeley (Norman: University of Oklahoma Press, 2014), 18–24, quote on 24.

8. Farriss, *Maya Society*, 158–61; Quezada, *Maya Lords*, 55–59.

9. Farriss, *Maya Society*, 39–55.

10. Farriss, *Maya Society*, 72–77; Farriss, "Nucleation and Dispersal"; Pedro Bracamonte y Sosa, *La conquista inconclusa de Yucatán: Los mayas de la montaña, 1560–1680* (México: Centro de Investigaciones y Estudios Superiores en Antropología Social/Universidad de Quintana Roo/Miguel Ángel Porrúa, 2001). On resettlement in the Ts'ulwiniko'ob region, see Jones, *Maya Resistance*, 9–10, 98; France V. Scholes and Sir Eric Thompson, "The Francisco Pérez *Probanza* of 1654–1656 and the *Matrícula* of Tipu (Belize)," in *Anthropology and History in Yucatán*, ed. Grant D. Jones (Austin: University of Texas Press, 1977), 43–68.

11. Mavis C. Campbell, *Becoming Belize: A History of an Outpost of Empire Searching for Identity, 1528–1823* (Kingston, Jamaica: University of West Indies Press, 2011), 1–87; Matthew Restall, "Creating 'Belize': The Mapping and Naming History of a Liminal Locale," *Terra Incognitae* 51, no. 1 (2019): 7, https://doi.org/10.1080/00822884.2019.1573962.

12. Scholes and Thompson, "The Francisco Pérez *Probanza*," 52.

13. Jones, *Maya Resistance*, 5, 10–11, 62.

14. Jones, *Maya Resistance*; Elizabeth Graham, *Maya Christians and Their Churches in Sixteenth-Century Belize* (Gainesville: University of Florida Press, 2011).

15. Jones, *Maya Resistance*, 102–5.

16. Church, Kray, and Yaeger, "Landscapes of Strategic Mobility," 318–19.

17. Jones, *Maya Resistance*, 270–73; Jones, *Conquest of the Last*, 408.

18. Thomas W. F. Gann, *Ancient Cities and Modern Tribes: Exploration and Adventure in Maya Lands* (London: Duckworth, 1926), 66.

19. Lentz, "Black Belizeans," 660–67.

20. "The Bay of Honduras. By Thomas Jefferys, Geographer to His Majesty," London, 1775, Colonial Office records, National Archives, United Kingdom (hereafter cited as CO) 700/BritishHonduras7. Just south of the region marked "Tipu" is one marked "Chanes." This may refer to a group of Itzá led by AjChan who, following the conquest of Nojpeten, escaped and established a small polity in southern Belize, where he was "made king over Mopans and Chols" (Jones, *Conquest of the Last*, xxvii, 418–21). The prefix Aj- means "masculine" and Chan is a surname.

21. Archibald Robertson Gibbs, *British Honduras: An Historical and Descriptive Account of the Colony from Its Settlement, 1670* (London: Sampson Low, Marston, Searle, & Rivington, 1883), 24–25. See also Barbara Bulmer-Thomas and Victor Bulmer-Thomas, *The Economic History of Belize: From the Seventeenth Century to Post-Independence* (Belize City: Cubola Press, 2012), 41–63.

22. Restall, "Creating 'Belize,'" 16–17; Gilbert M. Joseph, "British Loggers and Spanish Governors: The Logwood Trade and Its Settlements in the Yucatan Peninsula: Part I," *Caribbean Studies* 14, no. 2 (1974): 7–37, https://www.jstor.org/stable/25612609.

23. Campbell, *Becoming Belize*, 114, quote on 190.

24. Mary H. Helms, "Miskito Slaving and Culture Contact: Ethnicity and Opportunity in an Expanding Population," *Journal of Anthropological Research* 39, no. 2 (1983): 179–97, https://www.jstor.org/stable/3629966; Lawrence H. Feldman, ed. and trans., *Lost Shores, Forgotten Peoples: Spanish Explorations of the South East Maya Lowlands* (Durham, NC: Duke University Press, 2000), 217–20.

25. Victor Bulmer-Thomas and Barbara Bulmer-Thomas, "The Origins of the Belize Settlement," *Tempus: Revista en Historia General* 4 (2016): 137–60, https://revistas.udea .edu.co/index.php/tempus/article/view/326161; Restall, "Creating 'Belize.'"

26. Bolland, *Formation*, 49.

27. Restall, "Creating 'Belize,'" 8, 21.

28. Campbell, *Becoming Belize*, 155–210, 245–82.

29. Jennifer L. Anderson, *Mahogany: The Costs of Luxury in Early America* (Cambridge, MA: Harvard University Press, 2012), 18, 106. See also Bulmer-Thomas and Bulmer-Thomas, *Economic History*, 70–77.

30. Definitive Treaty of Paris, Paris, Article XVII, 10 Feb. 1763, ABH FSP.

31. Anderson, *Mahogany*, 90–91.

32. Definitive Treaty of Peace, Versailles, 3 Sept. 1783, ABH FSP.

33. Restall, "Creating 'Belize,'" 21.

34. Notice by Governor of Yucatán, 27 May 1784, ABH Alm. 1828.

35. Anderson, *Mahogany*, 104–8.

36. Convention of London, 14 July 1786, ABH FSP.

37. R. A. Humphreys, *The Diplomatic History of British Honduras, 1638–1901* (London: Oxford University Press, 1961), 6. The Spaniards used piles of stones (*mojoneras*) with

wooden crosses erected atop them to mark land boundaries in Yucatán as early as the sixteenth century (Quezada, *Maya Lords*, 59–60).

38. Lindsay W. Bristowe and Philip B. Wright, *The Handbook of British Honduras for 1888–89; Comprising Historical, Statistical, and General Information Concerning the Colony* (Edinburgh and London: William Blackwood and Sons, 1888), 26.

39. Humphreys, *Diplomatic History*, 10.

40. Restall, "Crossing," 387–88.

41. Anderson, *Mahogany*, 159. At this time, British population counts included only the British settlements.

42. Anderson, *Mahogany*, 5, 115, 121, 270.

43. Humphreys, *Diplomatic History*, 16.

44. O. Nigel Bolland and Assad Shoman, *Land in Belize, 1765–1871: The Origins of Land Tenure, Use, and Distribution in a Dependent Economy* (Kingston, Jamaica: Institute of Social and Economic Research, University of the West Indies, 1975), 9–10, 12, 15–17, 35–36.

45. Treaty of Amity, Commerce and Navigation, between Great Britain and Mexico, 26 Dec. 1826, ABH Treaty with Mexico.

46. Humphreys, *Diplomatic History*, 28.

47. P. K. Menon, "The Anglo-Guatemalan Territorial Dispute over the Colony of Belize (British Honduras)," *Journal of Latin American Studies* 11, no. 2 (1979): 343–71, http://www.jstor.org/stable/156309.

48. Anderson, *Mahogany*, 121.

49. Meeting of Superintendent Francis Cockburn with the Judges and Magistrates, 12 Sept. 1834, ABH MMJ.

50. Meeting of the Sup. and the Judges and Magistrates assembled as a Council, 5 Nov. 1834, ABH 2.

51. Humphreys, *Diplomatic History*, 22, 180.

52. Minette Church suggested the term "aspirational borders" and we discussed some of this territorial dispute in Minette C. Church, Jason Yaeger, and Christine A. Kray, "Re-Centering the Narrative: British Colonial Memory and the San Pedro Maya," in *Archaeologies of the British in Latin America*, ed. Charles E. Orser Jr. (Cham, Switzerland: Springer International, 2019), 73–76, 78.

53. See Bolland, *Formation*; Humphreys, *Diplomatic History*; Dutt, *Empire on Edge*.

54. Sup. Alexander MacDonald to Sec. of State, 25 Aug. 1837, ABH 14a.

55. Bolland and Shoman, *Land in Belize*, 47–48; Humphrey, *Diplomatic History*, 24.

56. Cal, "Anglo Maya Contact," 14.

57. Cockburn to SoS for the Colonies, 17 Apr. 1835, BARS 2.

58. In 1839, Messrs. Young, Toledo & Co. received a Crown license to harvest timber as far northwest as the Blue Creek, and in 1837, they received a license to work near Garbutt's Falls (Humphreys, *Diplomatic History*, 61).

59. John Hodge to Austin, 30 Nov. 1865, quoted in Austin to Gov. Henry Knight Stocks, 21 June 1866, no. 41, BARS 92.

60. Gann, *Ancient Cities*, 63.

61. Thomas Gann, *Mystery Cities of the Maya* (reprint, Kempton, IL: Adventures Unlimited Press, 1997; first published 1925), 94–95.

62. Bolland, *Formation*, 22.

63. Edward Rhys to Seymour, 3 Nov. 1862, BARS 78.

64. Major Luke Smith O'Connor, "An Exploring Ramble among the Indios Bravos, in British Honduras," *Living Age* 34, no. 434 (September 11, 1852): 513–17. The group's travel route was reconstructed by Jason Yaeger, email communication, 4 Oct. 2018.

65. Burdon, *Archives*, 1:4.

66. Stephen L. Caiger, *British Honduras: Past and Present* (London: G. Allen & Unwin, 1951), 30.

67. Bolland, "Maya Settlements"; Bolland, *Formation*, 20; Farriss, *Maya Society*, 57–62; Jones, *Maya Resistance*, 110–17.

68. Charles M. Woods Sr., J. Alexander Bennett, and Silvaana Udz, *Years of Grace: The History of Roman Catholic Evangelization in Belize* (Belize City: Roman Catholic Diocese of Belize City and Belmopan, 2015), 47.

69. Restall, "Creating 'Belize,'" 11–12.

70. Woods, Bennett, and Udz, *Years of Grace*.

71. Bolland, *Formation*, 21–23.

72. Captain George Henderson, *An Account of the British Settlement of Honduras; Being a View of Its Commercial and Agricultural Resources, Soil, Climate, Natural History, &c.* 2nd ed. (London: R. Baldwin, 1811), 26–27.

73. Redfield and Villa Rojas, *Chan Kom*, 24–27.

74. Seymour to Gov. Charles Henry Darling, Report on the Blue Book of the Settlement for the year 1858, 22 June 1859, ABH 65.

75. Farriss, *Maya Society*, 277.

76. Hodge to Austin, 30 Nov. 1865, quoted in Cal, "Anglo Maya Contact," 14.

77. "Some [other] Indian residents of British Honduras" were the ones who told Superintendent Seymour about the presence of Chichanhá-region migrants in the Booth's River region in 1857 (Seymour to Major Gen. Bell, 15 May 1857, Confidential no. 1, BARS 52).

78. William Coffin to Fancourt, 18 Mar. 1848, BARS 25; Merchants and mahogany cutters to Fancourt, 2 Mar. 1848, BARS 28.

CHAPTER 2: TO THE SOUTH OF THE UPRISING: BRITISH MUNITIONS, REFUGE, AND NEW LANDLORDS (1847–1850)

1. Census of 1835, 31 Dec. 1835, ABH Census 5. August 1, 1834, marked Emancipation Day in the British Empire, although there followed a four-year transition period (until 1838) in which enslaved people were to serve as "apprentices"; those people labeled as "slaves" in this census were likely in the apprentice phase.

2. Bolland, *Formation*, 3.

3. Farriss, *Maya Society*, 51–56, 84.

4. Farriss, *Maya Society*, 382–83.

5. Robert W. Patch, *Maya and Spaniard in Yucatan, 1648–1812* (Stanford, CA: Stanford University Press, 1993), 150, 200.

6. Stephens, *Incidents of Travel in Yucatan* (London: John Murray, 1843), 1:335, 2:171, 1:207.

7. Rugeley, *Yucatán's Maya Peasantry*, 68–69, 75.

8. Rugeley, *Yucatán's Maya Peasantry*, xv, 52–57, 68–69, quotes on xv and 52.

9. Rugeley, *Yucatán's Maya Peasantry*, 39–52, 134–41.

10. González Navarro, *Raza y tierra*, 60–62.

11. Quezada, *Maya Lords*, 61.

12. Restall, *Maya World*, 56.

13. Farriss, *Maya Society*, 276. On "conquest by purchase," see Restall, *Maya World*, 220–25.

14. Patch, *Maya and Spaniard*.

15. Farriss, *Maya Society*, 383.

16. Rugeley, *Yucatán's Maya Peasantry*, 63–68, 124–25.

17. Gilbert M. Joseph, *Rediscovering the Past at Mexico's Periphery: Essays on the History of Modern Yucatan* (Tuscaloosa: University of Alabama Press, 1986), 31–33.

18. Stephens, *Incidents of Travel*, 2:204.

19. B. M. Norman, *Rambles in Yucatan; Or, Notes of Travel through the Peninsula, Including a Visit to the Remarkable Ruins of Chi-Chen, Kaba, Zayi, and Uxmal* (New York: J. & H. G. Langley, 1843).

20. Edward Rhys to Seymour, 4 Jan. 1862, BARS 74.

21. Farriss, *Maya Society*, 383.

22. Bricker, *Indian Christ*, 224–53, quote on 224.

23. Paul Sullivan, *Unfinished Conversations: Mayas and Foreigners between Two Wars* (Berkeley: University of California Press, 1989), xiv–xv, 164.

24. Michael Hesson, email communication, 30 July 2021.

25. Allan F. Burns has discussed how Maya oral literature (including historical tales) commonly uses a couplet cadence, which serves as a mnemonic device as well as lending

poetic flourish (Burns, *An Epoch of Miracles: Oral Literature of the Yucatec Maya* [Austin: University of Texas Press, 1983]).

26. Rugeley, *Yucatán's Maya Peasantry*, 148–64.

27. Dumond, *Machete*, 80, 91–98; Reed, *Caste War* (rev.), 61–73.

28. Sec. of the Gov. of Yucatán to Fancourt, 31 Dec. 1847, ABH 28.

29. Matías Esteves to Fancourt, 18 Jan. 1848, BARS 28; Fancourt to Gov. Charles E. Grey, 7 June 1848, no. 30, BARS 25; Fancourt to Gov. of Yucatán, 1 Feb. 1848, ABH 22b; José Y. Perrera de Loria to Sup., 19 Feb. 1848, BARS 28.

30. Convention of London, 14 July 1786, ABH FSP.

31. Fancourt to Mends, 4 Mar. 1848, BARS 22.

32. Fancourt to Officer Commanding Troops, 23 Apr. 1848, ABH 22b; Earl Grey to Gov. Grey, 12 May 1848, no. 8, BARS Despatches Inwards 30; Earl Grey to Gov. Grey, 30 June 1848, no. 10, BARS Despatches Inwards 30; Comandante Juan Pablo Cocom and Secretary José Teodoro Villanueva to Fancourt, 6 May 1848, BARS 29.

33. Reprinted in Ancona, *Historia de Yucatán*, 4: Apéndice, X–XII.

34. Ancona, *Historia de Yucatán*, 4: Apéndice, X–XII. See also Dumond, *Machete*, 116–22. The relationship between labor exploitation, indebted servitude, and the rebellion is discussed in González Navarro, *Raza y tierra*.

35. Bricker, *Indian Christ*, 101.

36. Terry Rugeley, "The Caste War in Guatemala," *Saastun: Revista de Cultura Maya* 3, no. 3 (1997): 73–76, 83–84.

37. Cocom to Fancourt, 11 May 1848, BARS 28. See also Cocom to Fancourt, 21 June 1848, BARS 28.

38. Fancourt to Gray, 7 June 1848, no. 30, BARS 25. Dutt traced Fancourt's favorable view to information strategically provided to him by Austin Cox and Edward Rhys—merchants motivated by financial interests (Dutt, *Empire on Edge*, 23–50).

39. Fancourt to Gray, 7 June 1848, no. 30, BARS 25.

40. Comandante General Cecilio Chi et al. to Fancourt, 15 June 1848, BARS 29; Chi et al. to Fancourt, 8 July 1848, BARS 28.

41. Fancourt to Grey, 8 July 1848, no. 40, BARS 25; Fancourt to Grey, 11 Aug. 1848, no. 49, BARS 25.

42. Restall, "Crossing," 385.

43. Comandante General Venancio Pec and Secretary José Victor Reyes to Fancourt, 5 Oct. 1848, BARS 28.

44. Note by Richard Hill, 28 Sept. 1848, enclosed with Pec and Reyes to Fancourt, 5 Oct. 1848, BARS 28; Seymour to Eyre, 14 June 1863, no. 70, BARS 81.

45. Fancourt to Grey, 11 Jan. 1849, no. 1, BARS 25.

46. Comandante José María Tzuc to Fancourt, 29 Dec. 1848, BARS 28.

47. The full text of the treaty is found in the *Journals of the House of Commons*, vol. 42 (1787), 274–75. Article XIV is quoted in Percy W. Doyle to Fancourt, 21 Mar. 1849, BARS 29.

48. Francisco Antonio Cervera et al., 17 July 1848, enclosed with Doyle to Fancourt, 12 Sept. 1848, BARS 29.

49. Austin Cox and James LaCroix to Fancourt, 29 Dec. 1848, BARS 29.

50. W. Parish Robertson to Doyle, 14 Mar. 1849, BARS 30; Doyle to Viscount Palmerston, 16 Mar. 1849, BARS 30; Doyle to Fancourt, 21 Mar. 1849, BARS 29.

51. G. Lennox Conyngham to H. Merivale, 28 May 1849, BARS 30.

52. J. D. Cetina to Fancourt, 19 June 1849, BARS 28; Fancourt to Commandant at Bacalar, 27 June 1849, BARS 32; Grey to Fancourt, 21 July 1849, no. 28, BARS 30.

53. Fancourt to Grey, 10 Aug. 1849, no. 36, BARS 31.

54. Burdon, *Archives*, 1:156, 158.

55. Comandante General Jacinto Pat to John Kingdom and Edward Rhys, 18 Feb. 1849, BARS 28; Kingdom et al. to Chiefs of the Yucatecan Indians, 29 Feb. 1849, BARS 28.

56. Comandante General Cecilio Chi and Comandante de las Armas Venancio Pec and Comandante de las Tropas José Atanacio Espadas to Fancourt, 22 Mar. 1849, BARS 28.

57. Doyle to Min. for Foreign Affairs Luis G. Cuevas, 18 Apr. 1849, BARS 29; José María Lacunza to Doyle, 9 Aug. 1849, BARS 30; Fancourt to Pat, 17 Sept. 1849, BARS 33.

58. Colonel J. D. Cetina to Fancourt, 28 May 1849, BARS 29; General Consul Joseph T. Crawford to Fancourt, 29 June 1849, BARS 29.

59. Fancourt to Pat, 17 Sept. 1849, BARS 33.

60. Dumond, *Machete*, 153–54.

61. Fancourt to Magistrates at Santa Helena and Douglas, 3 Oct. 1849, BARS 32; Fancourt to Grey, 12 Oct. 1849, no. 43, BARS 31; Cetina to Captain G. W. Meehan, 5 Oct. 1849, BARS 33.

62. Dumond, *Machete*, 156–57.

63. Faber to Fancourt, 13 Oct. 1849, BARS 33; Florentino Chan and Venancio Pec to Fancourt, 10 Oct. 1849, BARS 33.

64. Document issued by Lacunza, 3 Oct. 1849, BARS 33; Barbachano to Fancourt, 12 Sept. 1849, BARS 33; Faber to Fancourt, 13 Oct. 1849, BARS 33.

65. Lacunza to Doyle, 3 Nov. 1849, BARS 33; Fancourt to Grey, 11 May 1850, no. 19, BARS 31.

66. Gabbert, *Violence and the Caste War*, 173–81. See also Rajeshwari Dutt, *Maya Caciques in Early National Yucatán* (Norman: University of Oklahoma Press, 2017).

67. Punta Consejo Magistrate J. H. Faber to Fancourt, 4 Dec. 1848a, BARS 29.

68. Rafael Chan and Marcos Canul to James Plumridge, c. 22 Jan. 1869, BARS 103; Venancio Pec, "One Hundred Blows or Death: Venancio Pec's Letter to Modesto Méndez," in *Maya Wars*, ed. Terry Rugeley, 57–58.

69. Rugeley, *Rebellion*, 131; Fancourt to Grey, 11 Jan. 1850, no. 2, BARS 31.

70. Cal, "Anglo Maya Contact," 216.

71. Sidney W. Mintz, *Sweetness and Power: The Place of Sugar in Modern History* (New York: Penguin Books, 1985), 47–49.

72. Thomas W. F. Gann, *The Maya Indians of Southern Yucatan and Northern British Honduras* (Smithsonian Institution, US Bureau of American Ethnology, Bulletin 64, Washington: Government Printing Office, 1918), 20–32.

73. Orange Walk Magistrate Robert Downer to Lt. Gov. J. R. Longden, 27 Jan. 1870, BARS 105.

74. Northern District Magistrate Edwin Adolphus to Longden, 15 Jan. 1870, BARS 105.

75. O. Nigel Bolland, "Labour Control and Resistance in Belize in the Century after 1838," in *Colonialism and Resistance: Essays in Historical Sociology*, 2nd rev. ed. (Benque Viejo del Carmen, Belize: Cubola Publications, 2003), quote on 160.

76. Bolland, "Labour Control." See also Bolland and Shoman, *Land in Belize*, 58–60.

77. Longden to Gov. J. P. Grant, "General Report on the Land Question," 6 Mar. 1868, BARS 98.

78. Bolland, "Labour Control," 161.

79. Cal, "Rural Society," 303.

80. Angel Cal, "The Corozal (Goshen) Estate: 1819–1887," *Belcast Journal of Belizean Affairs* 1, no. 1 (1984): 41. In another example, Roberto Lunas paid Phillip Toledo rent of $5/acre for the land at Spanish Lookout where he maintained a sugar mill (Lunas before Belize Magistrate Samuel Cockburn, 1 June 1867, BARS 96).

81. These amounts of land were standard when I conducted ethnographic fieldwork in Sisbicchen and Dzitnup in northern Yucatán in the 1990s, and fifty *mecates* was the standard milpa size in British Honduras in 1941 (Report of the Interdepartmental Committee on Maya Welfare, 10 Nov. 1941, CO 123/384/8).

82. Cal, "Rural Society," 301–11. A sample tenant lease agreement from Carmichael's estate is reprinted on 405–9.

83. Northern District Magistrate Edmund Burke to Sup. Frederick Seymour, 8 Jan. 1862, BARS 74; D. Morris, *The Colony of British Honduras, Its Resources and Prospects; With Particular Reference to Its Indigenous Plants and Economic Productions* (London: Edward Stanford, 1883), 120.

84. Adolphus to Longden, 15 Jan. 1870, BARS 105. Work in the sugarcane fields and tending milpa were not mutually exclusive activities. Sugarcane would be planted between June and August; subsequently, during the time it took to mature (15–18 months), only weeding was required, which in Yucatán was done by *luneros*. Larger numbers of workers were needed for cutting and hauling during the harvest time (December through May), which is a slower period in the milpa cycle (Rugeley, *Yucatán's Maya Peasantry*, 73).

85. Burke to Seymour, 8 Jan. 1862, BARS 74.

86. Bolland, "Labour Control," 160–62.

87. Burke to Seymour, 8 Jan. 1862, BARS 74; Morris, *Colony of British Honduras*, 120.

88. S. Cockburn, *Rough Notes and Official Reports on the River Belize, the Physical Features of British Honduras, Taken in 1867–1869* (Kingston, Jamaica: C. L. Campbell Printer, 1875), 37.

89. Adolphus to Longden, 15 Jan. 1870, BARS 105.

90. Burke to Seymour, 8 Jan. 1862, BARS 74. For substantially similar accounts, see also Adolphus to Longden, 15 Jan. 1870, BARS 105; Downer to Longden, 27 Jan. 1870, BARS 105; Cockburn to Sup., 24 Feb. 1870, BARS 106; Gibbs, *British Honduras*, 175–78; Morris, *Colony of British Honduras*, 120–23; Bristowe and Wright, *Handbook*, 196–99; Henry Fowler, *A Narrative of a Journey across the Unexplored Portion of British Honduras, with a Short Sketch of the History and Resources of the Colony* (Belize: Government Press, 1879), 52.

91. Adolphus to Longden, 15 Jan. 1870, BARS 105.

92. Cockburn, *Rough Notes*, 36–37.

93. Adolphus to Longden, 15 Jan. 1870, BARS 105; Downer to Longden, 27 Jan. 1870, BARS 105.

94. Burke to Seymour, 8 Jan. 1862, BARS 74.

95. Henderson, *Account of the Settlement*, 66–67.

96. Rugeley, *Yucatán's Maya Peasantry*, 73.

97. Adolphus to Longden, 15 Jan. 1870, BARS 105.

98. Cockburn, *Rough Notes*, 37.

99. Claudio Manríquez to Florencio Vega, 11 July 1866, BARS 93.

100. Doyle to Fancourt, 16 Jan. 1850, ABH 33; Santa Helena Mag. to Fancourt, 12 Apr. 1850, ABH 33; Fancourt to Doyle, 17 Sept. 1850, ABH 32b.

101. The settlement was referred to in different ways, depending upon the author of the communication, the language in which it was written, and its audience. In the original Maya-language "Proclamation of Juan de la Cruz" (1850), and in a letter written in Maya from Juan de la Cruz to Governor Barbachano (dated August 28, 1851), he called it "in Cahahal, Chan Sta. [sign of the cross]," meaning "my village, Little Holy Cross" (quoted in Bricker, *Indian Christ*, 188, 210). Elsewhere in rebel communications, it was referred to as Noj Kaj Santa Cruz, meaning "the main [or large or grand] village of the Holy Cross." In letters from rebel leaders to British officials, they typically referred to it simply as "Santa Cruz," which they might have done thinking that the British would not know the meaning of the Maya words "Chan" or "Noj Kaj."

102. Bricker, *Indian Christ*, 103–18. See also Richard Buhler, S. J., ed., *A Refugee of the War of the Castes Makes Belize His Home: The Memoirs of J. M. Rosado*. Occasional Publications No. 2 (Belize: Belize Institute for Social Research and Action, 1970). Nauat (meaning "interpreter") could have been Manuel Nauat's title rather than a surname.

103. Dumond, *Machete*, 408–9; Gabbert, "Of Friends and Foes."

CHAPTER 3: THE PACÍFICOS DEL SUR AND
COMPETING LAND CLAIMS (1851-1857)

1. Humphreys, *Diplomatic History*, 52–54. See also Bolland, *Formation*, 188–92.

2. Bolland, *Formation*, 184; Public Meeting, 23 Jan. 1851, ABH 20.

3. Sup. P. E. Wodehouse to Grey, 5 Dec. 1851, no. 36, BARS 38.

4. Dumond, *Machete*, 186–87; N.D. Mag. to Sup., 9 Sept. 1851, ABH 33.

5. Ancona, *Historia de Yucatán*, 325; Bricker, *Indian Christ*, 115; Dumond, *Machete*, 187.

6. Quoted in Dumond, *Machete*, 192.

7. Dumond, *Machete*, 190; Rugeley, *Maya Wars*, 60–61; Rugeley, *Rebellion*, 135.

8. Rugeley, *Rebellion*, 129–30.

9. Wodehouse to Grey, 11 June 1853, no. 20, BARS 48.

10. The Spanish version of the treaty is reprinted in Melchor Campos García, ed., *Guerra de Castas en Yucatán: Su origen, sus consecuencias y su estado actual, 1866* (Mérida, Yucatán, Mexico: Universidad Autónoma de Yucatán, 1997), 98–101. Acknowledging the multiethnic composition of Pacífico communities, Article 7 indicated that: "The whites can remain in the Indian villages." The "whites" probably included a combination of residents of the represented towns prior to the rebellion, refugees from towns still embroiled in conflict, and deserters from the Yucatecan armed forces.

11. Father George M. Avvaro to Austin, 25 Jan. 1867, BARS 89.

12. Austin to Gov. John Peter Grant, 7 Feb. 1867, no. 26, BARS 92.

13. Dumond, *Machete*, 194–97.

14. Wodehouse to Indian Commissioners, 12 Oct. 1853, ABH 40.

15. Tzuc to Wodehouse, 27 Oct. 1853, BARS 78.

16. Karl Sapper, "Independent Indian States of Yucatan," in *Mexican and Central American Antiquities, Calendar Systems, and History*, ed. and trans. by Charles P. Bowditch, 625–34 (Bulletin of the Bureau of American Ethnology 28. Washington, DC: Smithsonian Institution, 1904, first published in 1895), 626–27.

17. Bolland, *Formation*, 184, 189–90.

18. Stevenson to Gov. Henry Barkley, 16 Sept. 1854, no. 65, BARS 52.

19. Bolland, *Formation*, 182–87.

20. Longden to Grant, "General Report on the Land Question," 6 Mar. 1868, BARS 98.

21. Rugeley, *Rebellion*, 131; Bolland, *Formation*, 3.

22. Stevenson to Barkly, 17 Oct. 1855, no. 70, BARS 55.

23. Acting Sup. Thomas Price to Darling, 3 May 1860, BARS 68, Confidential; Seymour to Gov., Report on the Blue Book of the Settlement for the year 1858, 22 June 1859, ABH 65. The report noted: "More robust than the Spaniard, less addicted to pleasure than the negro they [the Maya] are admirably adapted to the monotonous drudgery of logwood cutting."

24. Cal, "Rural Society," 222–23.

25. R. Temple, "The Commercial Resources of British Honduras," *Journal of the Society of Arts* 3, no. 154 (2 Nov. 1855): 783–85, https://www.jstor.org/stable/41323582.

26. Cal, "Anglo Maya Contact," 219, 224–25. See also Downer to Longden, 27 Jan. 1870, BARS 105.

27. Rhys to Seymour, 3 Nov. 1862, BARS 78.

28. Joseph, "British Loggers," 15–16.

29. Downer to Longden, 27 Jan. 1870, BARS 105. See also Cal, "Rural Society," 221–24; Cockburn, *Rough Notes*, 36–37.

30. Cal, "Anglo Maya Contact," 142.

31. Luciano Tzuc, Fernando Chabel, and Marcos Canul to Toledo, 20 Aug. 1856, BARS 26. What is referred to here as "aniseed" was likely a crude, locally distilled rum (Spanish: *aguardiente*) that was "flavoured with anise for retailing to the Indians" (Stephens, *Incidents of Travel*, 2:183).

32. Tzuc to Toledo, 2 Sept. 1856, BARS 26. Separately, the Yucatecan Comandante at Bacalar confirmed that his command extended as far as Pucté, and Tzuc's command to the west of that. He further indicated that he had no influence over Tzuc as Tzuc reported directly to the state government (Mariano Trejo to Stevenson, 15 Sept. 1856, BARS 54). Panting's Bank was located on Blue Creek, just west of the point where it empties into the Hondo (Humphreys, *Diplomatic History*, Map V).

33. Stevenson to Acting Gov. Edward Wells Bell, 9 Sept. 1856, no. 72, BARS 55.

34. Stevenson to Doyle, 7 Oct. 1856, BARS 54.

35. Stevenson to Bell, 16 Oct. 1856, no. 76, BARS 55; Adolphus to Col. Sec. Greville Buckley-Mathew, 21 May 1866, BARS 93.

36. Stevenson to Bell, 15 Jan. 1857, BARS 52.

37. Dumond, *Machete*, 467 n. 53.

38. Pablo Encalada to Stevenson, 21 Sept. 1856, BARS 54. See also Cal, "Anglo Maya Contact," 141.

39. Stevenson to Bell, 15 Nov. 1856, BARS 52, Secret.

40. Stevenson to Sec. of State for the Colonies, Henry Labouchere, 16 Dec. 1856, BARS 52.

41. Seymour to Bell, 14 July 1857, BARS 52.

42. Seymour to Darling, 17 Dec. 1857, no. 37, BARS 55; Faber to Seymour, 20 Dec. 1857, BARS 58.

43. Rugeley, *Yucatán's Maya Peasantry*, 50, 106.

44. Seymour to Bell, 17 June 1857, Confidential no. 2, BARS 52.

45. Many deserters from the Yucatecan armed forces settled among the Pacíficos (Juan Bautista Águilar, "Letter of Juan Bautista Águilar," in *Maya Wars*, ed. Terry Rugeley, 125–27).

46. Seymour to Bell, 15 May 1857, Confidential no. 1, BARS 52.

47. Rugeley, "Caste War in Guatemala," 83–84.

48. Bolland and Shoman, *Land in Belize*, 79.

49. Seymour to Bell, 15 May 1857, Confidential no. 1, BARS 52. As will be explained in chapter 4, while Bolland ("Maya Settlements," 13) concluded that Asunción Ek led this 1857 Chichanhá migration, Ek's group did not arrive until 1861.

50. Henderson, *Account of the Settlement*, 57–64; Cal, "Rural Society," 152.

51. Seymour to Gov., Report on the Blue Book of the Settlement for the year 1858, 22 June 1859, ABH 65; Interviews with former San Jose residents; Cal, "Rural Society," 152.

52. Interviews with former San Jose residents. Engravings representing women and men carrying enormous bundles of grasses and breadnut leaves on their backs are found in Ober, *Traveling in Mexico*, 87, 115.

53. Seymour to Gov., Report on the Blue Book of the Settlement for the year 1858, 22 June 1859, ABH 65.

54. Jones identified the allied villages in Guatemala as the Holmul Minor Cluster (Jones, "Levels of Settlement Analysis," 162–68). In January 1859, the boundaries of an *alcalde* district (intended for villages of "Indians" or Yucatecans) were to be drawn in the Labouring Creek region (Meeting of Executive Council, 4 Jan. 1859, BARS 53).

55. Again, figure 1.4 shows the extent of private land claims throughout the western district at the time. The diagonal shading on the map indicates the western boundary of lands for which British Honduras Company (BHC) then claimed ownership. It may be that BHC purchased the stretch of land that included San Pedro soon after Hume drew his 1858 map. See also Humphreys, *Diplomatic History*, Map IV.

56. Captain Peter Herbert Delamere to Austin, 4 Oct. 1866, BARS 89.

57. In the 1930s, residents at San Jose similarly paid an average rent of $7.50/year for a milpa plot and $10/year for a house lot to the company/landlord (Belize Estate and Produce Company). Just as with logwood, work in mahogany did not preclude milpa cultivation, as the work of both is seasonal and milpa work can be divided among family members. While mahogany woodcutting crews typically headed out at farther distances and for longer periods than was the case for logwood work, even if the adult males in a family set out with a mahogany crew in late August, the remaining family members would have harvested the milpa produce. In addition, there were many tasks to be done closer to the bank, and if the Maya houses were nearby, they could have performed those tasks without needing to travel long distances.

58. While Maya tenants might have been required to provide a portion of their agricultural produce to the company crews, others might have engaged in trade with the crew members. The mahogany workers—from the eighteenth century through to the 1930s—were given food rations of flour and salt pork. The rations were often simply called "seven and four," because the amounts remained the same: seven quarts of flour and four pounds of salt pork per week. As was the case in San Jose in the 1930s, the mahogany workers in the 1850s–1860s might have traded a bit of their rations to villagers for a little peccary or deer meat, fish, yams,

cassava, sweet potatoes, or fruit, or some might have bought them directly. In the 1930s, the San Jose residents who worked for the company also received those rations, which some would sell or trade to other villagers to acquire other food products, and they would sometimes sell their rations to earn money for other consumer items, such as cloth fabric.

59. Seymour to Darling, 16 Nov. 1857, no. 35, BARS 55. A census of predominantly Catholic villages and mahogany works in the British settlement compiled by the Jesuit fathers in 1857 enumerated a total of nineteen thousand people. Notably, the census did not include settlements of Protestants, the coastal islands, "nor the forrest where thousands of Indians are believed to live" (Seymour to Darling, Report on the Bluebook of 1857, May 1858, no. 42, BARS 55). None of the settlements listed lie west of the New River, a sign that the Jesuits were not used to traveling in the western region.

60. Seymour to Bell, 17 June 1857, Confidential no. 2, BARS 52.

61. Toledo to Austin, 2 Aug. 1866, BARS 89.

62. Seymour to Bell, 17 June 1857, no. 20, BARS 55.

63. Seymour to Bell, 14 July 1857, BARS 52.

64. Faber to Seymour, 20 Dec. 1857, BARS 58.

65. Seymour to Bell, 14 July 1857, BARS 52. The fact that timber workers could not be relied upon as frontier soldiers, having no vested interest in protecting their employers' property, was a frequent complaint, pointing to a brittle relationship between workers and employers.

66. Seymour to Darling, 17 Aug. 1857, BARS 52.

67. Seymour to Darling, 16 Sept. 1857, no. 32, BARS 55.

68. Burke to Seymour, 2 Nov. 1857, BARS 58.

69. Darling to Seymour, 16 July 1857, BARS 55.

70. Seymour to Darling, 17 Nov. 1857, no. 36, BARS 55.

71. Seymour to Darling, 17 Dec. 1857, no. 37, BARS 55; Faber to Seymour, 20 Dec. 1857, BARS 58.

72. Seymour to Darling, 17 Aug. 1857, BARS 52.

CHAPTER 4: "WE FIND THE INDIANS VERY USEFUL" (1858–1863)

1. Captain William Anderson to Seymour, 15 Feb. 1858, BARS 61. Venancio Puc, referenced here, is not the same as Venancio Pec, mentioned in chapter 2.

2. Seymour to Darling, 17 Feb. 1858, no. 10, BARS 55.

3. Burke to Seymour, 26 Feb. 1858, BARS 61.

4. Seymour to Darling, 13 Mar. 1858, no. 11, BARS 55.

5. Seymour to Darling, 13 Mar. 1858, no. 11, BARS 55.

6. Seymour to Darling, 13 Mar. 1858, no. 11, BARS 55; Seymour to Darling, 17 Mar. 1858, no. 12, BARS 55; Seymour to Darling, 17 Apr. 1858, no. 27, BARS 55.

7. Seymour to Darling, 15 Aug. 1858, no. 53, BARS 55; Seymour to Darling, 17 Oct. 1858, no. 66, BARS 65.

8. Seymour to Darling, 13 Mar. 1858, no. 11, BARS 55.

9. Seymour to Darling, 17 May 1858, BARS 55.

10. Convention between Her Majesty and the Republic of Guatemala, relative to the Boundary of British Honduras, 30 Apr. 1859, ABH Convention with Guatemala; Menon, "Anglo-Guatemalan," 354–57. Guatemala failed to ratify the treaty by the deadline, and in 1867, both parties rejected its provisions.

11. Seymour to Darling, 17 Aug. 1859, no. 61, BARS 65.

12. Bolland, *Formation*, 182–87.

13. Paul Sullivan, "John Carmichael: Life and Design on the Frontier in Central America," *Revista Mexicana del Caribe* 5, no. 10 (2000): 29–32, http://www.redalyc.org/articulo .oa?id=12801001.

14. Sullivan, "John Carmichael," 32, 39; Bolland and Shoman, *Land in Belize*, 74–78.

15. Price to Darling, 3 May 1860, Confidential, BARS 68.

16. Price to Darling, 3 May 1860, BARS 68. The appointed alcalde in the district was the company foreman (Swasey), not a Maya leader.

17. Price to Darling, 3 May 1860, BARS 68. Price does not mention who was the alcalde at San Pedro at the time, nor does he mention Asunción Ek, who was presumably still at Chichanhá.

18. Dumond, *Machete*, 232–34; Reed, *Caste War* (rev.), 220–32.

19. Seymour to Darling, 8 Feb. 1860, no. 7, BARS 68; Toledo to Austin, 2 Aug. 1866, BARS 89.

20. Burke to Price, 24 June 1860, BARS 71.

21. Statement by Stephen Panting, 17 May 1866, BARS 93; Toledo to Austin, 2 Aug. 1866, BARS 89.

22. Cherrington to Burke, 24 June 1860, BARS 71; Burke to Price, 24 June 1860, BARS 71.

23. This probably refers to the 1853 Pacífico-Yucatán peace treaty, merely with the wrong date written.

24. General Asunción Ek to Burke, 6 June 1860, BARS 71.

25. Dumond, *Machete*, 486. Feliciano Yah succeeded Luciano Tzuc as Comandante General when he was deposed in 1857 (Faber to Seymour, 20 Dec. 1857, BARS 58); it is not clear if Yah held that position in June 1860 or if Ek in fact had succeeded him.

26. Dumond, *Machete*, 262; Adolphus to Longden, 17 Aug. 1868, BARS 102.

27. Cherrington to Burke, 24 June 1860, BARS 71; Crown Surveyor J. H. Faber to Sup. Price, 6 July 1860, BARS 71.

28. Statement by Basilio Grajales, enclosed in Burke to Austin, 6 June 1864, BARS 84.

29. Grajales to Mexican Consul in Belize, José María Martínez, 23 July 1860, BARS 71.

30. Austin to Eyre, 13 July 1864, no. 83, BARS 81.

31. Price to Darling, 15 Jan. 1861, no. 6, BARS 68; Price to Darling, 17 Jan. 1861, no. 8, BARS 68.

32. Price to Darling, 7 Feb. 1861, no. 10, BARS 68.

33. Humphreys, *Diplomatic History*, 103.

34. Census of British Honduras, 8 April 1861, BARS 74. The census also enumerated 5,067 people in Belize, 1,113 in Stann Creek, and 306 in Punta Gorda.

35. Faber to Price, 27 Apr. 1861, BARS 74.

36. Price to Darling, 12 Mar. 1861, no. 29, BARS 68.

37. Plumridge and Twigge to Price, 12 Apr. 1861, BARS 71; Deposition of Trejo, 12 Apr. 1861, BARS 71.

38. Plumridge and Twigge to Price, 12 Apr. 1861, BARS 71; Deposition of Trejo, 12 Apr. 1861, BARS 71.

39. Deposition of Trejo, 12 Apr. 1861, BARS 71.

40. Price to Darling, 13 Apr. 1861, BARS 68.

41. Burke to Price, 25 Apr. 1861, BARS 71.

42. Price to Darling, 12 Aug. 1861, no. 94, BARS 68.

43. Price to Darling, 27 Sept. 1861, no. 112, BARS 68.

44. Faber to Price, 27 Apr. 1861, BARS 74.

45. Pablo García to José Ulúac, 27 Nov. 1861, BARS 79; Seymour to Eyre, 13 Feb. 1863, no. 15, BARS 81.

46. Seymour to Eyre, 12 Nov. 1862, no. 187, BARS 81.

47. Ek to Burke, 6 June 1860, BARS 71.

48. Seymour to Eyre, 12 Nov. 1862, no. 187, BARS 81. In this 1862 letter, Seymour mentions the burning of Chichanhá and the plan to attack Bacalar with the support of the Campechano authorities as precipitating events for the departure of Ek's group. He says that these events occurred in 1857, but he was mistaken, since we know from other sources that they occurred in 1860 and in late 1861, respectively. In 1860 and the first half of 1861, Seymour had been on leave in England, and as we have seen, Price's reports during that period focused on the Kruso'ob, which would explain Seymour's mistake. In essence, there were two large-scale migrations from Chichanhá southward, both due in part to disagreements with Tzuc. Seymour appears simply to have conflated the two episodes. (See also Seymour to Eyre, 13 Feb. 1863, no. 15, BARS 81.) Jones similarly concluded that "Ek must have established his headquarters at San Pedro in 1861 or early 1862" ("Levels of Settlement Alliance," 146).

49. Recall that in April 1860, Juan Can, the leader at Santa Cruz near Yalbac, was politically aligned with Chichanhá. Early in 1861, Can was said to have "three hundred men under his orders" at Santa Rita (also near Yalbac) (Faber to Price, 27 Apr. 1861, BARS 74).

50. Seymour to Eyre, 12 Nov. 1862, no. 187, BARS 81.

51. Seymour to Eyre, 8 Oct. 1862, no. 117, BARS 81.

52. Seymour to Eyre, 30 Aug. 1862, no. 109, BARS 68.

53. Seymour to Eyre, 8 Oct. 1862, no. 117, BARS 81.

54. José E. Vidaurre to Lino Lara, 23 Aug. 1862, BARS 78.

55. Seymour to Eyre, 8 Oct. 1862, no. 117, BARS 81; Seymour to Eyre, 12 Nov. 1862, no. 187, BARS 81. At this time, logging foremen commonly doubled as magistrates of the districts in which they worked, demonstrating once again the close alliance between the timber companies and the colonial government.

56. Inspector Patrick Cunningham to Acting Col. Sec. A. W. Moir, c. 18 Sept. 1862, BARS 78.

57. G. W. Hulse to Cunningham, 14 Sept. 1862 (postscript added 18 Sept.), BARS 78.

58. Rhys to Seymour, 3 Nov. 1862, BARS 78.

59. Adolphus to Acting Col. Sec. Thomas Graham, 11 Sept. 1866, BARS 93.

60. Seymour to Eyre, 8 Oct. 1862, no. 117, BARS 81.

61. Superintendent's speech, 21 Jan. 1858, ABH Assembly. See also Bolland, "Alcaldes and Reservations."

62. Meeting of Executive Council, 4 Jan. 1859, ABH 53.

63. Seymour to Eyre, 8 Oct. 1862, no. 117, BARS 81; Bolland, "Alcaldes and Reservations," 42–47.

64. Rhys to Seymour, 3 Nov. 1862, BARS 78. Rhys did not visit the Holmul cluster villages in Guatemala at this time.

65. Seymour to Eyre, 12 Nov. 1862, no. 187, BARS 81.

66. Seymour to Eyre, 13 July 1863, no. 72, BARS 81.

67. Seymour to Eyre, 14 Jan. 1863, no. 7, BARS 81.

68. Seymour to Eyre, 8 Oct. 1862, no. 117, BARS 81.

69. Seymour to Eyre, 14 Jan. 1863, no. 7, BARS 81.

70. Rhys to Seymour, 3 Nov. 1862, BARS 78.

71. Seymour to Eyre, 12 Nov. 1862, no. 187, BARS 81.

72. Guatemalan Consul Antonio Mathé to Seymour, 29 Oct. 1862, BARS 78; Seymour to Eyre, 14 Feb. 1863, Confidential, BARS 81.

73. Ulúac to Panting, 15 Jan. 1863, BARS 79.

74. Ulúac to Panting, 16 Jan. 1863, BARS 79.

75. Seymour to Eyre, 13 Feb. 1863, no. 15, BARS 81.

76. John Carmichael Jr. to Longden, 15 Nov. 1867, BARS 93.

77. González Navarro, *Raza y tierra*, 195.

78. Corozal Magistrate James Hume Blake to Austin, 11 May 1866, BARS 93.

79. Blake to Seymour, 5 May 1863, BARS 83.

80. Seymour to Eyre, 13 April 1863, no. 29, BARS 81.

81. Seymour to Eyre, 1 May 1863, no. 42, BARS 81.

82. Seymour to Eyre, 14 June 1863, no. 70, BARS 81. See also Burke to Acting Lt. Gov. George Berkeley, 19 Dec. 1863, BARS 84.

83. Seymour to Eyre, 1 May 1863, no. 42, BARS 81.

84. Seymour to Eyre, 14 June 1863, no. 70, BARS 81.

85. Dumond, *Machete*, 272. Icaiché was located eight miles (thirteen kilometers) to the east of Chichanhá.

86. Tzuc to Seymour, 15 June 1863, BARS 83; Tzuc to Seymour, 20 June 1863, BARS 83. See also Statement by Santiago Cervera, 16 May 1866, BARS 93.

87. Seymour to Eyre, 13 July 1863, no. 72, BARS 81.

88. Barbachano to Seymour, 11 July 1863, BARS 83.

89. Barbachano to Tzuc, 11 July 1863, BARS 83.

90. Statement by Hodge, 30 July 1866, BARS 93.

91. Mathé to Seymour, 5 June 1863, BARS 83.

92. Seymour to Eyre, 13 July 1863, no. 72, BARS 83.

93. Ek to Seymour, 8 May 1863, BARS 83.

94. Seymour to Eyre, 13 July 1863, no. 72, BARS 81.

95. Seymour to Eyre, 13 July 1863, no. 72, BARS 81.

96. Ek to Belize Magistrate, 26 June 1863, BARS 83.

97. Seymour to Eyre, 13 July 1863, no. 72, BARS 81.

98. Seymour to SoS for the Colonies, 14 Sept. 1863, BARS 81.

CHAPTER 5: MAYA GENERALS, COMPANY SUBCONTRACTORS, AND THE BATTLE OF SAN PEDRO (1864–1866)

1. General D. Zapata, General Santos, and Secretary General Gerardo del Castillo to Berkeley, 1 Jan. 1864, BARS 84.

2. Austin to Eyre, 11 Apr. 1864, no. 28, BARS 81.

3. Burke to Berkeley, 4 Apr. 1864, BARS 84.

4. Austin to Eyre, 14 May 1864, no. 62, BARS 81.

5. Seymour to Darling, Report on the Bluebook of 1857, May 1858, no. 42, BARS 55.

6. Captain Warren Glubb to Fancourt, 27 Apr. 1848a, BARS 29.

7. Cetina to Fancourt, 19 June 1849, BARS 28.

8. Cockburn, *Rough Notes*, 31.

9. Burke to Austin, 16 June 1864a, BARS 86; Cal, "Rural Society," 232.

10. Burke to Berkeley, 20 May 1864, BARS 84; Statement by Grajales, 6 June 1864, BARS 84. Although the police magistrate initially reported that Canul had killed his own child, Grajales's later statement clarified that Vega's son is the one who was killed.

11. Tzuc to Pascual Ojeda, 11 May 1864, BARS 84; Statement by Grajales, 6 June 1864, BARS 84. Canul's compadre was Pascual Ojeda, whom we have seen previously, as a smuggler of munitions to the Kruso'ob.

12. Tzuc to Grajales, 11 May 1864, BARS 84.

13. Grajales to Burke, 18 May 1864, BARS 84.

14. Burke to Austin, 23 May 1864a, BARS 84.

15. Tzuc to Inhabitants of the English Territory, 31 May 1864a, BARS 84.

16. Burke to Austin, 16 June 1864a, BARS 86.

17. Burke to Austin, 23 May 1864, BARS 86.

18. Austin to Burke, 26 May 1864, BARS 84; Burke to Grajales, 28 May 1864, BARS 84.

19. Burke to Austin, 3 June 1864, BARS 84; Austin to Eyre, 7 June 1864, no. 70, BARS 81.

20. Austin to Eyre, 16 June 1864, no. 71, BARS 81.

21. Eyre to Gov. of Yucatán, 22 June 1864, BARS 86.

22. Antonio Meda to Eyre, 6 July 1864, BARS 86.

23. Panting to Austin, 30 July 1864, BARS 86.

24. Austin to Eyre, 16 June 1864, no. 71, BARS 81; Austin to Eyre, 13 July 1864, no. 83, BARS 81; Austin to Eyre, 12 Aug. 1864, no. 89, BARS 81; Blake to Austin, 22 Aug. 1864, BARS 86.

25. Austin to Eyre, 1 June 1864, no. 67, BARS 81; Austin to Eyre, 7 June 1864, no. 70, BARS 81.

26. Delamere to Berkeley, 7 June 1864, BARS 84.

27. Austin to Eyre, 12 July 1864, no. 82, BARS 81.

28. Austin to Eyre, 16 June 1864, no. 71, BARS 81.

29. Supreme Political Prefect F. Navarrete to Austin, 6 Aug. 1864, BARS 86.

30. Hodge to Austin, c. 20 July 1864, BARS 86.

31. Hodge to Austin, 5 May 1866, BARS 89.

32. Austin to Eyre, 14 Dec. 1864, no. 124, BARS 81.

33. See also Richmond, *Conflict and Carnage*, 76–77.

34. Extract and translation of a decree by the Imperial Commissioner of Yucatán, José Salazar Ilarrequé, 19 Sept. 1864, as published in the *Periódico del Gobierno de Yucatán*, 23 Sept. 1864, BARS 86.

35. Austin to Eyre, 14 Nov. 1864, no. 120, BARS 81.

36. Austin to Eyre, 14 Jan. 1865, no. 4, BARS 85.

37. Comandante General Marcos Canul and Comandante Rafael Chan to George W. Raboteau, 9 Feb. 1865, BARS 86.

38. Raboteau to BHC, 11 Feb. 1865, BARS 86.

39. Canul and Chan to Hodge, 15 Feb. 1865, BARS 86; Austin to Eyre, 18 Mar. 1865, no. 19, BARS 92.

40. Hodge to Canul, 21 Mar. 1865, BARS 93.

41. Capt. E. Rogers to Maj. Molesworth, 14 May 1866, BARS 93.

42. Statement by Cervera, 16 May 1866, BARS 93.

43. Juan Bautista Águilar, "Letter of Juan Bautista Águilar," in *Maya Wars*, ed. Terry Rugeley, 125–27.

44. Austin to Stocks, 8 May 1866, no. 21, BARS 92.

45. Hodge to Austin, 2 May 1866, BARS 93; Adolphus to Buckley-Mathew, 2 May 1866, BARS 93; Austin to Stocks, 8 May 1866, no. 21, BARS 92; Statement of Jesús Martínez before Adolphus, 14 May 1866, BARS 93; Canul and Chan to Austin, 18 May 1866, BARS 93.

46. Graham to Hodge, 17 May 1866, BARS 93.

47. Remarks on the report of Mr. Ohlafen by John Hodge, 30 July 1866, BARS 93.

48. Ohlafen to Graham, 15 June 1866, BARS 93.

49. Receipt acknowledged by Rafael Chan, 30 June 1866, BARS 93.

50. Statement by Cervera, 16 May 1866, BARS 93.

51. Austin to Stocks, 28 June 1866, unnumbered, BARS 92.

52. Austin to Stocks, 2 Aug. 1866, no. 56, BARS 92; Raboteau to Hodge, 19 July 1866, BARS 93.

53. Austin to Stocks, 8 May 1866, no. 21, BARS 92.

54. Austin to Stocks, 29 June 1866, no. 42, BARS 92; Austin to Stocks, 21 June 1866, no. 41, BARS 92; Austin to Plues, 31 May 1866, BARS 89; Austin to Stocks, 26 July 1866, no. 53, BARS 92.

55. Adolphus to Buckley-Mathew, 21 May 1866, BARS 93; Adolphus to Austin, 20 July 1866, BARS 89.

56. Austin to Stocks, 26 July 1866, no. 53, BARS 92.

57. Statement by Robert William Roberts, Sept. 1866, BARS 89.

58. Ohlafen to Austin, 1 June 1866, BARS 92; Austin to Stocks, 7 June 1866, no. 29, BARS 92.

59. Austin to Stocks, 2 Aug. 1866, no. 56, BARS 92.

60. Statement by Mariano Medina before Downer and Adolphus, 14 Dec. 1866, BARS 89.

61. Dumond, *Machete*, 197.

62. Austin to Stocks, 2 Aug. 1866, no. 56, BARS 92. See also Austin to Grant, 17 Apr. 1867, no. 67, BARS 98. The exact location of the canal cut by Messrs. Hyde & Co. is unknown, although it might correspond to the section marked "Canal" on figure 1.4, which probably also corresponds to the section marked as "Canal Bank" on Faber's 1867 map ("Map of British Honduras, compiled by Surveys by J. H. Faber, Crown Surveyor, E. L. Rhys, and others," 1867, CO 700/ BRITISHHONDURAS 22). The prior swampiness of the region is confirmed by a notation on an 1833 map, which is largely blank west of the New River, except for a point where Booth's River is now identifiable, the note reading, "The River Asia looses

[*sic*] itself in these Swamps" ("Map of Honduras … Compiled and drawn by L. Hebert, Senr, London, May, 1833," CO 700/ BRITISHHONDURAS 17).

63. Statement by James Phillips before Austin in Council, 14 Dec. 1866, BARS 93.

64. Austin to Stocks, 21 June 1866, no. 41, BARS 92.

65. Austin to Grant, 20 Nov. 1866, no. 116, BARS 92.

66. S. S. Plues to Graham, 30 Aug. 1866, BARS 89.

67. Ek to Austin, 10 May 1866, BARS 93; Resolutions of the Assembly, 23 May 1866, ABH Assembly 1866; Austin to Ek, 28 May 1866, BARS 93.

68. In 1868, the lieutenant governor noted that many if not all of the villages in the western district, including "San Pedro, Santa Cruz, Chumbalche, San Jose, Naranjal, Quam Hill &c." were on lands owned by BHC or YTC (Longden to Grant, 6 Mar. 1868, no. 39, BARS 98).

69. In a possible example, one of Vega's employees was transporting pigs from San Pedro to Vega's plantation at San Estevan via dorey (Hernández before Delamere, 29 Oct. 1866, BARS 93).

70. For example, Santiago Pech went from San Pedro to Icaiché and was expected to bring back cattle and hogs. These were likely intended for the mahogany crews (oxen to haul the timber and hogs for provisions), but whether he went as a tenant-employee of the company or on his own accord is unclear (Hernández before Delamere, 29 Oct. 1866, BARS 93).

71. Harley to Austin, 15 Feb. 1867, BARS 95.

72. Cockburn, *Rough Notes*, 29.

73. David M. Pendergast, "The Nineteenth-Century Sugar Mill at Indian Church, Belize," *The Journal of the Society for Industrial Archeology* 8, no. 1 (1982): 57–66, https://www.jstor.org/stable/40968027.

74. Austin to Stocks, 22 Aug. 1866, no. 59, BARS 92.

75. Manríquez to Vega, 11 July 1866, BARS 93.

76. Hodge to Graham, 28 July 1866, BARS 93.

77. Graham to Austin, 2 Aug. 1866, BARS 96, Statement by Austin, 28 Feb. 1867, BARS 96.

78. Adolphus to Graham, 11 Sept. 1866, BARS 93.

79. Adolphus to Graham, 14 Sept. 1866, BARS 93.

80. Austin to Stocks, 21 Sept. 1866, no. 81, BARS 92.

81. Delamere to Austin, 4 Oct. 1866, BARS 89.

82. Delamere to Austin, 4 Oct. 1866, BARS 89.

83. Austin to Stocks, 9 Oct. 1866, no. 90, BARS 92; Austin to Pablo Encalada, 21 Oct. 1866, BARS 89.

84. Encalada to Austin, 8 Nov. 1866, BARS 89.

85. Austin to Grant, 10 Nov. 1866, no. 104, BARS 92.

86. Statement of Father Eugenio Biffi, 23 Jan. 1867, BARS 89.

87. María Díaz before Delamere, 10 Nov. 1866, BARS 93.

88. Austin to Grant, 1 Nov. 1866, no. 100, BARS 92.

89. Ek to Austin, cosigned by Calisto Medina, 9 Nov. 1866, BARS 89.

90. José Martín Serrato before Downer, 26 Nov. 1866, BARS 93.

91. José Carmen Hernández before Delamere, 29 Oct. 1866, BARS 93.

92. Delamere to Austin, 29 Oct. 1866, BARS 93; Delamere to Molesworth, 29 Oct. 1866, BARS 93.

93. Austin to Grant, 1 Nov. 1866, no. 100, BARS 92.

94. Austin to Molesworth, 5 Nov. 1866, BARS 89.

95. Delamere to Austin, 11 Nov. 1866a, BARS 93.

96. Carmichael Jr. to Ek, 5 Nov. 1866, BARS 93.

97. Statement of Biffi, 23 Jan. 1867, BARS 89.

98. José Medina before Delamere, 10 Nov. 1866, BARS 93.

99. Ek to Carmichael Jr., 5 Nov. 1866, BARS 93.

100. Medina before Delamere, 10 Nov. 1866, BARS 93.

101. Delamere to Austin, 11 Nov. 1866, BARS 93. Calisto Medina's account is conveyed in Statement of Biffi, 23 Jan. 1867, BARS 89.

102. Statement of Biffi, 23 Jan. 1867, BARS 89.

103. Statement of Biffi, 23 Jan. 1867, BARS 89; Delamere to Austin, 11 Nov. 1866, BARS 93.

104. Statement of Biffi, 23 Jan. 1867, BARS 89.

105. Delamere to Austin, 11 Nov. 1866, BARS 93; Carmichael Jr. to Austin, 12 Nov. 1866, BARS 93.

106. Charles Savery before Delamere, 7 Nov. 1866, BARS 93.

107. Manuel Isama before Delamere, 10 Nov. 1866, BARS 93.

108. Ek to Austin, cosigned by Medina, 9 Nov. 1866, BARS 89.

109. BARS 93, Lorenzo Ortiz before Delamere, 10 Nov. 1866. Ortiz's statement was later corroborated by José Carmen Hernández, Vega's employee at Yalbac. When Hernández issued his statement in mid-December, there were about one hundred Icaiché men stationed at San Pedro; he insisted, however, that: "Asuncion Ek has nothing to do with this raid—but the Indians and also those in the neighborhood invited Canul to join them, some months ago, about four months ago" (Hernández before Rhys, 18 Dec. 1866, BARS 93). Hernández's October 29 statement to Delamere (about a conspiracy brewing at San Pedro and everyone, including Ek, asking him to keep quiet about it) was what had sent Delamere to San Pedro initially. Why did he implicate Ek in October and clear him in December?

110. María Díaz before Delamere, 10 Nov. 1866, BARS 93; Manríquez before Delamere, 10 Nov. 1866, BARS 93.

111. Carmichael Jr. to Austin, 12 Nov. 1866, BARS 93.

112. Ferguson and others to Austin, 21 Nov. 1866, BARS 89. At this time, there were only two large mahogany firms in the colony (BHC and YTC) and three smaller ones (Harley, Phillips, and Mathé) (Austin to Grant, 1 Nov. 1866, no. 100, BARS 92).

113. Ek and Medina to Austin, 13 Nov. 1866, BARS 89.

114. Austin to Ek, 20 Nov. 1866, BARS 89.

115. Austin to Grant, 20 Nov. 1866, no. 116, BARS 92.

116. Graham to Downer, 26 Nov. 1866, BARS 93.

117. Serrato before Downer, 26 Nov. 1866, BARS 93.

118. Lorenzo Santos before Rhys, 18 Dec. 1866, BARS 93. Although the word of someone who had been beaten and imprisoned by Comandante Ek for stealing money from Vega should not necessarily be taken at face value, it is in part corroborated by Medina's statement that Ek ultimately decided to reach out to Canul when he felt that he needed protection from the British (Statement of Biffi, 23 Jan. 1867, BARS 89). Similarly, of course, Medina's testimony is not entirely to be trusted.

119. Virginio Cámara was described as a "white man" (Phillips before Austin, 14 Dec. 1866, BARS 93). One more indication of the intertwining of the timber companies and their sometimes-antagonists is that Cámara had previously worked as a secretary for the BHC (Statement of Liberato Robelo before Adolphus, 28 Dec. 1867, BARS 96).

120. James Phillips before Austin, 14 Dec. 1866, BARS 93; Felipe Fuentes before Carmichael Jr., 25 Jan. 1867, BARS 89; José Carmen Hernández before Rhys, 18 Dec. 1866, BARS 93.

121. Faber to Austin, 10 May 1867, BARS 96.

122. Addressed from General Marcos Canul, Comandante Rafael Chan, and Secretary Virginio Cámara to Austin, 9 Dec. 1866, BARS 89. It seems likely that Rafael Chan directed the secretary to add Canul's name with the intention of intimidating Austin (in this letter and another dated December 26). Several pieces of evidence lead to the conclusion that Canul was not in San Pedro in December 1866. Canul was not on site during the time that James Phillips was held hostage in San Pedro (December 5–10) (Phillips before Austin, 14 Dec. 1866, BARS 93). One of Vega's employees who was in San Pedro in mid-December said that Canul was not there (Hernández before Rhys, 18 Dec. 1866, BARS 93). On December 18, Austin Cox said that Canul was at Icaiché (Cox to Graham, 18 Dec. 1866a, BARS 93). On December 25, Felipe Fuentes did not see Canul in San Pedro, and none of the stories he was told about the skirmish mentioned Canul (Fuentes before Carmichael Jr., 25 Jan. 1867, BARS 89). After the battle, in a letter with the dateline Santa Clara de Icaiché, Canul wrote that it was "a Commission that I sent to San Pedro" that "met up with the English troops and they met them with gun muzzle to muzzle" (Canul and Chan to Adolphus, 18 Jan. 1867a, BARS 89). Similarly, during the battle, it was the "Commandant" (Chan) who gave the ceasefire order (Avvaro to Austin, 25 Jan. 1867a, BARS 89). Not a single eyewitness account places Canul at San Pedro in December 1866 or January 1867.

123. Phillips before Austin, 14 Dec. 1866, BARS 93.

124. Phillips before Austin, 14 Dec. 1866, BARS 93; Canul, Chan, and Camara to Swasey, 3 Dec. 1866, BARS 93; Swasey to YTC, 5 Dec. 1866, BARS 89.

125. John Samuel August before Cockburn, 27 Dec. 1866, BARS 89.

126. Vidaurre to Austin, 15 Dec. 1866, BARS 89.

127. Statement by Savery, 28 Feb. 1867, BARS 96.

128. Austin to Grant, 12 Dec. 1866, no. 26, BARS 92; Austin to Major McKay, 17 Dec. 1866, BARS 89.

129. Austin to Grant, 12 Dec. 1866, no. 26, BARS 92. Austin's harsh condemnation of Delamere must be addressed. In the nineteenth century, the WIR were "negro" colonial forces recruited largely from the British colonies of Jamaica and Barbados, as well as some of the African colonies. Austin directed harsher judgment and language against the WIR commanders, including Captain Delamere (from Barbados), than he did any other members of the colonial government.

130. Austin to Grant, 12 Dec. 1866, no. 26, BARS 92.

131. James Haylock before Austin, 24 Dec. 1866, BARS 89; Canul and Chan to Austin, 18 Jan. 1867b, BARS 89. One of those detained was apparently José Carmen Hernández, who was questioned by Rhys and explained that he had been forced to deliver a letter from San Pedro to Swasey (Hernández before Rhys, 18 Dec. 1866, BARS 93).

132. Minutes of a meeting of the principal inhabitants of Belize, 17 Dec. 1866, BARS 93.

133. Carmichael Jr. to Austin, 14 Dec. 1866, BARS 89.

134. Austin to Grant, 12 Dec. 1866, no. 26, BARS 92.

135. R. Williamson to Austin, 26 Dec. 1866, BARS 89; Downer to Austin, 27 Dec. 1866a, BARS 89.

136. Rhys to Austin, 20 Dec. 1866, BARS 89.

137. Canul and Chan to Adolphus, 18 Jan. 1867a, BARS 89; Canul and Chan to Austin, 18 Jan. 1867b, BARS 89. In these letters, Canul indicates that he was not present, saying "a Commission that I sent to San Pedro . . . met up with the English troops."

138. Canul and Chan to Adolphus, 18 Jan. 1867a, BARS 89; Canul and Chan to Austin, 18 Jan. 1867b, BARS 89; Canul and Chan to Austin, 26 Dec. 1866, BARS 89; Fuentes before Carmichael Jr., 25 Jan. 1867b, BARS 89.

139. Williamson to Austin, 26 Dec. 1866, BARS 89.

140. Fuentes before Carmichael Jr., 25 Jan. 1867, BARS 89; Haylock before Austin, 24 Dec. 1866, BARS 89.

141. Haylock before Austin, 24 Dec. 1866, BARS 89; Williamson to Austin, 26 Dec. 1866, BARS 89.

142. Austin to Grant, 28 Dec. 1866, no. 133, BARS 92; Avvaro to Austin, 25 Jan. 1867a, BARS 89.

143. Austin to Grant, 28 Dec. 1866, no. 133, BARS 92; Fuentes before Carmichael Jr., 25 Jan. 1867, BARS 89.

144. José María Trejo before Adolphus, 23 Dec. 1866, BARS 89.

CHAPTER 6: FLIGHT, DESERTERS, AND CANUL'S LAST STAND (1867–1872)

1. Minutes of Executive Council, 3 Jan. 1867, BARS 89.

2. Austin to Carmichael, 7 Jan. 1867, BARS 89.

3. Austin to Grant, 1 Feb. 1867, no. 22, BARS 92.

4. Austin to Carmichael, 2 Feb. 1867, BARS 89.

5. Notes from meeting between commissioners of Encalada and Austin, 4 Feb. 1867, BARS 89.

6. Austin to Grant, 18 Jan. 1867, no. 11, BARS 92; Austin to Grant, 24 Jan. 1867, no. 14, BARS 92; Austin to Carmichael, 2 Feb. 1867, BARS 89.

7. Avvaro to Austin, 25 Jan. 1867, BARS 89. Avvaro, an Italian Jesuit, was Superior of the Jesuit mission from Jamaica, and had been in British Honduras since 1853. Father Eugenio Biffi, an Italian secular priest, aided the Jesuit mission in British Honduras between 1862–1867 (Anonymous, "Historical Sketch of the Catholic Mission in British Honduras," *The Pilgrim of Our Lady of Martyrs* 19, no. 11 [1903]: 282–83; Frederick C. Hopkins, "The Catholic Church in British Honduras [1851–1918]," *The Catholic Historical Review* 4, no. 3 [1918]: 305, 308, https://www.jstor.org/stable/25011583).

8. Balam to Austin, 19 Jan. 1867, BARS 86.

9. Statement of Biffi, 23 Jan. 1867, BARS 89.

10. Avvaro to Austin, 25 Jan. 1867, BARS 89.

11. Austin and Grant, 7 Feb. 1867, no. 26, BARS 92.

12. Adolphus to Austin, 17 Feb. 1867, BARS 89.

13. Austin to Carmichael, 2 Feb. 1867, BARS 89.

14. Austin to Grant, 11 Feb. 1867, no. 31, BARS 92.

15. Austin to Grant, 11 Feb. 1867, no. 31, BARS 92.

16. Downer to Graham, 7 Feb. 1867, BARS 89; Austin to Grant, 8 Apr. 1867, no. 53, BARS 98; Chief Justice Richard James to Austin, 18 May 1867, BARS 96.

17. Downer to Graham, 7 Feb. 1867, BARS 89; Austin to Grant, 8 Apr. 1867, no. 53, BARS 98; Corner to Austin, 18 May 1867, BARS 96.

18. Austin to Grant, 11 Feb. 1867, no. 31, BARS 92.

19. Williamson to Austin, 21 Feb. 1867, BARS 89.

20. Austin to Grant, 25 Feb. 1867, no. 35, BARS 92.

21. Harley to Austin, 9 Feb. 1867, BARS 95.

22. Austin to Grant, 25 Feb. 1867, no. 35, BARS 92.

23. Harley to Ek, 9 Feb. 1867, BARS 95.

24. Harley to Austin, 15 Feb. 1867, BARS 95.

25. Resolutions passed by the Legislative Assembly, 11 Feb. 1867, BARS 89.

26. Austin to Grant, 25 Feb. 1867, no. 35, BARS 92. I often think about the women at San Jose who were preparing meals for their families when the British arrived. Did they all escape? How long did they have to run before they found food?

27. Capt. Thomas Edmunds to Harley, 13 Feb. 1867, BARS 95.

28. Adolphus to Graham, 16 Feb. 1867, BARS 89.

29. Carmichael to Austin, 19 Feb. 1867, BARS 89.

30. Harley to Austin, 21 Feb. 1867b, BARS 89.

31. Downer to Graham, 26 Feb. 1867, BARS 89.

32. Statement by Austin, 28 Feb. 1867, BARS 96.

33. Statement by Austin, 28 Feb. 1867, BARS 96. It would in fact be decades before villages in the western region were assigned schoolteachers.

34. Biffi to Asunción and Irenies Ek, 1 Mar. 1867, BARS 96. Women are so rarely mentioned in these official colonial documents that when one is mentioned, she stands out.

35. Biffi to Asunción and Irenies Ek, 1 Mar. 1867, BARS 96.

36. When the San Pedro Maya Project team headed by Richard Leventhal conducted survey and excavation in the early 2000s, the location where San Pedro had been was situated on private property. The village of San Jose was still on Belize Estate and Produce Company (the successor to BHC) lands in 1936.

37. Delamere to Harley, 9 Mar. 1867, BARS 95.

38. Carmichael to Graham, 30 Mar. 1867, BARS 95.

39. Encalada to Austin, 4 Mar. 1867, BARS 89.

40. Austin to Earl of Carnarvon, 6 Apr. 1867, BARS 98, Separate.

41. Passport signed by Faber and Cockburn, 10 May 1867, BARS 96; Edmunds to Cockburn, 31 May 1867, BARS 96.

42. Austin to Grant, 13 July 1867, no. 119, BARS 98.

43. Austin to Grant, 13 Mar. 1867, no, 46, BARS 92. See also Austin to Eyre, 20 May 1865, no. 36, BARS 92; Austin to Grant, c. June 1867, no. 85, BARS 98.

44. Austin to Grant, c. June 1867, no. 85, BARS 98.

45. Austin to Grant, 16 Apr. 1867, no. 66, BARS 98.

46. Austin to Grant, 17 Apr. 1867, no. 67, BARS 98.

47. Austin to Grant, 30 Apr. 1867, no. 71, BARS 98.

48. Harley to Longden, 26 Dec. 1867, CO 123/132.

49. Edmunds to Cockburn, 31 May 1867, BARS 96; Carvajal to Cockburn, 27 Apr. 1867, BARS 96. Santa Rita lay somewhat to the north of the villages that were named in 1862 as having been under Ek's leadership.

50. Austin to Grant, 30 Apr. 1867, no. 69, BARS 98.

51. Austin to Grant, 30 Apr. 1867, no. 69, BARS 98.

52. Faber to Austin, 10 May 1867, BARS 96.

53. Edmunds to Cockburn, 31 May 1867, BARS 96; Cockburn, *Rough Notes*, 3.

54. Corner to Austin, 18 May 1867, BARS 96.

55. Longden to Grant, Reports on the Blue Book for the year 1867, 19 June 1868, ABH 98.

56. Austin to Grant, Report on Blue Book of 1866, 10 Aug. 1867, no. 130, BARS 98.

57. Plumridge to Longden, 29 Jan. 1869, BARS 103.

58. Cockburn, *Rough Notes*, 31.

59. Cal, "Rural Society," 232.

60. Canul to Castillo, 3 May 1867, BARS 96. Canul's supply order reveals something about his priorities: "eight demijohns aniseed, half a ream of white paper, one ream of yellow ditto, one box of Soap, eight lbs cocoa, 2 pieces of manta cuida [brown cotton cloth], half a box sperm candles, eight lbs pepper and one doz handkerchief." See also Canul to Castillo, 7 May 1867, BARS 96. Yo Creek is located to the west of Orange Walk (New River).

61. Austin to Grant, 17 May 1867, no. 84, BARS 98.

62. Comandantes Marcos Panti and Juan Bautista Yam to Downer, 23 May 1867, BARS 96.

63. Downer to Graham, 24 May 1867, BARS 96.

64. Carmichael to Austin, 17 June 1867a, BARS 96.

65. Carmichael to Austin, 8 Aug. 1867, BARS 96.

66. Austin to Grant, 16 Aug. 1867, no. 132, BARS 98.

67. Carmichael Jr. to Longden, 15 Nov. 1867, BARS 93.

68. Bonifacio Novelo, Bernardino Cen, and José Crescencio Poot to Carmichael, 30 Oct. 1867, BARS 93.

69. Longden to Grant, 5 Nov. 1867, no. 3, BARS 98.

70. Carmichael Jr. to Longden, 15 Nov. 1867, BARS 93.

71. Longden to Grant, 28 Nov. 1867, no. 6, BARS 93.

72. Novelo, Cen, and Poot to Longden, 9 Jan. 1868, BARS 97; Longden to Grant, 11 Jan. 1868, no. 5, BARS 98.

73. Interview with María Torres, 9 July 2005, Santa Familia.

74. Interview with Pedro Ortega, 7 July 2005, Santa Familia.

75. Interview with Anonymous, 13 July 2005, Branch Mouth.

76. Adolphus to Col. Sec. Hankin, 26 Dec. 1867, BARS 96.

77. Downer to Hankin, 27 Dec. 1867, BARS 96.

78. Carmichael Sr. to Longden, c. 23 Dec. 1867, BARS 96.

79. Carmichael to Longden, 31 Dec. 1867, BARS 96; Carmichael to Longden, 6 Jan. 1868, BARS 96.

80. Longden to Grant, 11 Jan. 1868, no. 5, BARS 98.

81. Longden to Grant, 6 Mar. 1868, no. 39, BARS 98.

82. Faber to Hankin, 30 Dec. 1867, BARS 96.

83. Humphreys, *Diplomatic History*, 138.

84. Longden to Grant, 22 Jan. 1868, no. 9, BARS 98.

85. Harley to Longden, 26 Dec. 1867, CO 123/132.

86. Longden to Grant, 22 Jan. 1868, no. 9, BARS 98.

87. Carmichael to Longden, 4 Feb. 1868, BARS 97.

88. Longden to Grant, 6 Jan. 1868, no. 2, CO 123/132; Harley to Longden, 26 Dec. 1867, CO 123/132.

89. Longden to Grant, 25 Feb. 1868, no. 33, BARS 98. The Secretary of State for the Colonies nixed the first clause of the Peace of the Frontier Bill saying that the legislature could not render it illegal for a resident to cultivate land beyond its borders (Longden to Grant, 5 May 1868, no. 67, BARS 98).

90. Lt. L. D. Crookenden to Lt. Col. Edmunds, 26 Feb. 1868, BARS 97; Plumridge to Longden, 21 Mar. 1868, BARS 97.

91. Hodge to Longden, 4 May 1868, CO 123/133.

92. Robelo to Downer, 8 Feb. 1868, BARS 97; Longden to Grant, 26 Feb. 1868, no. 36, BARS 98.

93. J. I. Blockley to Longden, 10 July 1868, BARS 102.

94. Longden to Grant, 25 July 1868, no. 111, BARS 98.

95. Longden to Grant, 4 May 1868, no. 62, CO 123/133. See also Hodge to Longden, 17 July 1868a, BARS 102.

96. George Gillett to YTC, 19 Apr. 1868, CO 123/133; Harley to Longden, 24 Apr. 1868, Private, BARS 97.

97. Plumridge to Longden, 26 Apr. 1868, CO 123/133; Account of the banks that are worked on Yucatecan lands, Canul and Chan, 20 Apr. 1868, CO 123/133; Enclosure with Plumridge to Longden, 2 May 1868, CO 123/133; Robelo to BHC, 27 Apr. 1868, CO 123/133.

98. Hodge to Longden, 4 May 1868, CO 123/133.

99. Pablo García to Longden, 20 June 1868, BARS 102.

100. García to Canul, 20 June 1868, BARS 102.

101. Longden to Grant, 25 July 1868, no. 111, BARS 98.

102. Blockley to Longden, 10 July 1868, BARS 102.

103. "Passport for Citizens Collu, Flor, and Canto," issued by Canul and Chan, 15 June 1868, BARS 102.

104. Plumridge to Austin, 5 July 1868, BARS 102.

105. Longden to Grant, 30 July 1868, no. 113, BARS 98; Raboteau's testimony, 13 July 1868, BARS 102.

106. Plumridge to Longden, 31 July 1868, BARS 102; Canul to Longden, 3 Aug. 1868, BARS 102.

107. Captain José Justo Chan to John August, 20 Sept. 1868, BARS 102.

108. Longden to Grant, 30 July 1868, no. 113, BARS 98.

109. Hodge to Longden, 3 Aug. 1868, BARS 102.

110. Hodge to Longden, 3 Aug. 1868, BARS 102.

111. Longden to Grant, 12 Aug. 1868, no. 127, BARS 98.

112. Chan to August, 20 Sept. 1868, BARS 102.

113. Hodge to Longden, 10 Oct. 1868, BARS 102; Hodge to Longden, 13 Oct. 1868, BARS 102.

114. Longden to Grant, 2 Oct. 1868, no. 149, BARS 98.

115. Longden to Grant, 21 Jan. 1869, no. 5, BARS 98.

116. Cockburn, *Rough Notes*, 25–26, 36–37.

117. Cockburn, *Rough Notes*, 37.

118. "Ley de 3 de noviembre de 1868 para el servicio en los establecimientos del campo del estado de Campeche," reprinted in González Navarro, *Raza y tierra*, 324–29.

119. Plumridge to Longden, 29 Jan. 1869, BARS 103.

120. Plumridge to Longden, 30 Nov. 1868, BARS 103.

121. Chan and Canul to Plumridge, c. 22 Jan. 1869, BARS 103.

122. Plumridge to Longden, 29 Jan. 1869, BARS 103.

123. Plumridge to Longden, 30 Jan. 1869, BARS 103; Plumridge to Longden, 14 Mar. 1869, BARS 103.

124. Plumridge to Longden, 27 June 1869, BARS 103.

125. Plumridge to Longden, 3 Aug. 1869, BARS 103.

126. Longden to Grant, 13 Nov. 1869, no. 128, BARS 98; Adolphus to Longden, 26 Nov. 1869, BARS 105.

127. Adolphus to Longden, 1 Dec. 1869, BARS 105.

128. Longden to Grant, 29 Jan. 1870, no. 24, BARS 98.

129. Plumridge to Longden, 28 Nov. 1869, BARS 105; Adolphus to Longden, 1 Dec. 1869, BARS 105.

130. @AyeshaASiddiqi, Twitter post, 2 September 2015.

131. Adolphus to Longden, 15 Jan. 1870, BARS 105.

132. Downer to Longden, 27 Jan. 1870, BARS 105.

133. Adolphus to Longden, 15 Jan. 1870, BARS 105.

134. Longden to Grant, 28 Feb. 1870, no. 28, BARS 105.

135. Adolphus to Longden, 15 Jan. 1870, BARS 105.

136. Longden to Grant, 28 Feb. 1870, no. 28, BARS 105.

137. Longden to Grant, 28 Mar. 1870, no. 40, BARS 98.

138. Canul and Chan to Lt. Gov., 4 May 1870, BARS 106.

139. Canul and Chan to Lt. Gov., 4 May 1870, BARS 106; Memorial of Mr. Downer, 16 Dec. 1872, CO 123/150.

140. Bristowe and Wright, *Handbook*, 28.

141. Canul and Chan to Lt. Gov., 4 May 1870, BARS 106.

142. Carmichael et al. to Administrator and Exec. Council, c. 27 May 1870, BARS 106; Memorial of Mr. Downer, 16 Dec. 1872, CO 123/150; Adolphus to Lt. Gov. William Wellington Cairns, June 1870, BARS 106.

143. Minute paper with Cairns to Rushworth, 15 Sept. 1872, no. 169, CO 123/149.

144. Bolland, *Formation*, 191–92.

145. Statements of the principal inhabitants of Orange Walk before Capt. White, 11 Sept. 1872, CO 123/149.

146. Statement of Lt. Smith before White, 7 Sept. 1872, CO 123/149.

147. Harley to Grant, 6 April 1872, no. 61, CO 123/148.

148. Canul et al. to Cairns, 10 Apr. 1871, BARS 109.

149. Downer to Col. Sec. Mitchell, 20 Nov. 1871, BARS 109.

150. Capt. F. le Breton Butler to Fort Adjutant, 6 Dec. 1871, BARS 109.

151. Icaiché Chiefs to Harley, 2 Jan. 1872, BARS 110. They also mentioned a "Sucalil," which is unknown.

152. Harley to Icaiché Chiefs, 8 Feb. 1872, BARS 110.

153. Harley to Grant, 6 Apr. 1872, no. 61, CO 128/148.

154. Statements of the principal inhabitants before Capt. White, 11 Sept. 1872, CO 123/149.

155. Statement by Downer, 11 Sept. 1872, CO 123/149. The prisoner escaped when he was tasked with cutting brush at the graveyard; he needed to relieve himself, and ran away once he reached the woods.

156. General in Chief José Luis Moo to Lt. Gov., 20 Jan. 1874, BARS 113.

157. Maj. Johnston to Cairns, 11 Sept. 1872, CO 123/149; Statement by Downer, 11 Sept. 1872, CO 123/149; Memorial of Mr. Downer, 16 Dec. 1872, CO 123/150.

158. Statement of Cerapio Ramos, 15 Sept. 1872, BARS 111; Chan and Moo to Cairns, 26 Sept. 1872, CO 123/150.

159. Johnston to Cairns, 13 Sept. 1872, CO 123/150.

160. William Miller, "Notes on a Part of the Western Frontier of British Honduras," *Proceedings of the Royal Geographical Society and Monthly Record of Geography* 9, no. 6 (1887): 422.

161. Cairns to Rushworth, 13 Sept. 1872, no. 110, CO 123/150.

162. Mitchell to Cairns, 30 Oct. 1872, CO 123/150.

163. Bolland, *Formation*, 3, 188.

EPILOGUE: PLACING BOUNDARY MARKERS

1. Bolland, "Alcaldes and Reservations," 52–53. See also Bristowe and Wright, *Handbook*, 79–81.

2. Odile Hoffman, *Property and Territory: Origins of a Colonial Order in Belize in the Nineteenth and Twentieth Centuries* (Benque Viejo del Carmen, Belize: Cubola Publishers, 2021), quote on 53.

3. Report of the Interdepartmental Committee on Maya Welfare, 10 Nov. 1941, CO 123/384/8.

4. Report of the Interdepartmental Committee on Maya Welfare, 10 Nov. 1941, CO 123/384/8.

5. Bolland, "Alcaldes and Reservations," 52–55; Hoffman, *Property and Territory*, 55–62; Joel Wainwright, *Decolonizing Development: Colonial Power and the Maya* (Malden, MA: Blackwell, 2008). 51–54.

6. Bolland and Shoman, *Land in Belize*, 91.

7. Report of the Interdepartmental Committee on Maya Welfare, 10 Nov. 1941, CO 123/384/8.

8. Bolland, "Alcaldes and Reservations," 56–57.

9. Dumond, *Machete*, 340.

10. Dumond, *Machete*, 342. Asunción Ek was still first *alcalde* at San Pedro in 1888, representing an awkward correspondence of Icaiché-appointed and British-recognized *alcaldes* (Bristowe and Wright, *Handbook*, 113).

11. Mundy to Arana, 3 Mar. 1875, BARS 114; Messrs. Phillips and Co. to Graham, 22 Mar. 1875, BARS 119; Faber to Messrs. Phillips and Co., 19 Mar. 1875, BARS 119; Smith to Messrs. Phillips and Co., 14 Apr. 1875, BARS 119.

12. Faber to Messrs. Phillips and Co., 19 Mar. 1875, BARS 119; Arana et al. to Lt. Gov., 13 Apr. 1875, BARS 114.

13. Dumond, *Machete*, 342–50.

14. Dumond, *Machete*, 362–63, 399, 424.

15. Karl Sapper, "Independent Indian States of Yucatan," in *Mexican and Central American Antiquities, Calendar Systems, and History*, ed. and trans. Charles P. Bowditch, 625–34 (Bulletin of the Bureau of American Ethnology 28. Washington, DC: Smithsonian Institution, 1904. First published 1895).

16. Dumond, *Machete*, 402.

17. Allen Wells and Gilbert M. Joseph, *Summer of Discontent, Seasons of Upheaval: Elite Politics and Rural Insurgency in Yucatán, 1876–1915* (Stanford, CA: Stanford University Press, 1996), 151.

18. Allen Wells, *Yucatán's Gilded Age: Haciendas, Henequen, and International Harvester, 1860–1915* (Albuquerque: University of New Mexico Press, 1985), 160–62, quote on 160.

19. González Navarro, *Raza y tierra*, 226–32; Wells and Joseph, *Summer of Discontent*, 270–71.

20. Interview with Tomasa Ortega, 6 July 2005, Santa Familia.

21. Interview with María Torres, 9 July 2005, Santa Familia.

22. Interview with Jorge Tun, 5 July 2005, Branch Mouth.

23. Interview with Pedro Ortega, 7 July 2005, Santa Familia.

24. Belize Estate and Produce Co., Claims to Lands on Western Frontier, 1935, CO 123/350/3.

Bibliography

ARCHIVES AND COLLECTIONS

ABH: Major Sir John Alder Burdon, ed. *Archives of British Honduras*, 3 vols. London: Sifton Praed, 1931–1935.

BARS: Belize Archives and Record Service, Belmopan, Belize

CO: Colonial Office records, National Archives, Kew, United Kingdom

SECONDARY AND PRINTED PRIMARY SOURCES

Abu-Lughod, Lila. "Writing against Culture." In *Recapturing Anthropology: Working in the Present*, edited by Richard G. Fox, 137–62. Santa Fe, NM: School of American Research Press, 1991.

Ancona, Eligio. *Historia de Yucatán desde la época mas remota hasta nuestros días*. Vol. 4, *La guerra social*. Mérida, Yucatán: Imprenta de M. Heredía Argüelles, 1880.

Anderson, Jennifer L. *Mahogany: The Costs of Luxury in Early America*. Cambridge, MA: Harvard University Press, 2012.

Anonymous. "Historical Sketch of the Catholic Mission in British Honduras." *The Pilgrim of Our Lady of Martyrs* 19, no. 11 (1903): 274–88.

Badillo Sánchez, Alejandra. "Memorial de la Guerra Social Maya." Accessed June 15, 2022. https://memorialguerrasocialmaya.org.

https://doi.org/10.5876/9781646424634.c009

Baqueiro, Serapio. *Ensayo histórico sobre las revoluciones de Yucatán desde el año de 1840 hasta 1864, tomo I*. Mérida, Yucatán: Imprenta de M. Heredía Argüelles, 1878.

Berzunza Pinto, Ramón. *Guerra social en Yucatán (Guerra de Castas)*. Mérida, Yucatán: Maldonado Editores/Gobierno del Estado de Yucatán, Secretaría de Educación, 1997.

Blair, Robert Wallace. "Yucatec Maya Noun and Verb Morpho-Syntax." PhD diss., University of Chicago, 1964.

Bolland, O. Nigel. "Maya Settlements in the Upper Belize River Valley and Yalbac Hills: An Ethnohistorical View." *Journal of Belizean Affairs* 3 (1974): 3–23.

Bolland, O. Nigel. *The Formation of a Colonial Society: Belize, from Conquest to Crown Colony*. Baltimore: Johns Hopkins University Press, 1977.

Bolland, O. Nigel. "The Maya and the Colonization of Belize in the Nineteenth Century." In *Anthropology and History in Yucatán*, edited by Grant D. Jones, 69–99. Austin: University of Texas Press, 1977.

Bolland, O. Nigel. "Alcaldes and Reservations: British Policy towards the Maya in Late Nineteenth Century Belize." *América Indígena* 57, no. 1 (1987): 33–75.

Bolland, O. Nigel. "Labour Control and Resistance in Belize in the Century after 1838," in *Colonialism and Resistance: Essays in Historical Sociology*, 159–71. 2nd rev. ed. Benque Viejo del Carmen, Belize: Cubola Publications, 2003.

Bolland, O. Nigel, and Assad Shoman. *Land in Belize, 1765–1871: The Origins of Land Tenure, Use, and Distribution in a Dependent Economy*. Kingston, Jamaica: Institute of Social and Economic Research, University of the West Indies, 1975.

Bracamonte y Sosa, Pedro. *Amos y sirvientes: Las haciendas de Yucatán, 1789–1860*. Mérida, Yucatán, México: Universidad Autónoma de Yucatán, 1993.

Bracamonte y Sosa, Pedro. *La conquista inconclusa de Yucatán: Los mayas de la montaña, 1560–1680*. México: Centro de Investigaciones y Estudios Superiores en Antropología Social/Universidad de Quintana Roo/Miguel Ángel Porrúa, 2001.

Briceño Chel, Fidencio, and Gerónimo Ricardo Can Tec, eds. *U nu'ukbesajil u ts'íibta'al maayat'aan: Normas de escritura para la lengua maya*. México: Secretaría de Cultura, Instituto Nacional de Lenguas Indígenas, 2014.

Bricker, Victoria Reifler. *The Indian Christ, the Indian King: The Historical Substrate of Maya Myth and Ritual*. Austin: University of Texas Press, 1981.

Bristowe, Lindsay W., and Philip B. Wright. *The Handbook of British Honduras for 1888–89; Comprising Historical, Statistical, and General Information Concerning the Colony*. Edinburgh and London: William Blackwood and Sons, 1888.

Buhler, Richard, S. J., ed. *A Refugee of the War of the Castes Makes Belize His Home: The Memoirs of J. M. Rosado*. Occasional Publications No. 2. Belize City: Belize Institute for Social Research and Action, 1970.

Bulmer-Thomas, Barbara, and Victor Bulmer-Thomas. *The Economic History of Belize: From the Seventeenth Century to Post-Independence.* Belize City: Cubola Press, 2012.

Bulmer-Thomas, Victor, and Barbara Bulmer-Thomas. "The Origins of the Belize Settlement." *Tempus: Revista en Historia General* 4 (2016): 137–60. https://revistas.udea .edu.co/index.php/tempus/article/view/326161.

Burns, Allan F. *An Epoch of Miracles: Oral Literature of the Yucatec Maya.* Austin: University of Texas Press, 1983.

Caiger, Stephen L. *British Honduras: Past and Present.* London: G. Allen & Unwin, 1951.

Cal, Angel Eduardo. "Anglo Maya Contact in Northern Belize: A Study of British Policy toward the Maya during the Caste War of Yucatán, 1847–1872." MA thesis, University of Calgary, 1983.

Cal, Angel Eduardo. "The Corozal (Goshen) Estate: 1819–1887." *Belcast Journal of Belizean Affairs,* 1, no. 1 (1984): 41–47.

Cal, Angel Eduardo. "Rural Society and Economic Development: British Mercantile Capital in Nineteenth-Century Belize." PhD diss., University of Arizona, 1991.

Campbell, Mavis C. *Becoming Belize: A History of an Outpost of Empire Searching for Identity, 1528–1823.* Kingston, Jamaica: University of West Indies Press, 2011.

Campos García, Melchor, ed. *Guerra de Castas en Yucatán: Su origen, sus consecuencias y su estado actual, 1866.* Mérida, Yucatán, Mexico: Universidad Autónoma de Yucatán, 1997.

Canto Alcocer, Jorge Alberto. "Las otras castas de la guerra: Bonifacio Novelo y los mestizos de Valladolid en la guerra social de 1847." In *La ventana de Zací: Otras miradas de la Guerra de Castas,* edited by Jorge Alberto Canto Alcocer and Terry Rugeley. Valladolid, Yucatán: Universidad de Oriente, 2013.

Church, Minette C., Christine A. Kray, and Jason Yaeger. "Landscapes of Strategic Mobility in Central America: San Pedro Siris during the Caste War." In *Routledge Handbook of the Archaeology of Indigenous-Colonial Interaction in the Americas,* edited by Lee M. Panich and Sara L. Gonzalez, 308–23. New York: Routledge, 2021.

Church, Minette C., Jason Yaeger, and Christine A. Kray. "Re-Centering the Narrative: British Colonial Memory and the San Pedro Maya." In *Archaeologies of the British in Latin America,* edited by Charles E. Orser Jr., 73–97. Cham, Switzerland: Springer International, 2019.

Cobain, Ian. *The History Thieves: Secrets, Lies and the Shaping of a Modern Nation.* London: Portobello Books, 2016.

Cockburn, S. *Rough Notes and Official Reports on the River Belize, the Physical Features of British Honduras, Taken in 1867–1869.* Kingston, Jamaica: C. L. Campbell Printer, 1875.

Dumond, Don E. *The Machete and the Cross: Campesino Rebellion in Yucatán.* Lincoln: University of Nebraska Press, 1997.

Dutt, Rajeshwari. *Maya Caciques in Early National Yucatán.* Norman: University of
  Oklahoma Press, 2017.

Dutt, Rajeshwari. *Empire on Edge: The British Struggle for Order in Belize during Yucatán's
  Caste War, 1847–1901.* Cambridge: Cambridge University Press, 2020.

Farriss, Nancy M. "Nucleation versus Dispersal: The Dynamics of Population Movement
  in Colonial Yucatan." *Hispanic American Historical Review* 58, no. 2 (1978): 187–216.
  http://www.jstor.org/stable/2513085.

Farriss, Nancy M. *Maya Society under Colonial Rule: The Collective Enterprise of Survival.*
  Princeton, NJ: Princeton University Press, 1984.

Feldman, Lawrence H., ed. and trans. *Lost Shores, Forgotten Peoples: Spanish Explorations of
  the South East Maya Lowlands.* Durham, NC: Duke University Press, 2000.

Fowler, Henry. *A Narrative of a Journey Across the Unexplored Portion of British Honduras,
  with a Short Sketch of the History and Resources of the Colony.* Belize: Government Press,
  1879.

Gabbert, Wolfgang. "Of Friends and Foes: The Caste War and Ethnicity in Yucatan."
  Journal of Latin American Anthropology 9, no. 1 (2004): 90–118. https://doi.org/10.1525
  /jlca.2004.9.1.90.

Gabbert, Wolfgang. *Violence and the Caste War of Yucatán.* Cambridge: Cambridge
  University Press, 2019.

Gann, Thomas W. F. *The Maya Indians of Southern Yucatan and Northern British Honduras.*
  Smithsonian Institution, US Bureau of American Ethnology, Bulletin 64. Washington,
  DC: Government Printing Office, 1918.

Gann, Thomas W. F. *Ancient Cities and Modern Tribes: Exploration and Adventure in
  Maya Lands.* London: Duckworth, 1926.

Gann, Thomas W. F. *Mystery Cities of the Maya.* Reprint, Kempton, IL: Adventures
  Unlimited Press, 1997. First published 1925.

Gibbs, Archibald Robertson. *British Honduras: An Historical and Descriptive Account
  of the Colony from Its Settlement, 1670.* London: Sampson Low, Marston, Searle, &
  Rivington, 1883.

González Navarro, Moisés. *Raza y tierra: La guerra de castas y el henequén.* México, D. F.:
  Colegio de México, 1970.

Graham, Elizabeth. *Maya Christians and Their Churches in Sixteenth-Century Belize.*
  Gainesville: University of Florida Press, 2011.

Helms, Mary H. "Miskito Slaving and Culture Contact: Ethnicity and Opportunity in
  an Expanding Population." *Journal of Anthropological Research* 39, no. 2 (1983): 179–97.
  https://www.jstor.org/stable/3629966.

Henderson, Captain George. *An Account of the British Settlement of Honduras; Being a
  View of Its Commercial and Agricultural Resources, Soil, Climate, Natural History, &c.*
  2nd ed. London: R. Baldwin, 1811.

Hoffman, Odile. *British Honduras: The Invention of a Colonial Territory; Mapping and Spatial Knowledge in the Nineteenth Century*. Benque Viejo del Carmen, Belize: Cubola Productions, 2014. https://hal.archives-ouvertes.fr/hal-01287334.

Hoffman, Odile. *Property and Territory: Origins of a Colonial Order in Belize in the Nineteenth and Twentieth Centuries*. Benque Viejo del Carmen, Belize: Cubola Publishers, 2021.

Hopkins, Frederick C. "The Catholic Church in British Honduras (1851–1918)." *The Catholic Historical Review* 4, no. 3 (1918): 304–14. https://www.jstor.org/stable/2501 1583.

Humphreys, R. A. *The Diplomatic History of British Honduras, 1638–1901*. London: Oxford University Press, 1961.

Ingold, Tim. *Being Alive: Essays on Movement, Knowledge and Description*. London: Routledge, 2011.

Jones, Grant D. "Levels of Settlement Alliance among the San Pedro Maya of Western Belize and Eastern Petén, 1857–1936." In *Anthropology and History in Yucatán*, edited by Grant D. Jones, 139–89. Austin: University of Texas Press, 1977.

Jones, Grant D. *Maya Resistance to Spanish Rule: Time and History on a Colonial Frontier*. Albuquerque: University of New Mexico Press, 1989.

Jones, Grant D. *The Conquest of the Last Maya Kingdom*. Stanford, CA: Stanford University Press, 1998.

Joseph, Gilbert M. "British Loggers and Spanish Governors: The Logwood Trade and Its Settlements in the Yucatan Peninsula: Part I." *Caribbean Studies* 14, no. 2 (1974): 7–37. https://www.jstor.org/stable/25612609.

Joseph, Gilbert M. *Rediscovering the Past at Mexico's Periphery: Essays on the History of Modern Yucatan*. Tuscaloosa: University of Alabama Press, 1986.

Kray, Christine A., Minette C. Church, and Jason Yaeger. "Designs on/of the Land: Competing Visions, Displacement, and Landscape Memory in Colonial British Honduras." In *Legacies of Space and Intangible Heritage: Archaeology, Ethnohistory, and the Politics of Cultural Continuity in the Americas*, edited by Fernando Armstrong-Fumero and Julio Hoil Gutiérrez, 53–77. Boulder: University Press of Colorado, 2017.

Krech, Shepard, III. *The Ecological Indian: Myth and History*. New York: W. W. Norton, 1999.

Lapointe, Marie. *Los mayas rebeldes de Yucatán*. Mérida, Yucatán: Maldonado Editores, 1997.

Lentz, Mark W. "Black Belizeans and Fugitive Mayas: Interracial Encounters on the Edge of Empire, 1750–1803." *Americas* 70, no. 4 (2014): 645–75. https://www.jstor.org/stable /43189294.

Menon, P. K. "The Anglo-Guatemalan Territorial Dispute over the Colony of Belize (British Honduras)." *Journal of Latin American Studies* 11, no. 2 (1979): 343–71. http://www.jstor.org/stable/156309.

Miller, William. "Notes on a Part of the Western Frontier of British Honduras." *Proceedings of the Royal Geographical Society and Monthly Record of Geography* 9, no. 6 (1887): 420–23.

Mintz, Sidney W. *Sweetness and Power: The Place of Sugar in Modern History*. New York: Penguin Books, 1985.

Morris, D. *The Colony of British Honduras, Its Resources and Prospects; With Particular Reference to Its Indigenous Plants and Economic Productions*. London: Edward Stanford, 1883.

Nordstrom, Carolyn. *A Different Kind of War Story*. Philadelphia: University of Pennsylvania Press, 1997.

Norman, B. M. *Rambles in Yucatan; Or, Notes of Travel through the Peninsula, Including a Visit to the Remarkable Ruins of Chi-Chen, Kaba, Zayi, and Uxmal*. New York: J. & H. G. Langley, 1843.

Ober, Frederick A. *Travels in Mexico and Life among the Mexicans*. San Francisco: J. Dewing, 1884.

O'Connor, Major Luke Smith. "An Exploring Ramble among the Indios Bravos, in British Honduras." *Living Age* 34, no. 434 (September 11, 1852): 513–17.

Patch, Robert W. *Maya and Spaniard in Yucatan, 1648–1812*. Stanford, CA: Stanford University Press, 1993.

Pendergast, David M. "The Nineteenth-Century Sugar Mill at Indian Church, Belize." *The Journal of the Society for Industrial Archeology* 8, no. 1 (1982): 57–66. https://www.jstor.org/stable/40968027.

Quezada, Sergio. *Maya Lords and Lordship: The Formation of Colonial Society in Yucatán, 1350–1600*. Translated by Terry Rugeley. Norman: University of Oklahoma Press, 2014.

Redfield, Robert, and Alfonso Villa Rojas. *Chan Kom: A Maya Village*. Reprint, Chicago: Chicago University Press, 1962. First published 1934.

Reed, Nelson. *The Caste War of Yucatán*. Stanford, CA: Stanford University Press, 1964.

Reed, Nelson A. "White and Mestizo Leadership of the Cruzoob." *Saastun: Revista de Cultura Maya* 9 (1997): 63–88.

Reed, Nelson A. *The Caste War of Yucatán*. Rev. ed. Stanford, CA: Stanford University Press, 2001.

Restall, Matthew. *The Maya World: Yucatec Culture and Society, 1550–1850*. Stanford, CA: Stanford University Press, 1997.

Restall, Matthew. "Crossing to Safety? Frontier Flight in Eighteenth-Century Belize and Yucatan." *Hispanic American Historical Review* 94, no. 3 (2014): 381–419. https://doi.org/10.1215/00182168-2694300.

Restall, Matthew. "Creating 'Belize': The Mapping and Naming History of a Liminal Locale." *Terra Incognitae* 51, no. 1 (2019): 5–35. https://doi.org/10.1080/00822884.2019 .1573962.

Restall, Matthew, and Wolfgang Gabbert. "Maya Ethnogenesis and Group Identity in Yucatán, 1500–1900." In *"The Only True People": Linking Maya Identities Past and Present*, edited by Bethany J. Beyyette and Lisa J. LeCount, 91–131. Boulder: University Press of Colorado, 2017.

Richmond, Douglas W. *Conflict and Carnage in Yucatán: Liberals, the Second Empire, and Maya Revolutionaries, 1855–1876*. Tuscaloosa: University of Alabama Press, 2015.

Roys, Ralph L. *The Political Geography of the Yucatan Maya*. Publication 613. Washington, DC: Carnegie Institution of Washington, 1957.

Rugeley, Terry. *Yucatán's Maya Peasantry and the Origins of the Caste War*. Austin: University of Texas Press, 1996.

Rugeley, Terry. "The Caste War in Guatemala." *Saastun: Revista de Cultura Maya* 3, no. 3 (1997): 67–96.

Rugeley, Terry. *Rebellion Now and Forever: Mayas, Hispanics, and Caste War Violence in Yucatán, 1800–1880*. Stanford, CA: Stanford University Press, 2009.

Rugeley, Terry, ed. *Maya Wars: Ethnographic Accounts from Nineteenth-Century Yucatán*. Norman: University of Oklahoma Press, 2001.

Sapper, Karl. "Independent Indian States of Yucatan." In *Mexican and Central American Antiquities, Calendar Systems, and History*, edited and translated by Charles P. Bowditch, 625–34. Bulletin of the Bureau of American Ethnology 28. Washington, DC: Smithsonian Institution, 1904. First published 1895.

Scholes, France V., and Sir Eric Thompson. "The Francisco Pérez *Probanza* of 1654–1656 and the *Matrícula* of Tipu (Belize)." In *Anthropology and History in Yucatán*, edited by Grant D. Jones, 43–68. Austin: University of Texas Press, 1977.

Stephens, John L. *Incidents of Travel in Yucatan*, 2 vols. London: John Murray, 1843.

Sullivan, Paul. *Unfinished Conversations: Mayas and Foreigners between Two Wars*. Berkeley: University of California Press, 1989.

Sullivan, Paul. "John Carmichael: Life and Design on the Frontier in Central America." *Revista Mexicana del Caribe* 5, no. 10 (2000): 6–88. http://www.redalyc.org/articulo.oa ?id=12801001.

Sweeney, Lean. *La supervivencia de los bandidos: Los mayas icaichés y la política fronteriza del sureste de la peninsula de Yucatán, 1847–1904*. Mérida, Yucatán, Mexico: Universidad Nacional Autónoma de México, 2006.

Temple, R. "The Commercial Resources of British Honduras." *Journal of the Society of Arts* 3, no. 154 (1855, Nov. 2): 783–85. https://www.jstor.org/stable/41323582.

Van Maanen, John. *Tales of the Field: On Writing Ethnography*. 2nd ed. Chicago: University of Chicago Press, 2011.

Wainwright, Joel. *Decolonizing Development: Colonial Power and the Maya*. Malden, MA: Blackwell, 2008.

Wells, Allen. *Yucatán's Gilded Age: Haciendas, Henequen, and International Harvester, 1860–1915*. Albuquerque: University of New Mexico Press, 1985.

Wells, Allen, and Gilbert M. Joseph. *Summer of Discontent, Seasons of Upheaval: Elite Politics and Rural Insurgency in Yucatán, 1876–1915*. Stanford, CA: Stanford University Press, 1996.

White, Hayden. *The Content of the Form: Narrative Discourse and Historical Representation*. Baltimore: Johns Hopkins University Press, 1987.

Woods, Charles M., Sr., J. Alexander Bennett, and Silvaana Udz. *Years of Grace: The History of Roman Catholic Evangelization in Belize*. Belize City: Roman Catholic Diocese of Belize City and Belmopan, 2015.

Index

Locators followed by *f* indicate figures, followed by *n* indicate notes, and followed by *t* indicate tables.